Think Like Paul

Searching for the Message that Changed the World

Studies #1-25

Perry Lewis Stiltz IV

ISBN-13: 978-1986830584
ISBN-10: 1986830586

To the development of Christ within

ACKNOWLEDGMENTS

I'd like to give a special thanks to several people who have given me spiritual tools
or helped and encouraged me throughout this puzzle:

To my grandparents, Perry and Alberta Stiltz: you took care of my brother and I when we
were at the most impressionable ages of 3 and 6. We came into your lives at a time of
difficult circumstances, and yet you adopted us as your own. Thank you for teaching us
love, strength, humility and a bit of healthy skepticism.

To my parents, Perry and Diane: You left our worlds when we were small. But the stories
of your love for life did not. They were imprinted deep on my soul. And they became a
driving force for understanding the goodness of God and what He would have for us here
in this world.

Thank you Don Buo. Thanks for your friendship, encouragement, and heart. Thank you
Wah, and Mew, the Cain family, the Dalkes, and my Citivision brothers and sisters, and
all of you whose hearts who have impacted me so deeply.

Much appreciation for my brother,
for being a follower of the Spirit of Christ.

Table of Contents

"But this is the covenant which I will make with the house of Israel after those days," declares the Lord, "I will put My law within them and on their heart I will write it; and I will be their God, and they shall be My people. They will not teach again, each man his neighbor and each man his brother, saying, 'Know the Lord,' for they will all know Me, from the least of them to the greatest of them," declares the Lord, "for I will forgive their iniquity, and their sin I will remember no more."
—Jeremiah 31:33–34 NASB

www.ThinkLikePaul.com

Preface

We were in a college class studying the letter to the Hebrews. We came upon Hebrews 4:12 (the passage that describes the Word of God as "living and active and sharper than a two-edged sword..."), and I started wondering what that meant to those in the first century (Over the previous years, I had been striving to think as those in the first century may have thought). But this time, it was different, for there seemed to be no good answers.

"What was the 'Word of God'?" "What did that mean for those in the first century?" And for this passage, the question was a little more specific: "What specifically was the 'Word of God' to those in the first century who do not have a New Testament?" (It's not like Jesus handed out New Testaments so that everyone knew what to follow!)

Simple enough. Right? I mean, if we really understand this passage, then we should understand it in the manner they did. Right? ...But these were greater questions than I was able to answer. These questions would give birth to scores of other questions that would both challenge and befuddle me, in one fashion or another, for a couple of years.

At first, everything became less clear. Was the "Word" the Bible? If so, was it just the Old Testament? Or the New Testament? Or both? Would those in the first century have thought of this "Word" as Jesus or the Spirit? Was it a message *inside* the Bible? If so, what exactly does that mean? Or was it just a general nonspecific "message of God"? Which of these, if any, actually make sense for any individual passage?

I didn't want to regurgitate the thinking of my teachers. I didn't want peoples opinions. I wanted to know what Paul thought. I didn't want to know just his thoughts on the "Word of God." I wanted to know why he was so passionate. I wanted to know why and how he was able to sing songs of praise after being thrown into prison. I mean, who does that?!? I wanted his spiritual riches. I wanted the knowledge that made him alive. If God's message was so powerful in those first few centuries, then wouldn't it be just as powerful now?!? And if it isn't as powerful as it was then, then what changed?

I had to know. And so I committed myself to *one thing*. I had committed myself to one goal: *To determine the first century perspective of the "Word of God."* I had to figure this out. What was that message that changed the world? What was that message that changed peoples hearts everywhere it went? Do we already have that message? If so, then why are we so ineffective in teaching how good God is? What specifically is the difference between their "Word of God" and our "Word of God"?

This book is the result of many things. On one level this book is the result of some of my basic assumptions. I have always believed that *if* there is a God:[1]

    A. He must be good.
    B. He must really care about humanity.
    C. He has made available spiritual and emotional riches for all of us.
    D. His message is just as powerful today as it was in the first few centuries (where it transformed the known world).

But on another level, this book is the result of my own struggles and doubts. When I was 3 my father was struck by a car and killed while working for the highway department. I only have a couple of vague memories of him. And when I was 6, my mother also died in a car accident. They were both physically active and loving individuals, and from what I remember and the stories that I heard about them, they were both in love with each other and with life itself. But as a result of their deaths, I grew up with many doubts and questions. I wondered about the purpose of those events, the purpose of life itself, and of course, the existence of God… And now, as I reflect upon these things, I have come to realize that this is the reason why I am so inquisitive, skeptical, and interested in answering the question of "Why?"

Ultimately, this study is about helping us get greater clarity with regards to the first century terminologies and purposes. Today, we are so vague with our terminology that we each may have our own meanings and concepts. This series is an effort to get us to put aside our differences and trainings, and strive to align with the "following Christ" that those NT writers understood. I wanted this, not just for the sake of clarity and Truth, but also for the sake of being able to communicate God's greatness to the world.

And due to this research, I have also come to the belief that in several significant ways, most of us do not have clarity around some important first century concepts. We have hazy, vague notions of the Word, and we confuse that with the Bible, and thus do not understand the role of the Bible. This has also led us to confusion with what it means to "follow Christ" and be led by the Holy Spirit (though this varies greatly from person to person). This book is intended to help us contemplate, discern, and get clarity with the faith of those first followers, for the purposes of aligning with the faith they had and being able to explain it to nonbelievers.

While these studies were challenging, they were small potatoes compared to my own programming. I was continually going back to the training that most of us have been given: "the Bible is the Word of God." This undoubtedly was my greatest obstacle to understanding the "word" (By the way, If you are conservative Christian, like myself, this will likely be your

---

[1] While I had some notion or sense of God as a small child, as I got older and made negative meanings about life (re: my parents deaths), I was essentially agnostic, until college where I was converted by the love of a minister and His family… Thank you Cain family.

biggest stumbling block). I, like many of you, had been trained to think "Bible" when the phrase "Word of God" is used.[2]

And, as you will see, the use of these terms interchangeably is a major source of today's confusion. But the solution to this, at least in part, is relatively simple. It is in committing ourselves to Truth. It is in valuing Truth more than our previous learnings or feelings. And it is committing ourselves to *reason and exegetics*, while also striving to understand *the Spirit of Christ*.

Surely, the paradigm that will be uncovered will seem "new" to many of you, at least in some regards, but ultimately it has all the markings of being very old. As you will see, this perspective will clearly point us toward God's answer to everything—Christ. And this will consistently fit with the specific circumstances and purposes of the first century church. Here, we will find that the *Spirit of Christ (the Word of God)* is much more powerful than any set of letters… And it will be in that Spirit that our spirit will be able to overcome every circumstance.

Essentially, this "new" paradigm will be built up from a foundation of understanding their definitions and purposes. And this will help us reconsider several important topics for the church today:

- The overarching purpose and goal of the Bible,
- How they consider Christ to be the answer to everything,
- What specifically is God's purpose for mankind,
- How Paul "followed Christ,"
- What is a covenant, and what is God's covenant for today,
- And the one commitment we can make that will radically change our lives, our relationships, and our churches.

I know this message is powerful today, because I have experienced it. Looking back, I realize now, that this message was what initially drew me to Christianity. For I saw this Word working in the Christians who converted me. And this is my hope for us today, that we each get clarity around the first century "Word of God," so that we can effectively spread it to the world around us.

I'm not trying to convert you to my way of thinking. I'm trying to help all of us align with His way of thinking. I don't really care if you trust me. I want you to trust Him. I don't really care if

---

[2] (Many of you may consider the notion of "the Bible is *not* the Word of God" as blasphemous or an affront to Christianity. Neither is the case. Blasphemy is speaking against God or sacred things (like the scriptures). **I am not challenging the scriptures. I am challenging modern christianity's approach to the scriptures.** I am convinced of the scriptures inspiration and authenticity. I am simply looking to understand the scriptures (and the Word) from the perspective of those who wrote the New Testament.)

you appreciate, honor, or respect me. My desire is for each of us to appreciate, honor, and respect Him.

My goal is for you to think. I want all of us to have a faith that is akin to Jesus' and Paul's. I want us each to have clarity on how Christ is our *Way* back to the Creator. Ultimately, my goal is for people to see the love, joy, strength, humility, compassion, forgiveness, and peace of Jesus *in you*… For this, I have become convinced, is God's most compelling message of all.

Be skeptical. Don't accept my assertions because they are published. Do your homework. Study it. Search your heart. Consider what would make sense to those in the first century. Are the studies here consistent with the writings and purposes of the New Testament authors? Are they consistent with our infinite Creator?

I want you to challenge the ideas developed in this book. But I also want you to challenge your own views. In fact, since you don't know me and my motivations, you *should* be skeptical, and I *should* be challenged. Likewise, *you should also examine and challenge the views you have been taught*. The battle is not between our perspectives, but between God's eternal truths and everything else.

I want these studies to be about both Truth and Spirit. Much of today's Christianity is deeply rooted in emotionalism, and only uses reason and logic where it supports their assertions. I am convinced that if we truly understand the first century perspectives, we will understand "following Christ" with our hearts *and* our minds. And while much of these studies bring our attention to exegetics and reason, ultimately, my own personal goal is to align our hearts with God Himself.

I hope these studies find you well. I hope they find you at a time of curiosity, humility and thoughtfulness. Ultimately, my hope is for His light to shine bright in you, so that others may want to know about this wonderful and amazing Creator.

…And yes, ultimately, everything seems to point to *one* thing. And it is this "one thing" that has dramatically changed my life… In every way. I wish this blessing upon you, and the people you come into contact with.

May we each find the heart and motivation of Christ Himself.
—Perry Stiltz

Then he said to me,
"This is the word of the LORD
to Zerubbabel saying,
'Not by might nor by power,
but by My Spirit,'
says the LORD of hosts."
—Zechariah 4:6

Introduction

A powerful king envisioned a beautiful city. He commissioned his master architect to build a city that would represent his majesty. The architect and his engineers got to work and built a beautiful and prosperous city that was unmatched in the world. This city came to symbolize the enduring greatness of the king and the design set forth by his architect.

The secret to the architect's success was not in the outward facades, or even a particular style or design, but in the material that held everything together. His secret was in the foundation — a new kind of construction— a material that was significantly stronger and more malleable than their traditional materials of clay or stone. They called this new thousand-year-material —"cement."

After the king and his original engineers died, greed came into both the government and the engineering guilds. This led to massive corruption, shortcuts, and a disregard of the king's blueprints. And though they professed obedience to the ancient king and his designs, they did not continue to follow his expensive methods—but they were not able to do this openly, as the citizens remembered and loved the king. So the government and the engineers simply started to refer to "cement" as anything in the foundation.

Centuries later, and after several wars and much destruction within the city, a new government of the people came into power. With this government came a movement to build according to the king's original plans. Many of the engineers believed that a strict adherence to the original blueprints was critical, and that if they followed them exactly, they could bring back the glorious civilization.

Everyone thought they were following the king's plans. They thought they were constructing the same buildings that the master did centuries before. The city planners, engineers, and the general public were excited and proud that they were recreating the city of the ancient king. With this construction came praise and popularity for those leading the charge.

But even after centuries of following these ancient blueprints, their buildings didn't have the draw and intrigue of the ancient city. While a few of the newer buildings were beautiful and popular, they always seemed to degrade and lose their glory within just a few decades... As a result, there was little appreciation for the ancient king and growing doubts for his architect and designs.

Many citizens knew something was wrong, but were not sure what the problem was. Some asked for new methods, while the majority were content with the opinions of their neighborhood engineers.

Some of the citizens would occasionally asked their engineers "Is this what the ancient city looked like?" The engineers (who had spent their lives studying the blueprints and constructing the city) would often respond defensively with a "Of course it is! We have the blueprints, and we are following them exactly!" And while the engineers were so confident and intent on defending their constructions, many others seemed to notice that the quality of their buildings were virtually indistinguishable from the neighboring cities. This led many to become their own architects for their own buildings, as they had decided that the king's designs were not that impressive.

… …But few seemed to care, as their materials seemed to be correct, and everybody was so busy with their designs, constructions, and the thought of increasing the king's kingdom.

These Studies
This is an effort to understand first century notion of "following Christ." This is simply an effort to see how Paul and the other Apostles considered "Christ" and what they thought it meant to follow Him.

Here we will spend much of our time striving to understand the foundation of their faith—the *word of God* (Studies #11-20). But before we get there, we will need to understand the how Christ was their pathway back to God (#1-5), and the role of the Scriptures (#6-10). And finally we will look at how these concepts relate to Paul's perspective of the Spirit, the New Covenant, and dying with Christ (#21-25).

> Are we drinking from the purity of the first century word?
>
> Or are we drinking downstream from our ancestral religions?

> What if we had the clarity and purpose of Paul?
>
> What if we were teaching the same message that he taught?
>
> What if God's Message was just as powerful now as it was in the first few centuries?

Essentially these studies are a concentrated effort to understand four basic questions, which will help us understand the 5th area of study:

1. What exactly was the church's purpose and goal?
2. What exactly was the role and purpose of the Scriptures?
3. What exactly was the "Word of God"?
4. What exactly was the "New Covenant"?
5. What exactly is the "Holy Spirit"?

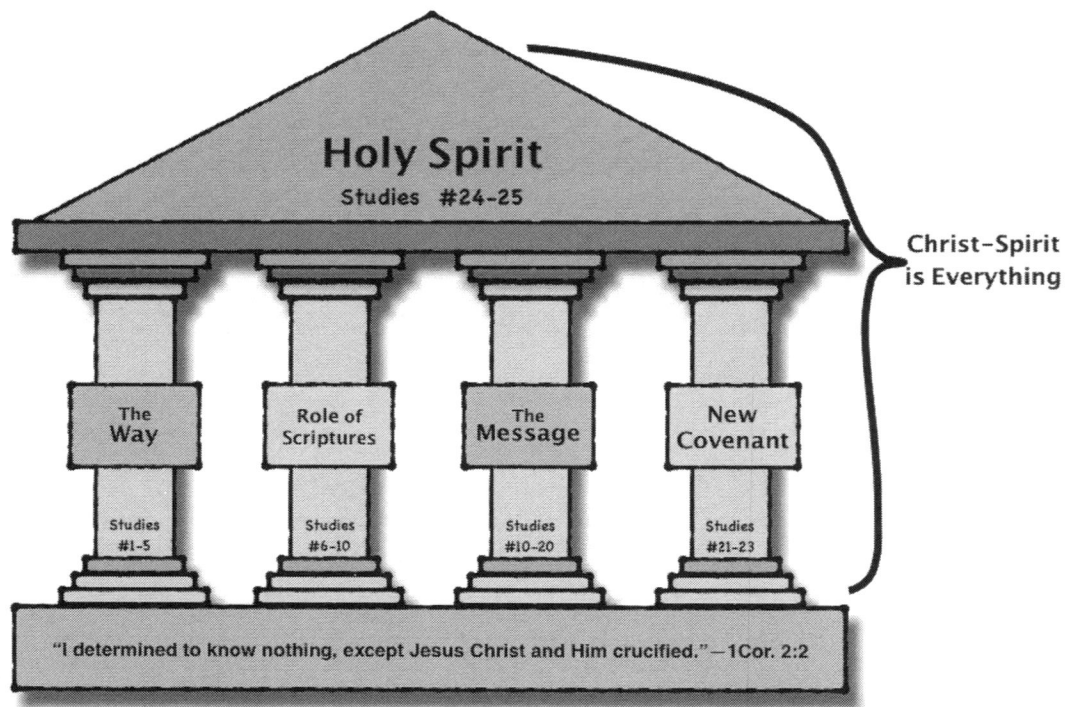

What we will find is that Paul's model of "following Christ" is a clear focus on the spiritual, rather than traditions, rules, and the religiousness that is common today. As we will see, his priority is in growing the church into Christ's image.

The Ultimate Conclusion— Christlikeness is Everything
Ultimately, this study is about understanding *their* terminologies and *their* purposes. It is about figuring out *their* concept of Christ, and what *they* thought it meant to *follow Him*. On this journey we will uncover how their traditions, rules, and doctrines were used to grow the Christ-Spirit within. We will also examine passages that reveal the priorities of both Jesus and Paul, and how those priorities can give us insight into the force that is guiding them—the Holy Spirit.

My studies have consistently pointed me toward a cohesive and all-encompassing message that directs us toward the Messiah and growing into His likeness. Here we will see how the Scriptures are, in some form or fashion, directing their readers (and us) toward God's image within us.

> **The truth is like a lion. You don't have to defend it.**
> **Let it loose. It will defend itself.**
> **—St. Augustine**

	Today's Perspective	Christ = God's Message
How the "Christ is Everything" Model can Clarify many of Today's Unclear and Confusing Teachings		
What is the "Word of God"?	Bible?!? Christ?!?	Christ's Spirit
What is the Purpose of the New Testament?	Instruction Manual	Teach/remind recipients of Christ (likeness)
What is our standard?	Bible?!? Christ?!?	Spirit in Jesus
What exactly doe it mean to "follow Christ"?	???	adopt the heart and mind of Jesus
What is the New Covenant?	???	Promise to love one another as He loved us (Growing in Christlikeness)
What exactly is the purpose of church?	???	Christ's Spirit within
Purpose of man?	???	To be the image of God (Love)
What specifically is our WAY back to God?	???	Following Christ's likeness (love, joy, peace···)
What is the Holy Spirit?	???	Love (revealed in Jesus)
Leads the church to···	Ambiguity and Confusion (private interpretations of Scripture)	Being recognized as followers of Christ (John 13:34–35)

Concision in style, precision in thought, decision in life.
—Victor Hugo

Lifting the Fog

Unfortunately, much of today's Christian tenets are trapped in a fog of vagueness and ambiguity. Everybody preaches: "faith in Christ," "He is the way," and that "we should love others."

Did God send His Son to continue His mysteriousness? Or did He come to reveal God's Spirit?

—But what do we mean by *faith?* And what do we mean by *Christ?* Do we understand "*faith in Christ*" the way Paul did? How can a person be "the way"? And what is *love?* Do we really understand this in the same way they would have?

These studies will only look for clues within the Bible. We want to understand the apostles "cement." We want to understand their terminology with as little ambiguity as possible. And we don't want to conflate their foundational concepts with today's thinking. These studies will thoroughly examine specific topics for the purpose of "finding Truth" and leaving doubt behind. Ultimately, we want to understand the concepts that *grew* their churches so dramatically.

Why are there so many churches?

Paul said that we should be "united in Christ". What did he mean?

Why do we all explain Christianity differently?

> There is no greater impediment to the advancement of knowledge than the ambiguity of words
> —Thomas Reid

So what will we learn from these studies? What exactly was "the faith" that those first prophets were teaching? Here are some of the conclusions that these studies will reveal. (For more details go to *Paul's "Christ is Everything" Faith* in the Final Thoughts section p.177)

Christianity was the commitment to "following the Spirit in Jesus". It was *not* blind obedience to a religion, a church, or organization. The ecclesia (church/assembly/'called out') was a group of people committed to following Christ and building each other up in His likeness, for "**Christ**" **was their answer for everything.** "Aligning" with the Spirit (in Jesus) was their method of "following Him."

Christ's faith was to be their faith. The first century Christians were teaching Jesus' faith (His spirit of love, forgiveness, joy, hope, courage...). They were striving to understand His priorities, mindset, and values. He was the one that authored and finished the faith. "Unity in Christ" was not about a common place of worship, or the commitment to a specific set of traditions or rules, but rather was simply the Spirit that was revealed with Jesus and the cross.

Christ's Spirit is an infinite resource for life and godliness. The Spirit in Jesus is a spirit of infinite love, joy, forgiveness, compassion, strength, courage, peace, boldness, determination, self-control, patience... And "in the development of Jesus' spirit within us" God would provide whatever was needed for any situation, even torture and death.

Christ's Spirit was their goal. Christ was the end of the Law. His spiritual likeness was the goal and purpose of the Law. The purpose of the Scriptures(and the church) was the building up of each other in the Spirit of Jesus.

Christianity was about seeing the image of God in others. In the first century there was an emphasis placed on valuing others as Christ valued us. It wasn't about passing judgment on people, but rather teaching them about the image/Spirit that is within them.

God's message(word) cannot be contained within writings. His message is beyond both language and thought, and thus cannot fully be conveyed through words or writings. God's message is Spirit. It is a message that speaks directly to our hearts.

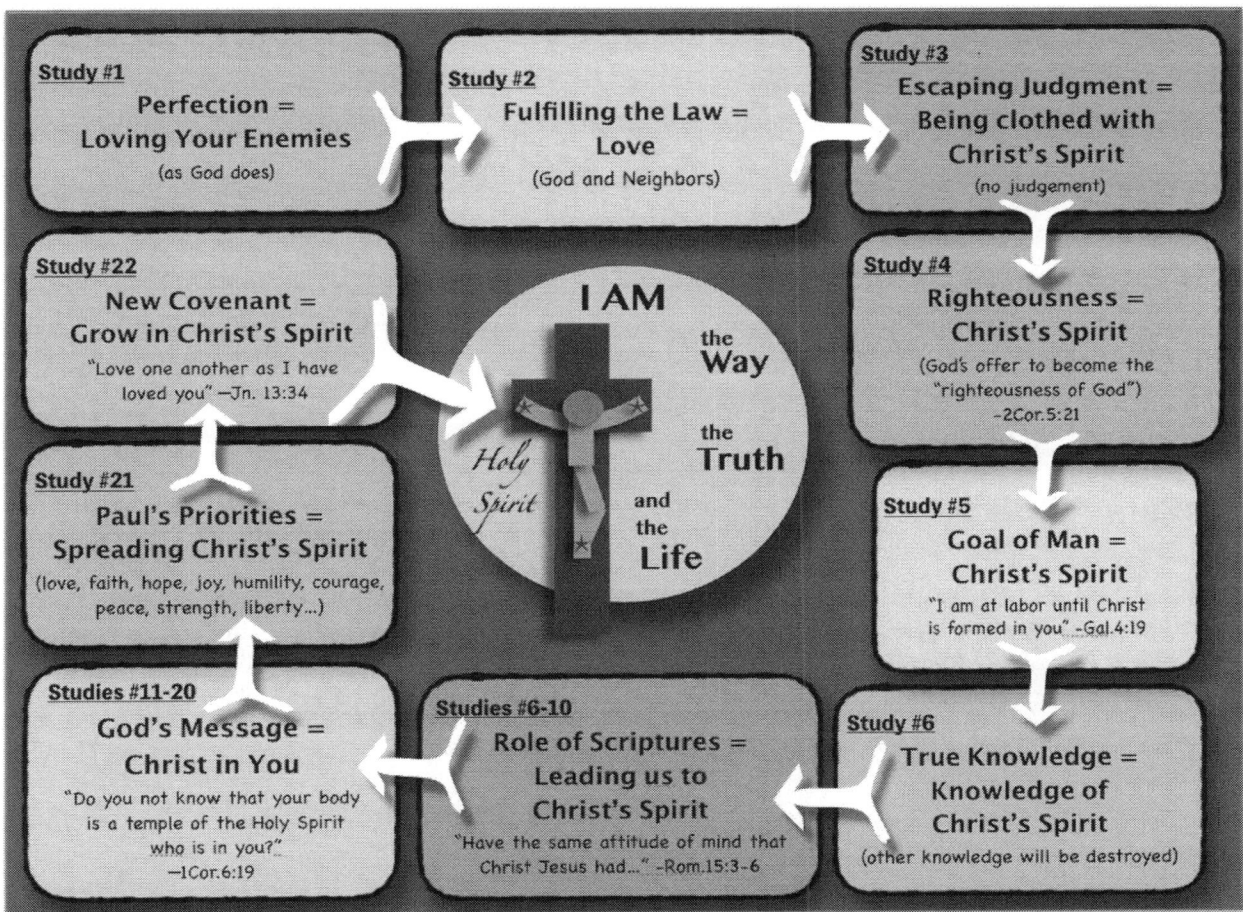

God's message is the Spirit that goes to the cross. God's message is a spirit that is willing to give up everything for you.

God's message is "Christ in you". This Christ-in-you spirit is living, enduring, nurturing and imperishable. It is thankful, compassionate, honest, and sincere. This "message of God" has the ability to change and sanctify the heart of man.

> Just as a math book teaches mathematics and **is not** "math" itself...
>
> the Bible teaches the "Word" but is not the "Word" itself.

This Christ-in-you-message is God's ultimate message to humanity. Jesus states God's message in the "New Commandment" which He gave His apostles at the Passover with His followers:

> "A new commandment I give to you, that you love one another, even as I have loved you, that you also love one another. By this all men will know that you are My disciples, if you have love for one another." —John 13:34-35 NASB

Having Christ's Spirit is being the "righteousness of God". Righteousness was revealed in Christ. He gave us an opportunity to come and know God, and be His righteousness on earth.

The Christ-Spirit is Truth and Knowledge. Jesus proclaims that He is the Truth. Paul proclaims that knowing Christ's Spirit is "real knowledge." The first century notions for Truth and Knowledge were simply the Spirit of Jesus.

The Purpose of the Scriptures was to Lead us to Christ. Christ was the promised Messiah, and the pouring out of God's Spirit onto the world. The ultimate purpose for both the Old and New Testaments was: directing their readers toward Christ (the image of God within).

The Spirit in Jesus was everything to those first followers. He is the Alpha and Omega. His Spirit is the Way, the Truth, and the Life. The purpose of the church was to remind and encourage the Spirit of Jesus within each other, for that Spirit is God's Answer for everything.

Spirit of God

in mankind

= the Way, the Truth, and the Life
= the Righteousness of God
= the Goal of the Church
= the Purpose of the Bible
= the Message of God
= the Purpose of Paul
= the New Covenant
= the Holy Spirit

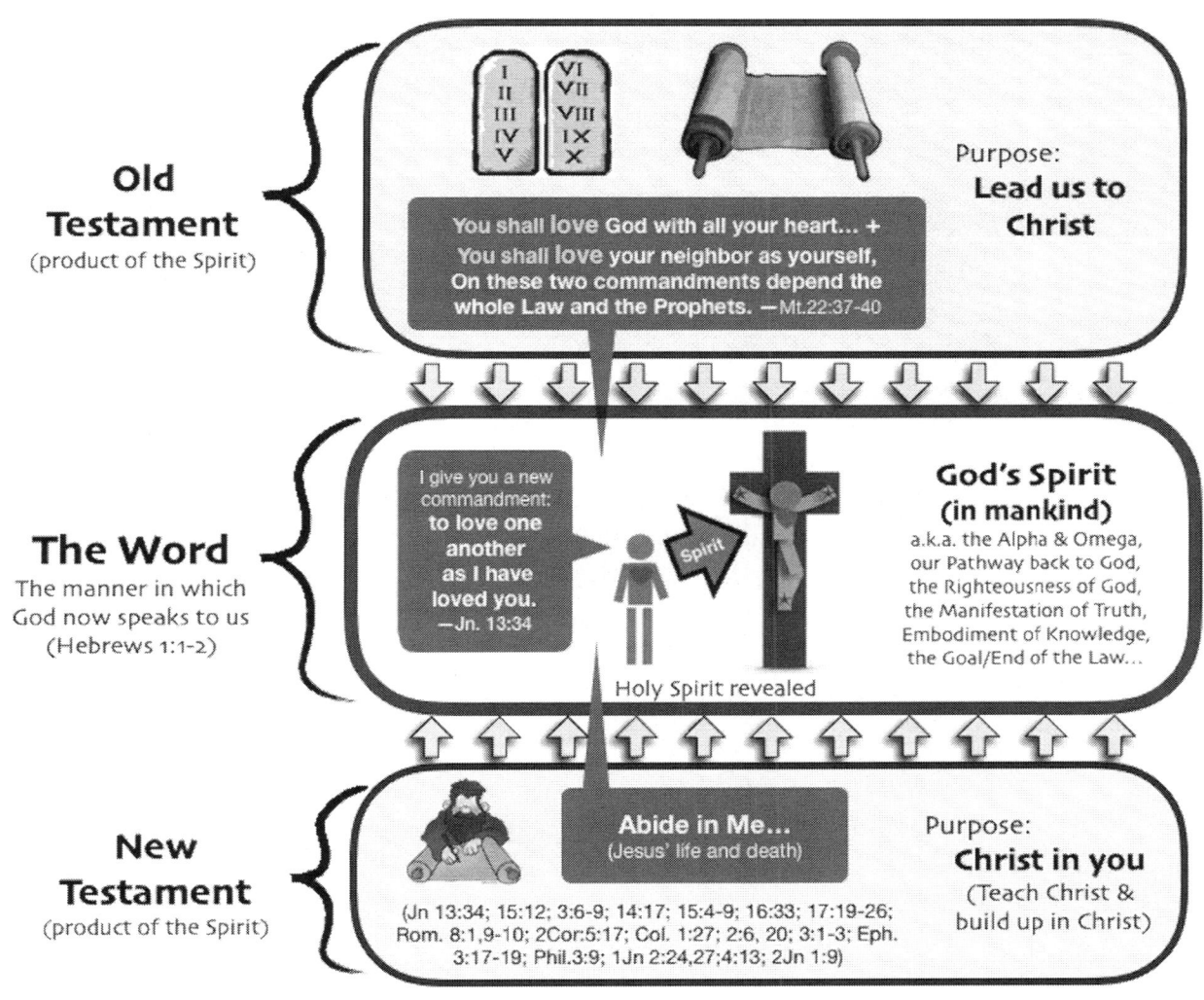

Old Testament
(product of the Spirit)

Purpose:
Lead us to Christ

You shall love God with all your heart... +
You shall love your neighbor as yourself,
On these two commandments depend the
whole Law and the Prophets. —Mt.22:37-40

The Word

The manner in which
God now speaks to us
(Hebrews 1:1-2)

I give you a new
commandment:
**to love one
another
as I have
loved you.**
—Jn. 13:34

Spirit

**God's Spirit
(in mankind)**
a.k.a. the Alpha & Omega,
our Pathway back to God,
the Righteousness of God,
the Manifestation of Truth,
Embodiment of Knowledge,
the Goal/End of the Law...

Holy Spirit revealed

New Testament
(product of the Spirit)

Abide in Me...
(Jesus' life and death)

Purpose:
Christ in you
(Teach Christ &
build up in Christ)

(Jn 13:34; 15:12; 3:6-9; 14:17; 15:4-9; 16:33; 17:19-26;
Rom. 8:1,9-10; 2Cor:5:17; Col. 1:27; 2:6, 20; 3:1-3; Eph.
3:17-19; Phil.3:9; 1Jn 2:24,27;4:13; 2Jn 1:9)

Preparing for the First Century

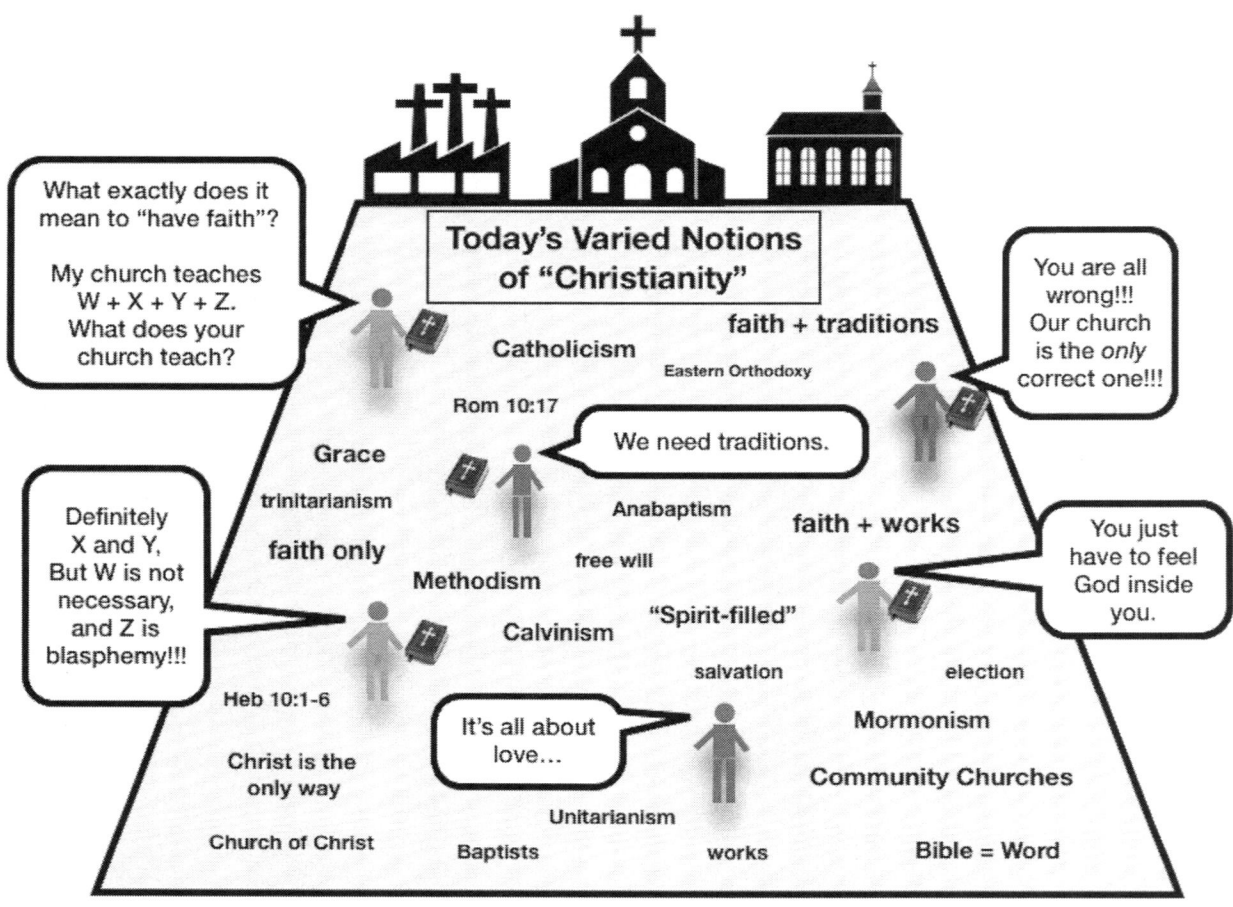

Our Lenses

We have each learned the Bible and its language through a particular set of lenses. These lenses both *create*, and are *created by*, our belief structures. They are constantly organizing and building upon our previous understandings, whether they are correct or not.

This study is an effort to remove our religious lenses, and contemplate the Bible from a first century perspective. Here we will strive to get underneath today's religious constructs and unearth the original foundations of "Christ," and what that meant to those first believers. While this will at times be critical of today's practices, ultimately I want it to be an encouragement to contemplate the "following of Christ" that was taught by those first messengers.

> **Confirmation Bias**
> The tendency to interpret new evidence as confirmation of one's existing beliefs or theories.

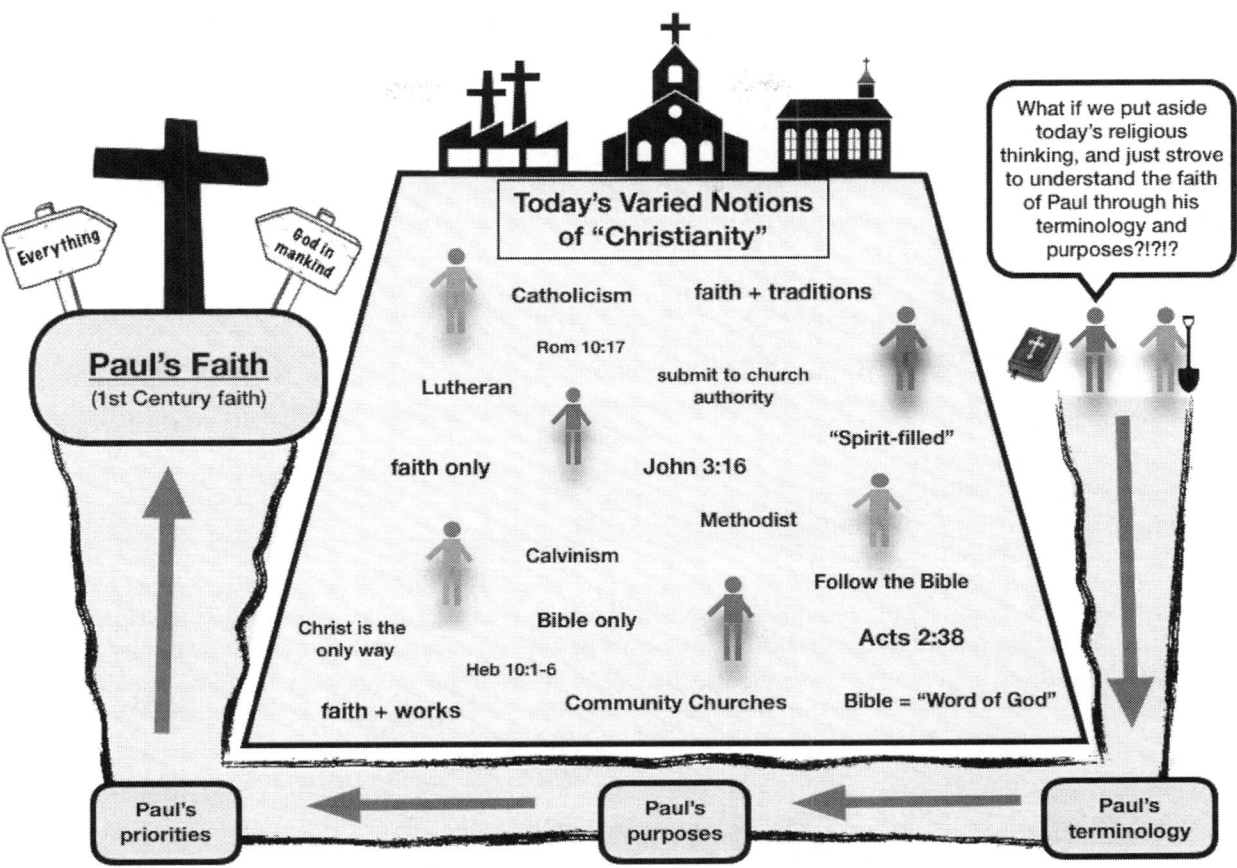

Paul's Answer to Everything

What if we took off our religious lenses and endeavored to understand Paul's purpose for his letters? What if we strove to understand the time and perspective of those first century recipients? What if we allowed Paul and the other New Testament writers to define the words they used? What if our solutions really were, as Paul stated, "in Christ"?

Years ago I decided to filter everything through one verse:

> For I determined to know nothing, but Jesus Christ and Him crucified.—1 Corinthians 2:2 NASB

Consider the three statements Paul makes in this verse:
- (1) He is determined to know Jesus Christ.
- (2) He is determined to know Christ crucified.
- (3) He has determined to know nothing else.

Paul writes this statement to a very divisive and broken church. The Corinthians were arrogant, boastful, jealous, fleshly, and spiritually immature. But Paul knows the Truth, and repeatedly

For I determined to know nothing, except for Jesus and Him crucified.
(1 Corinthians 2:2)

offers Christ as the solution. He believes that *Christ is the answer to everything*. These studies are built on this premise.

Role of the Bible

The first century letters (the New Testament) are our most significant and trusted record of the first century Christian perspective. We will trust their authenticity and accuracy as those first followers did, but will also not be afraid to challenge some of *today's* thinking. Again, **we are not challenging the Bible, but rather are challenging some of our traditional thoughts and approaches** *regarding* **the Bible**… So be prepared, for at times, we may need to reevaluate today's teachings that are not aligned with the thoughts and perspectives of what the Apostles taught.

The Purpose of These Studies

These studies are designed to allow the New Testament to speak for itself, so that we may understand the faith, psychology, and mindset of the Apostles. And ultimately, their mindset will help us better understand the nature and *superiority* of Christ, and what it meant to follow Him.

My purposes for these studies are:
1. to find the Truth
2. to understand the first-century perspective
3. to encourage a Christlike spirit
4. and to encourage you to think

The structure of these studies are primarily:
* a series of contextual passages
* questions
* commentary (to tie the ideas together)
* homework (in the back of book)

> **What Are Your Purposes for these Studies?**
>
> Are you looking for *the Truth*?
> Are you looking to grow?
> Are you looking for tools to help others?
> Or grow the church?
>
> _____
> _____
> _____
> _____

So Many Questions

At some point you will probably ask yourself "Why are there so many questions?" Well, I'm not really interested in your ability to repeat my thoughts. I want your faith to be *your* faith, and not a recording of mine. And the questions are going to be the key to opening the door to some new answers. I will tell you some of my theories, but I'd rather you understand it through your ability to think exegetically (also, we have too many people teaching their theories without understanding basic exegetical principles). Your growth and your faith need to come from answers that *you* find. My hope is that these questions and studies will stimulate both your mind and heart.

The art and science of asking questions is the source of all knowledge.

—Thomas Berger

Searching for Their Purpose

There are a few key words that can help us understand their purpose for a particular set of instructions. Noticing the key words of: **_Therefore_**, **_so that_**, **_in order that_**, and **_that_**— will help us understand the purpose of their lessons. This will ultimately help us comprehend the role of specific instructions and the spiritual likeness the author wants us to adopt.

Language vs. Meaning

Differences in opinions are never truly reconciled when we are defining our terms differently. We may say 'baptism', 'The Word', or 'Christ', but if I define them differently than you, then we may only agree in the verbiage, and not in what they actually represent.

This is also one of our biggest difficulties with evangelism. We may say things like "repentance is essential" or "we should love others," but if our definitions for "repentance" and "love" are different than theirs, then we are not going to be able to come to a real agreement. These studies will help remedy this …if we strive to understand the meanings of those first followers.

> This is one of the chief reasons that new Bible translations appear: language is never static, but fluid, alive, and changeable. What makes sense in one time may not make sense in another; usage of a particular word may disappear, or a word's meaning may change entirely…
> –Charles Spurgeoun

The message of Christ was an extremely effective message in the first four centuries. It spread like wildfire without any of today's technologies. This powerful message was conveyed from one person to another. They didn't need the internet, TV evangelists, radio ministries, or even a printing press… and yet the message they taught changed the world.

> For who hath known the mind of the Lord, that he should instruct him? But we have the mind of Christ.
> —1 Cor. 2:16 NASB

This study is about understanding _that_ message. We want to understand more than their terminology. We want to understand what that terminology represented to them. We want _their_ internal constructs.

Language is continually changing, so our verbiage must continue to change if we are going to communicate the original ideas. Much of today's difficulties are the result of clinging to terminology rather than their meanings. In these studies we will strive to remedy these linguistic hurdles with a constant questioning of their meanings and purposes.

Christos = Messiah = God in Man

In the New Testament, Christ not only refers to the person/ spirit that is in Jesus, but it is also a reference to the spirit that lives in His followers. Christ is found to be active in men prior to the physical existence of Jesus (1Cor. 10:4–5;1Pet. 1:10-11), and is consistently used in contexts where the Spirit is working in man.

> The Greek word "Christos" can mean
> Christ (or Christlikeness)
> Messiah (or messiah-ness)
> Anointed (or anointed-ness)

Also, the Greek word *Christos* may be translated to either Christ or Christlikeness. So depending upon the context or the need for clarification, I may refer to Christ as "Christlikeness" or the "Spirit of God in man."

The Holy Spirit

What if Holy Spirit was more simple and yet more powerful than anything we have been taught? What if we could recognize this Spirit within ourselves or others? Today, there is much confusion and mystery regarding the Holy Spirit. Some teach it as an internal "knowing" or "feeling," while others teach it as *a following of certain rules or examples*. These studies will not delve into the Holy Spirit until we define their terms and understand their purposes. Once we understand their basic notions and what it meant to *follow Christ*... then we will have a solid foundation for understanding the Holy Spirit.

When we do arrive at the subject of the Holy Spirit and its purposes (Studies #24-25), we will not rely upon opinions or feelings. We will rely upon the emphasis of the Bible —the Alpha and Omega—the person of Christ—the one who has *revealed* and *poured out* the Spirit of God.

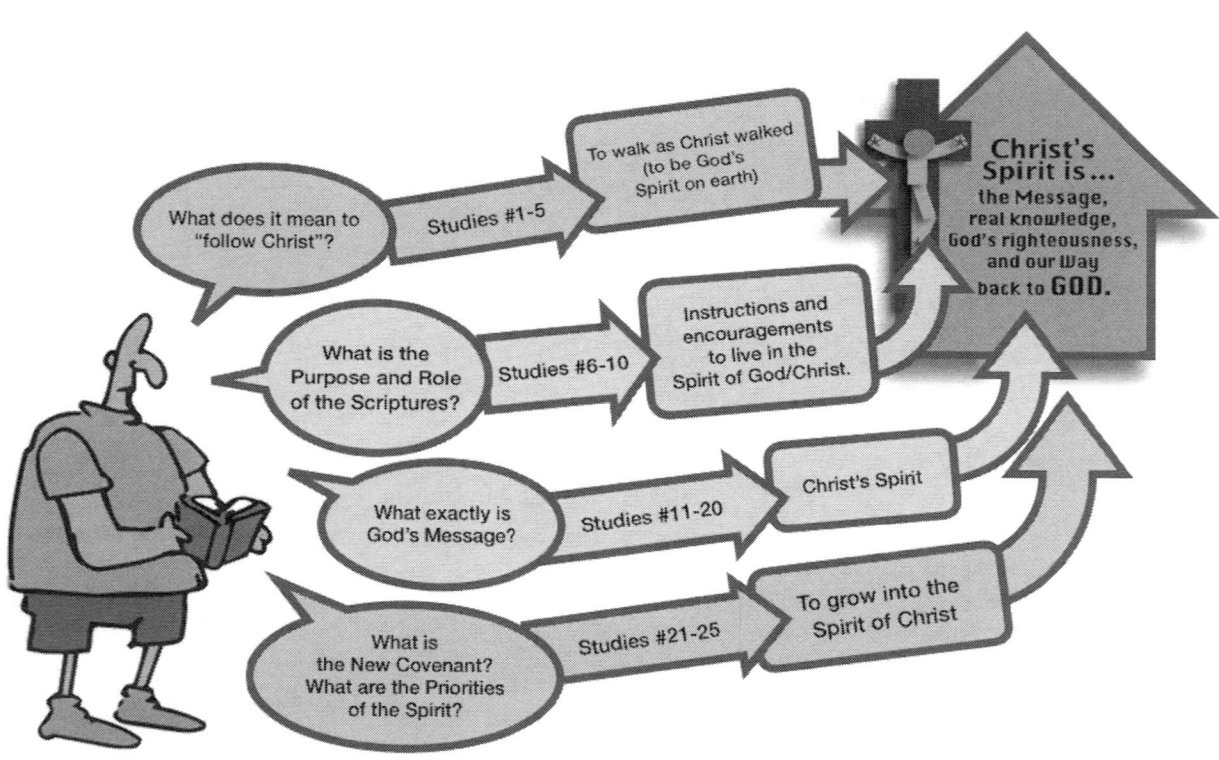

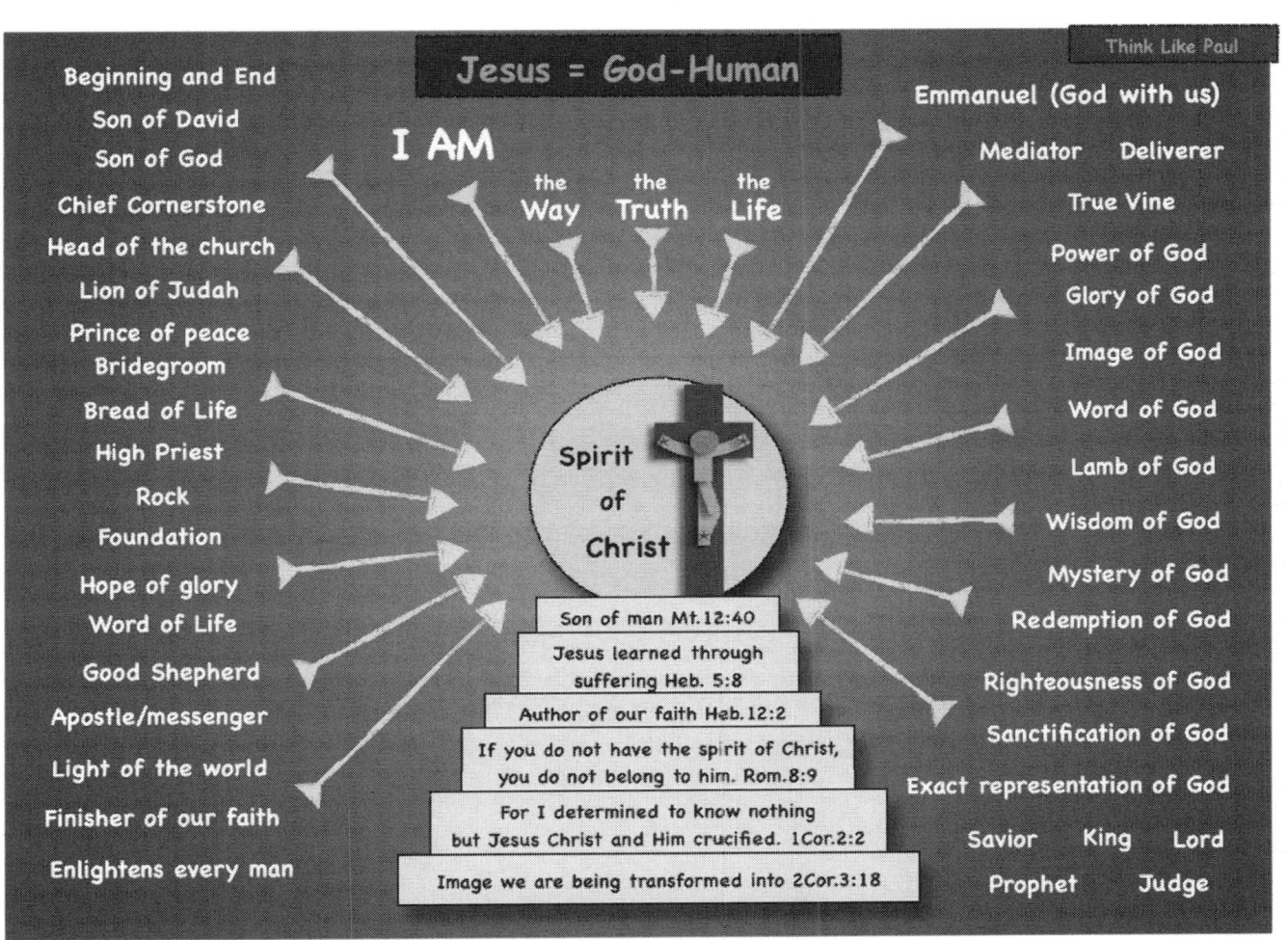

Part 1: How Would Paul Explain "Christianity"?

How is Jesus "the Way"?

Study #1: How Would Jesus Explain "Being Perfect"?
What did they call "perfect"? In what manner was Jesus perfect?

Study #2: How Would Paul Explain "Fulfilling the Law"?
Is it possible to fulfill the Law? If so, how?

Study #3: How Would Paul Explain "Avoiding Judgment"?
What is our standard? What protects us from judgement?

Study #4: How Would Paul Explain "Becoming Righteous"?
What exactly is righteousness? Can we be righteous? If so, how?

Study #5: How Would Paul Explain the "Goal of the Church"?
Why are we here? What is the purpose of man?

Conclusion: Christianity is Following Christ's Spirit

How is Jesus "the Way"?

When Jesus says "I am the Way," what exactly does He mean? How can a person be a "way"? Is it confessing that He is the Son of God? Is it attendance to a particular church? Is it obedience to a specific set of rules or traditions? What precisely does that mean? How would we know if we are in the "Way"?

> **I am the way,** and the truth, and the life. No one comes to the Father except through me. —John 14:6 ESV

The other day I saw the side of a container truck with the words "Christ is the answer" painted on the side. We Christians confess statements like these regularly… But what do we mean by a statement like that? How would we explain this "Christ is the answer" statement to someone who is suffering with drug addiction, lust, greed, or depression? Or more importantly, how would Jesus or Paul have explained this "Christ as the answer" notion?

> But this I confess to you, that according to **the Way,** which they call a sect, I worship the God of our fathers, believing everything laid down by the Law and written in the Prophets, having a hope in God, which these men themselves accept, that there will be a resurrection of both the just and the unjust.
> Acts 24:14-15 ESV

Literally Christos means "Messiah" or "Anointed One," which certainly describes their thoughts of Jesus … But what does Paul mean when he says: "It is no longer I who live, but Christ who lives in me"? How can the Messiah (or Anointed One) live in him? What does that really mean? One of the breakthroughs that really helped me understand the nature of Christ and what it means to "follow Him," came when I decided to chart the names and descriptions of Christ, and what that may have meant to those who walked with Him.

> But be doers of the word, and not hearers only, deceiving yourselves.
>
> James 1:22 ESV

I started to see that Paul was referring to something internal—not just internal in himself, but also, in the likeness of Jesus. There was an alignment of priorities and values that they had in common.[3] There was an internal framework that Paul had applied to himself. And it was this framework (set of priorities) that was the force that guided his decisions.

But one of the ideas that became clear was that Jesus was *more* than God. He was also a *very human* being. Not a "human" in a sinful or negative sense, but a human in his heart's capacities, a human in the manner for which God designed us, and maybe even a human in the Garden of Eden sense.

This helped me understand one particular question I've always struggled with: "How can the person of Jesus be 'the way'?"… I mean, what does that really mean? Every church claims that

---

[3] We will look into deeper into this framework in the "Priorities of Christ" and "Testing the Spirits." (studies #21 and #25)

"He is the way," but again, what do they mean by that? Do they mean attendance to their church? Do they mean believing that Jesus came from God? What specifically does that mean? Or more importantly, What did it mean to those in the first century? Is it thinking certain thoughts? If so, which ones? Is it doing certain things? If so, which ones? What does it really mean to "follow Christ"?

From this place I started to see more clearly that Christ represented three notions simultaneously:

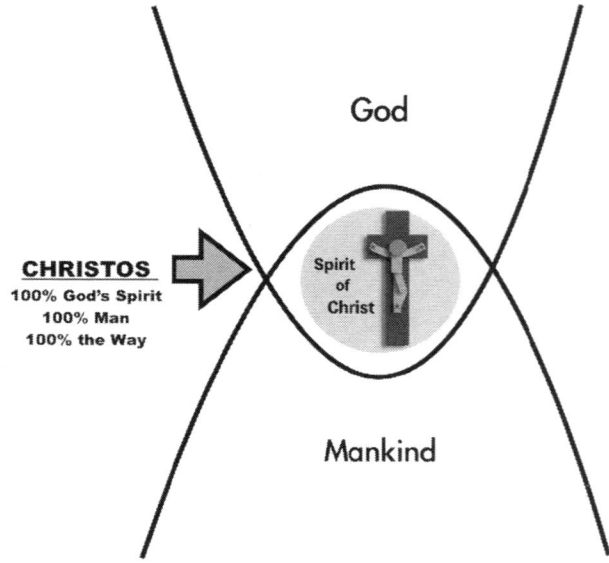

1) **100% the likeness of God** (exact representation of God)

2) **100% human** (flesh and blood, learned obedience, suffered, bled, and died)

3) **100% the Way** (our path back to alignment/intimacy with God)

From this notion, "Christ" was/is a spiritual being that we can intimately know, where His likeness *is* "the way." [4]

Today, we tend to place Him as an unknowable being and a likeness that cannot be attained. But these notions seem to demean one of His missions of coming to earth:

> I made known to them your name, and I will continue to make it known, that the love with which you have loved me may be in them, and I in them." —John 17:26 ESV

Christ was clearly their answer, and in these first 5 studies we will contemplate their perspective of certain notions, and juxtapose them against some of today's teachings.

---

[4] Okay… Then what does that mean? … At the time, my best guess was that it was developing His priorities and values (love, joy, forgiveness…). And though this didn't make Christianity any easier for me, it did seem to make sense with the style and nature of their letters … And pretty much everything else I'd come to understand. In the final studies (21-25), we will contemplate how this Christ-Spirit is more than a set of virtues.

Study #1: How Would Jesus Explain "Being Perfect"?

Would you want to hang out with someone who was "perfect"? Would you want to play chess or *Call of Duty* with someone who was perfect? Is this what we mean when we say Jesus was "perfect"?

> What is perfection?
> What specifically made Jesus "perfect"?
> How specifically did they describe it?

Today we may describe a meal or a baseball game as "perfect". The dictionary defines it as flawless or free from defect. But is that the manner in which Jesus or the Apostles considered it? Does our definition carry the same meaning as the original Greek?

Strong's Concordance states that perfect (Gr. teleios) means complete in all its parts; full grown; of age; especially of the completeness of Christian character.

As far as the New Testament records, Jesus only used the word "perfect" (*teleioi*) twice. In Matthew 5:43-48, Jesus teaches that we should be perfect as God is perfect.

> You have heard that it was said, 'You shall love your neighbor and hate your enemy.' But I say to you, **love your enemies** and **pray for those who persecute you**, so that you may be **sons of your Father** who is in heaven. For he makes his sun rise on the evil and on the good, and sends rain on the just and on the unjust. For if you love those who love you, what reward do you have? Do not even the tax collectors do the same? And if you greet only your brothers, what more are you doing than others? Do not even the Gentiles do the same? **therefore be perfect, as your heavenly Father is perfect**. NASB

Questions:
1. "And" and "so that" connects what three ideas?

2. What does Jesus equate with the perfection of the Heavenly Father?

3. How was Jesus perfect?

4. How is the modern notion of perfection different than Jesus'?

5. Is perfection a "doing," or a way of the Spirit?

6. Is this consistent with our previous studies?

God, help me understand the Spirit of Your Son

so that I may know You

Here Jesus is clearly equating "perfection" to loving your enemies as God does. Jesus also uses "perfect" (*teleios*) when talking to the rich young ruler in Matthew 19:16-22.

And behold, a man came up to him, saying, 'Teacher, what good deed must I do to have eternal life?' And he said to him, 'Why do you ask me about what is good? There is only one who is good. If you would enter life, keep the commandments.' He said to him, 'Which ones?' And Jesus said, 'You shall not murder, You shall not commit adultery, You shall not steal, You shall not bear false witness, Honor your father and mother, and, You shall love your neighbor as yourself.' The young man said to him, 'All these I have kept. What do I still lack?' Jesus said to him, 'If you would be **perfect** (*teleios*), go, sell what you possess and give to the poor, and you will have treasure in heaven; and come, follow me.' When the young man heard this he went away sorrowful, for he had great possessions. —Matthew 19:16-22 ESV

Questions:

7.   In Matthew 19, what actions does Jesus connect with "being perfect"?

8.   Is this consistent with the Matthew 5:43-48?

9.   Jesus demonstrated another level of love by dying on the cross for his enemies. Does this include you? Why would He love humanity so much?

10. How did Christ handle suffering?

Therefore, since Christ has suffered in the flesh, **arm yourselves also with the same purpose**, because he who has suffered in the flesh has ceased from sin, so as to live the rest of the time in the flesh no longer for the lusts of men, but for the will of God. —1 Peter 4:1–2 NASB

11. What purpose was Peter referring to? How can we "arm ourselves with the same purpose" of Christ?

God, help me understand how I may be a child of God

What would Jesus say?
Perfection is loving your enemies as God does. As it is seen in Jesus, it is a commitment to love regardless of circumstances.

and love my enemies as You do

Be Perfect as God is Perfect?!?

Therefore you are to be perfect, as your heavenly Father is perfect.
—Matthew 5:48 NASB

Let's look at the context.

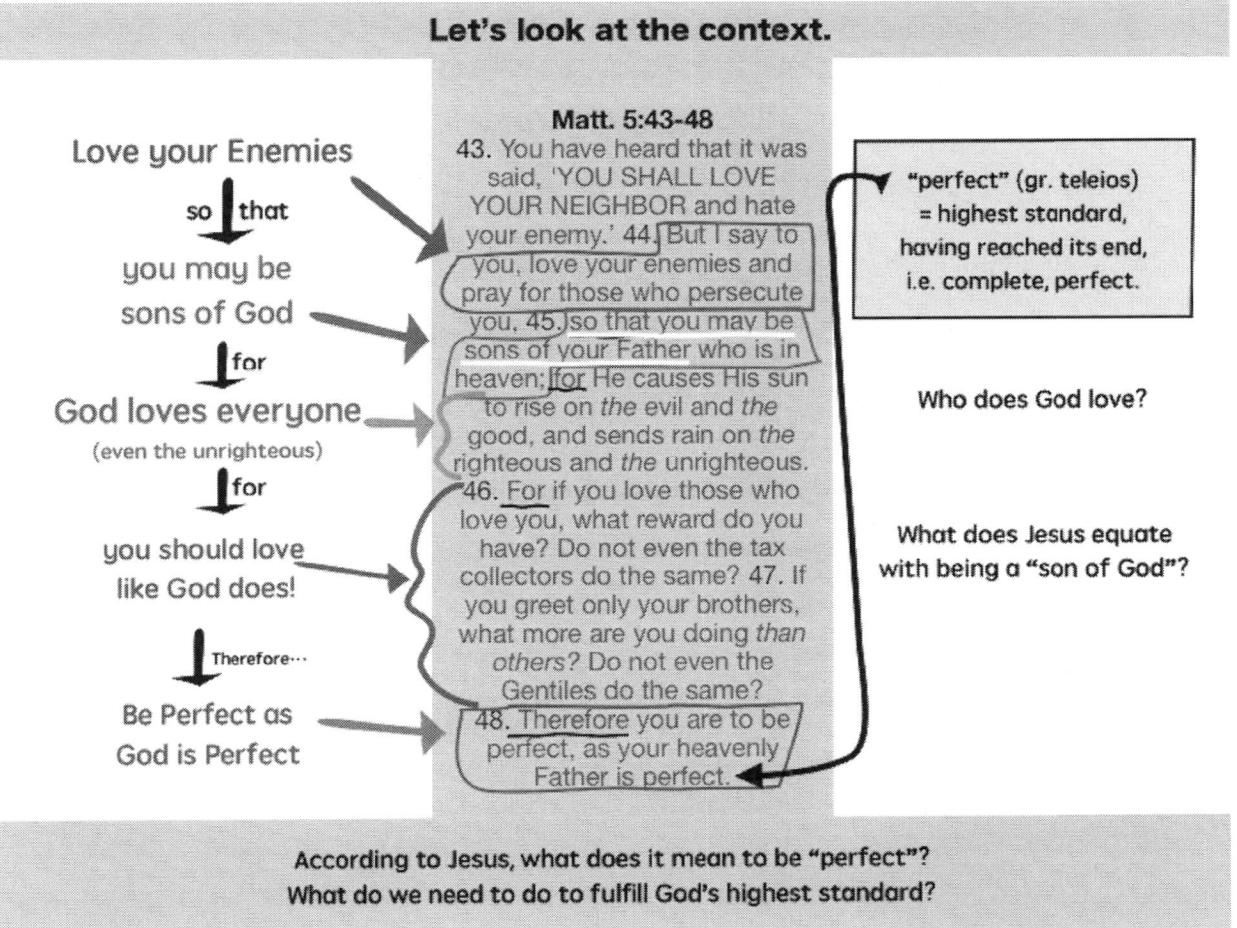

Love your Enemies

so ↓ that

you may be sons of God

↓ for

God loves everyone
(even the unrighteous)

↓ for

you should love like God does!

↓ Therefore···

Be Perfect as God is Perfect

Matt. 5:43-48
43. You have heard that it was said, 'YOU SHALL LOVE YOUR NEIGHBOR and hate your enemy.' 44. But I say to you, love your enemies and pray for those who persecute you. 45. so that you may be sons of your Father who is in heaven; for He causes His sun to rise on *the* evil and *the* good, and sends rain on *the* righteous and *the* unrighteous. 46. For if you love those who love you, what reward do you have? Do not even the tax collectors do the same? 47. If you greet only your brothers, what more are you doing *than others*? Do not even the Gentiles do the same? 48. Therefore you are to be perfect, as your heavenly Father is perfect.

"perfect" (gr. teleios) = highest standard, having reached its end, i.e. complete, perfect.

Who does God love?

What does Jesus equate with being a "son of God"?

According to Jesus, what does it mean to be "perfect"?
What do we need to do to fulfill God's highest standard?

Perry Stiltz   *Think Like Paul: Searching for the Message that Changed the World*

Love is the only force capable of transforming an enemy into a friend.
—Martin Luther King Jr.

Study #2: How Would Paul Explain "Fulfilling the Law"?

> Do not think that I came to abolish the Law or the Prophets; I did not come to abolish but to fulfill. —Matthew 5:17 NIV

What Jesus declares in regard to the Old Testament laws:

> Then one of them, a lawyer, asked *Him a question,* testing Him, and saying, "Teacher, which *is* the great commandment in the law?" Jesus said to him, "'You shall love the Lord your God with all your heart, with all your soul, and with all your mind.' This is *the* first and great commandment. And *the* second *is* like it: 'You shall love your neighbor as yourself.' On these two commandments hang **all** the Law and the Prophets."
> —Matthew 22:35-40 NKJV

Questions:

1. What verb does He use in these commandments?

2. Which law(s) is Jesus talking about?

Paul and James are the only New Testament writers who use the terminology of "fulfilling the law" in the following references:

> **Owe nothing to anyone except to love one another; for he who loves his neighbor has fulfilled the law.** For this, 'You shall not commit adultery, You shall not murder, You shall not steal, You shall not covet,' and if there is any other commandment, it is summed up in this saying, 'You shall love your neighbor as yourself.' Love does no wrong to a neighbor; therefore **love is the fulfillment of the law.** —Romans 13:8–10 NASB

> For you were called to freedom, brethren; only do not turn your freedom into an opportunity for the flesh, but through love serve one another. For **the whole Law is fulfilled in one word, in the statement, 'You shall love your neighbor as yourself.'** —Galatians 5:13–14 NASB

> Bare one another's burdens, and **thus fulfill the law of Christ.**
> —Galatians 6:2 ESV

> If you really **fulfill** *the* **royal law**[5] according to the Scripture, "You shall love your neighbor as yourself," you do well. —James 2:8 NKJV

---

[5] (note: 'royal law' literally means 'law of the king' in the original Greek)

3. What is the theme for "fulfilling the law"?

4. Which of the following is probably the way that Jesus fulfilled the law?
    a) Studying the law, then making sure He lived within its regulations
    b) Striving to not sin
    c) Following all the ordinances of Leviticus
    d) Loving all people, even enemies, despite experiencing humiliation, beatings, scourging, and crucifixion

5. Does fulfilling the law conflict with Jesus' definition of being perfect in Matthew 5:44–48? (Study #1)

Consider some of Paul's thoughts on "law" in relation to the Spirit:

I love because

He first loved me

> But the fruit of the Spirit is love, joy, peace, patience, kindness, goodness, faithfulness, gentleness, self-control; against such things there is no law. —Galatians 5:22 NASB

> All things are lawful for me, but not all things are profitable. All things are lawful for me, but I will not be mastered by anything.—1 Corinthians. 6:12 NASB

> All things are lawful, but not all things are profitable. All things are lawful, but not all things edify. Let no one seek his own *good,* but that of his neighbor. —1 Corinthians 10:23 NASB

> But if you are led by the Spirit, you are not under the Law. —Galatians 5:18 NASB

6. According to these passages, what types of activities are lawful for Paul?

7. What do you think is the mindset Paul wants the Galatians and the Corinthians to have?

> Therefore there is now no condemnation for those who are in Christ Jesus. For the **law of the Spirit of life in Christ Jesus has set you free** from the law of sin and of death. For what the Law could not do, weak as it was through the flesh, God *did:* sending His own Son in the likeness of sinful flesh and *as an offering* for sin, He condemned sin in the flesh, **so that the requirement of the Law might be fulfilled in us**, who do not walk according to the flesh but according to the Spirit. —Romans 8:1–4 NASB

Let's review how Paul connects some of these ideas:
> **so that** - connects a concept with its purpose
> **might be** - declares a potentiality

8. What is the law that sets us free?

9. How does he describe this "law of sin and death"?

10. According to this passage "the requirement of the Law might be fulfilled in_____."
    c) Paul
    d) Jesus
    e) us

11. How can the requirement of the Law be fulfilled in us?
    a) by following the examples of the New Testament
    b) by believing that Jesus is the Son of God
    c) by walking according to the Spirit of Christ

What would Paul say?
Jesus "fulfilled the Law" by fully loving God and His neighbor
(despite torture and death).

God, help me
understand
your kind of love

So that I may
fulfill the Law

Oh, I don't reject Christ. I love Christ.
It's just that so many of you Christians are so unlike Christ…
If Christians would really live according to the teachings of Christ,
as found in the Bible, all of India would be Christian today.
—Mahatma Gandhi

How are We Going to be Judged?

2Cor. 5.1-10 NASB

if our physical life is destroyed, we have house from God

↓ for

we want to be clothed spiritually (Spirit of Christ)

↓ inasmuch

to the degree we have clothed ourselves w/the Spirit of Christ we will not be found naked

so ↓ that

Our physical life will be overtaken by the Spirit of Christ

We were made for this PURPOSE

↓ Therefore...

be courageous, walk by faith, not by the physical we want to be pleasing to Him

↓ for

We must all appear before the judgment seat of Christ

so ↓ that

we may receive according to what we have done (good or bad)

¹For we know that if the earthly tent which is our house is torn down, we have a building from God, a house not made with hands, eternal in the heavens. ²For indeed in this *house* we groan, longing to be clothed with our dwelling from heaven, ³inasmuch as we, having put it on, will not be found naked. ⁴For indeed while we are in this tent, we groan, being burdened, because we do not want to be unclothed but to be clothed, so that what is mortal will be swallowed up by life. ⁵Now He who prepared us for this very purpose is God, who gave to us the Spirit as a pledge. ⁶Therefore, being always of good courage, and knowing that while we are at home in the body we are absent from the Lord —⁷for we walk by faith, not by sight—⁸we are of good courage, I say, and prefer rather to be absent from the body and to be at home with the Lord. ⁹Therefore we also have as our ambition, whether at home or absent, to be pleasing to Him. ¹⁰For we must all appear before the judgment seat of Christ, so that each one may be recompensed for his deeds in the body, according to what he has done, whether good or bad.

How do we clothe ourselves with the "dwelling from Heaven"?

Could this be the idea of "putting on Christ"?

Could this be the idea of "building each other up in Christ"?

Why is it so important for the church to grow into Christ's Spirit?

Could committing ourselves to the Spirit in Jesus this be the manner in which we escape judgment?

Could this be the manner our "mortal will be swallowed up by life"?

Think Like Paul: Searching for the Message that Changed the World

Study #3: How Would Paul Explain "Avoiding Judgment"?

For just as the Father raises the dead and gives them life, even so the Son gives life to whom he is pleased to give it. Moreover, **the Father judges no one, but has entrusted all judgment to the Son.**—John 5:21-22 NIV

Let's inspect some passages that may give us some insight into God's judgment.

Clothed with Christ

2 Corinthians 5:1–10

> What is the standard by which we will be judged? Is it the Bible? Is it Christ? Is it attendance to a particular church? Is it a particular set of actions, doctrines, thoughts or feelings? How can we have confidence for the day of judgment?

For we know that if the earthly tent which is our house is torn down, we have a building from God, a house not made with hands, eternal in the heavens. For indeed in this *house* we groan, longing to be clothed with our dwelling from heaven, **inasmuch** as we, having put it on, will not be found naked. For indeed while we are in this tent, we groan, being burdened, because we do not want to be unclothed but to be clothed, so that what is mortal will be swallowed up by life. Now He who prepared us for this very purpose is God, who gave to us the Spirit as a pledge. Therefore, being always of good courage, and knowing that while we are at home in the body we are absent from the Lord— for we walk by faith, not by sight— we are of good courage, I say, and prefer rather to be absent from the body and to be at home with the Lord. Therefore we also have as our ambition, whether at home or absent, to be pleasing to Him. For we must all appear before the **judgment seat of Christ**, so that each one may be recompensed for his deeds in the body, according to what he has done, whether good or bad. ESV

Questions:

1. Paul walks by _____, and not by _____.

2. What is the "earthly tent"? What is the "building from God"?

3. According to 5:10, we will all appear before the judgment seat of _____.

4. To what degree will we be found naked? What does our nakedness represent in regard to judgment day?

5. Does "inasmuch" imply varying levels of nakedness or clothing?

God, help me to walk by faith in the

Spirit of

Jesus

6. With what are we to be clothed? What does that likely mean?

> Speak and act as those who are going to be judged by the law that gives freedom, because judgment without mercy will be shown to anyone who has not been merciful. Mercy triumphs over judgment. —James 2:12-13 NIV

> Therefore do not pronounce judgment before the time, before the Lord comes, who will bring to light the things now hidden in darkness and will disclose the purposes of the heart. Then each one will receive his commendation from God. —1 Corinthians 4:5

7. What is greater than judgment?

8. What will be disclosed at the time of judgment?

Confidence in the Day of Judgment
Notice what gives John "confidence in the day of judgment."

> No one has ever seen God; if we love one another, God abides in us and his love is perfected in us. By this we know that we abide in him and he in us, because he has given us of his Spirit. And we have seen and testify that the Father has sent his Son to be the Savior of the world. Whoever confesses that Jesus is the Son of God, God abides in him, and he in God. So we have come to know and to believe the love that God has for us. God is love, and whoever abides in love abides in God, and God abides in him. By this is love perfected with us, **<u>so that</u> we may have confidence for the day of judgment**, because as he is so also are we in this world. —1 John 4:12-17 ESV

Questions:
9. What does he equate with "God abiding in us"?

10. How do we know that we abide in God?

11. What gives John "confidence for the day of judgment"?

> But he who is spiritual appraises all things, yet he himself is appraised by no one.
>
> 1 Cor. 2:15
> NASB

What does "living in Christ" mean?
In the following passages we have notions of "living in Christ."

From a very practical standpoint these passages never made sense to me. I mean… How can I live in another person? What exactly does that mean?

> **I can do all things through him** who strengthens me.
> —Philippians 4:13 ESV

> I have been crucified with Christ and I no longer live, but **Christ lives in me.** The life I now live in the body, I live by faith in the Son of God, who loved me and gave himself for me. —Galatians 2:20 NIV

> Likewise, my brothers, you also have died to the law through the **body of Christ,** so that[6] you <u>may</u> belong to another, to him who has been raised from the dead, <u>in order that</u> we <u>may</u> bear fruit for God. —Romans 7:4 ESV

Reread the previous statements of Paul with the notion that "Christ" represents a measure of godly qualities (like love, strength, courage, compassion, joy…) that is seen in Jesus… Then answer the following questions:

12. Can you see how "Christ" can live in Paul?

13. Can you see how "Christ" can live in us?

14. Do these passages fit Paul's situation?

15. Are they practical teachings for both the recipients and us?

What would Paul say?
We are going to be judged by Christ and what is within our hearts. And as we have put on Christ (likeness), we will be clothed on judgment day (because our sins will be covered by Christ).

The Apostle John explicitly teaches **love** "so that we may have confidence for the day of judgment."

Clothed with Jesus' Spirit = Avoiding Judgment

God, help me understand how I may clothe myself in the Spirit of Jesus

so that I may be confident in the day of Judgment

---

[6]Note: "so that" and "in order that" signifies a purpose, while "may" denotes a potentiality.

More Passages on Judgment

Judgment on those who:
>   have murderous intentions (Mt.5:21)
>   calling someone a "fool" (Mt.5:22)
>   do evil (Jn.5:29)
>   resist authority (Rom.13:2)
>   eating and drinking w/o discerning the body (1Cor.11:29) (Study #22)

Passing Judgment
>   Do not pass Judgment…
>> by appearances, but by righteous judgment (Jn. 7:24)
>> on the servant of another (Rom. 14:4)
>> on your brother (Rom.14:10)
>   Passing judgment = condemning yourselves (Rom. 2:1-2)

Jesus' Judgment:
>   Jesus' Judgment is: **just** (because He seeks the will of God - Jn 5:30) and **true** (because it is the Father's judgment Jn:8:16) for the purpose of causing the blind to see, and the seeing to be blind (Jn.9:39).

Judgment on the World and the Devil:
>   Now is the judgment of this world; the ruler will be cast out (Jn.12:31)
>   Jesus sends the Spirit to convict the world and the devil (Jn.16:8, 11)
>   Heavens and earth are being reserved for fire for the ungodly (2Pet.3.7)
>   God comes with thousands of "holy ones" to execute judgment (Jude 1:15)

Judgment on Israel:
>   Mt. 10:15;11:22-25; 12:41-42; Jn. 3:19

No Judgment
>   Believe in Jesus = no judgment (Jn 5:24)

Study #4: How Would Paul Explain "Becoming Righteous"?

What causes us to be righteous? Is it certain actions, thoughts, or feelings? Let's consider some of Paul's thoughts on righteousness:

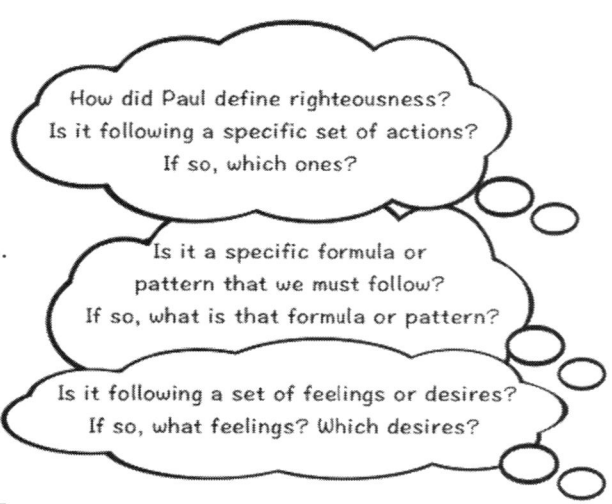

> But now apart from the Law the **righteousness of God has been manifested**, being witnessed by the Law and the Prophets.
> —Romans 3:21 NASB

> But by His doing you are in Christ Jesus, who became to us **wisdom** from God, and **righteousness**, and **sanctification**, and **redemption**, so that, just as it is written, "LET HIM WHO BOASTS, BOAST IN THE LORD." —1Corinthians 1:30-31 NASB

> For **Christ is the end (goal) of the law for righteousness** to everyone who believes.
> —Romans 10:4 NASB

Questions:

1. What is the difference between righteous and righteousness?

2. According to the previous passages, what/who is the "righteousness of God"?

is the Goal of Law

3. What/Who is the "end(goal) of the law of righteousness"?

4. If Christ is righteousness itself, then how can we become righteous?

Paul equates Christ with righteousness. He not only is righteous, but *is* righteousness itself. The New Testament writers consistently equated righteousness with God, Christ, and living in His Spirit:

> He made Him who knew no sin to be sin on our behalf, so that we might become the righteousness of God in Him.—2 Corinthians 5:21 NASB

Notice the two parts that connect Christ and us: "so that" and "we might." "So that" indicates God's purpose, and "we might" refers to a potentiality. This is **not** a consequential sentence of:

"Christ became sin on our behalf, *therefore* we are the righteousness of God." But rather, **this is an offer for us *to become* the righteousness of God.** God did His part by sending His Son to become sin on our behalf. If we wish to take Him up on his offer of righteousness, we choose to live in His Spirit.

Christlikeness is Righteousness

Now let us organize a few of these ideas regarding Law, righteousness, sin, and Christ, and see if we can come out with a theme:

God, help my heart understand how

the Spirit in Jesus

= Righteousness

1. Christ = righteousness of God (Rom. 3:21; 1 Cor. 1:30)
2. Christ = the goal of the law of righteousness (Rom. 10:4)
3. We should have the mind of Christ. (1 Cor. 2:16)
4. We can become the righteousness of God in Christ. (2 Cor. 5:21)
5. If you don't have the Spirit of Christ, you do not belong to Him. (Rom. 8:9)
6. Since we have put on our spiritual clothing (Christ), we will not be found naked ... Before the judgment seat of Christ. (2 Cor. 5:3–10) (Study #3)
7. Sin in Hebrew comes from the notion of "missing the target."

While these are just a few, notice a consistent

theme: **Living in Christ = Righteousness**

The righteousness displayed by Jesus challenged the Jews' concept of righteousness. They had believed that righteousness was about executing the rules correctly. But the righteousness in Jesus is not meticulous obedience to law. What we see in both Christ, and the apostles, is an all-consuming focus on the Spirit and its development in people.[7]

How Do We Hit the Target?!?

If sin = missing the target,
and Christ = Righteousness, then...
Don't we need to be like Christ to be righteous?
Wouldn't that make us the righteousness of God?
Wouldn't being Christlike be hitting the target?

Sin (missing the mark)

Righteousness (christlikeness)

Jesus is the son of God because He has the same spiritual likeness as God. He is not *the* Son because of His physical body. He is God's Son because of His Spirit. He is *the* Son because He is aligned with the infinite Spirit that created all things.

The Substance Belongs to Christ

Christ, the Spirit of God, contains the only substance that matters:

---

[7] This is reinforced by the authors of the gospels, for they make no mention of Jesus' obedience to the Law.

Therefore no one is to act as your judge in regard to food or drink or in respect to a festival or a new moon or a Sabbath day—things **which are a mere shadow** of what is to come; but **the substance belongs to Christ**. —Colossians 2:16–17 NASB

Traditions, festivals, Sabbaths, and some crazy new moon thing are all just shadows. This fits with Paul's notion that things that are not *of Christ* are insignificant, and will eventually be burned up (1Cor. 3:9-15). This Christ-Spirit that they were striving to grow into was *the real thing* and *the only thing*.

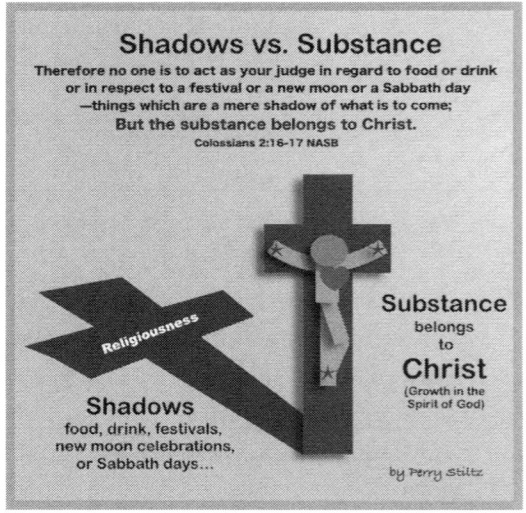

Either make the tree good and its fruit good, or make the tree bad and its fruit bad; for the tree is known by its fruit. You brood of vipers, how can you, being evil, speak what is good? For the mouth speaks out of that which fills the heart. —Mark 12:33-34 NASB

And Jesus said to him, "Why do you call Me good? No one is good except God alone." —Mark 10:18 NASB

Each word and every action spring from our hearts. Everything that is good is *of* God. In fact, He is the only one that is good. Their emphasis was not on traditions or regulations, but rather on the Christ-Spirit that was revealed in the person of Jesus.

What is our Motivation?
But what about giving, prayer and other things we consider "good"? Aren't those things "good" in the sight of God? In Jesus' sermon on the mount, He refers to 3 common religious acts that were associated with being godly, giving, prayer, and fasting:

Beware of practicing your righteousness before men **to be noticed by them**; otherwise **you have no reward with your Father** who is in heaven. So when you give to the poor, do not sound a trumpet before you, as the hypocrites do in the synagogues and in the streets, so that they may be honored by men. Truly I say to you, **they have their reward in full**.
—Matthew 6:1–2 NASB

When you pray, you are not to be like the hypocrites; for they love to stand and pray in the synagogues and on the street corners **so that they may be seen by men**. Truly I say to you, **they have their reward in full**. —Matthew 6:5 NASB

Whenever you fast, do not put on a gloomy face as the hypocrites *do,* for they neglect their appearance **so that they will be noticed by men** when they are fasting. Truly I say to you, **they have their reward in full**. —Matthew 6:16 NASB

Questions:

5. What are the common phrases in each of these verses in Matthew chapter 6?

6. Did they receive a reward from God? Why or why not?

7. Was their giving righteous?

8. Was their praying righteous?

9. Was their fasting righteous?

10. Is being crucified righteous?

Christ is Not a System
We human beings have a tendency to turn that which is spiritual into some repeatable physical form. We want to ritualize and systematize our faith. We would rather think "what do I have to do?" rather than "who do I need to be?" We make *righteousness* = X + Y + Z. This can be church attendance, donations, Bible study, or whatever.

One of the problems in equating righteousness with a formula is that over time our "righteousness" tends to become routine and unconscious. We act from habit rather than compassion and service. All actions, if they are to be righteous, must be rooted in the right motivation. Christianity is about being alive and awake and providing the encouragement that causes others to think positively of God and His spiritual Messenger—Christ.

> **Is Professing Belief Enough?!?**
>
> Today many profess that because they "believe," that they have salvation.
>
> **But what is "belief"?**
>
> Is it simply a cognitive awareness of Christ and what He did?
>
> Or is "belief" a confidence that Christ's Spirit is **our pathway** back to God?
>
> On that day many will say to me, 'Lord, Lord, did we not prophesy in your name, and cast out demons in your name, and do many mighty works in your name?' And then will I declare to them, 'I never knew you; depart from me, you workers of lawlessness.'
> — Matthew 7:22–23 ESV

Let your light shine before men in such a way <u>that</u> **they may see your good works**, and **glorify your Father** who is in heaven. —Matthew 5:16 NASB

But Israel, which **followed after the law** of righteousness, hath not attained to the law of righteousness. —Romans 9:31 KJV

11. What was Israel striving for?

The Son is the radiance of God's glory and the exact representation of his being.
—Hebrews 1:3 NIV

Now **the Lord is the Spirit**, and where the Spirit of the Lord is, there is liberty. But we all, with unveiled face, beholding as in a mirror the glory of the Lord, are being transformed into the same image from glory to glory, just as from the Lord, the Spirit.
—2 Corinthians 3:17–18NASB

Those who think they know something do not yet know as they ought to know. But whoever loves God is known by God.
—1 Corinthians 8:2–3 NIV

12. What were Paul and Jesus *striving for*? How is their striving different than Israel's "following after the Law of righteousness"?

13. If we are going to strive for something, what should we be striving for?

His Spirit = Our Pathway

Many teach that we just need to "believe," without understanding that the first century notion of "believing in Christ" conveyed the idea of following His Spirit... Remember, Christ taught God's forgiveness for those spirits <u>who would give that forgiveness</u> to others.

"but if you do not forgive others their trespasses, neither will your Father forgive your trespasses."—Mathew 6:15 ESV

"...Then his master summoned him and said to him, 'You wicked servant! I forgave you all that debt because you pleaded with me. And should not you have had mercy on your fellow servant, as I had mercy on you?' And in anger his master delivered him to the jailers, until he should pay all his debt. So also my heavenly Father will do to every one of you, if you do not forgive your brother from your heart."
—Matthew 18:32-35 ESV

What would Paul say?
The Jews equated righteousness with a fleshly(physical) obedience to the Law, rather than the Spirit(of God) that the Law was pointing toward. But now, through Christ (the adopting of Jesus' Spirit) God has given us the *opportunity* to be the *righteousness of God*.

In Jesus' Spirit = we are Righteous

Through growth in

I may become the righteousness of God

When I understand that everything happening to me
is to make me more Christlike, it resolves a great deal of anxiety.
—A. W. Tozer

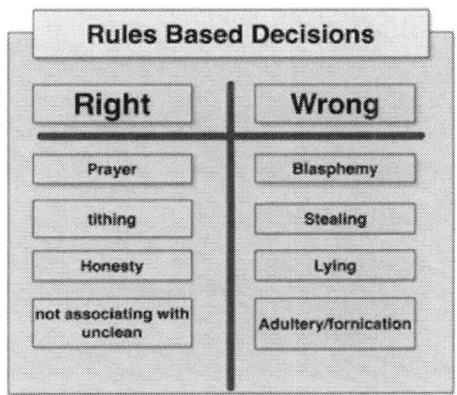

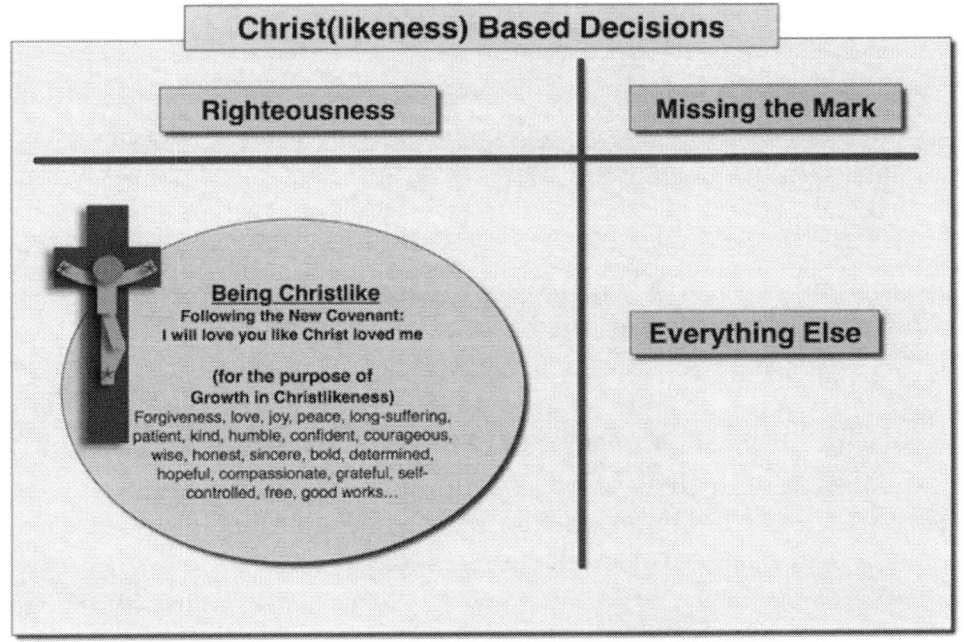

Study #5: How Would Paul Explain the "Goal of the Church"?

What is the end goal? What did Paul want the readers to see? What did he want them to do? Is there a specific set of rituals or actions to perform? What would *obedience to God* mean to Paul? Was there a specific set of actions, feelings, or thoughts that Paul and the other New Testament writers wanted others to take?

Consider these passages to the arrogant immature church in Corinth:

Do you not know that you are God's temple and that **God's Spirit dwells in you?**—1 Corinthians 3:16 ESV

Or do you not know that your body is a temple of the **Holy Spirit within you**, whom you have from God?—1 Corinthians 6:19 ESV

Therefore I exhort you, **be imitators of me.** For this reason I have sent to you Timothy, who is my beloved and faithful child in the Lord, and **he will remind you of my ways which are in Christ,** just as I teach everywhere in every church. —1 Corinthians 4:16-17 NASB

And we all, with unveiled face, beholding the glory of the Lord, **are being transformed into the same image** from one degree of glory to another. For this comes from the Lord who is the Spirit. —2 Corinthians 3:18 ESV

Always bearing about in the body the dying of the Lord Jesus, **that the life also of Jesus might be made manifest in our body.** —2 Corinthians 4:10 KJV

And what agreement hath the temple of God with idols? **For ye are the temple of the living God**; as God hath said, **I will dwell in them, and walk in** *them;* and I will be their God, and they shall be my people. —2 Corinthians 6:16 KJV

I am here to have the same mind and faith as

For who hath known the mind of the Lord, that he may instruct Him? But **we have the mind of Christ.** —1 Corinthians 2:16 KJV

Now consider these verses to the more judgmental and legalistic churches of Rome, Galatia and others:

However, you are not in the flesh but in the Spirit, if indeed the Spirit of God dwells in you. But **if anyone does not have the Spirit of Christ, he does not belong to Him**. —Romans 8:9 NASB

For those whom He foreknew, He also predestined *to become* **conformed to the image of His Son**, so that He would be the firstborn among many brethren. —Romans 8:29 NASB

Now the God of patience and of comfort grant you to **be of the same mind one with another according to Christ Jesus**. —Romans 15:5 ASV

But when He who had set me apart, even from my mother's womb, and called me through His grace, **was pleased to reveal His Son in me,** so that I might preach Him among the Gentiles, I did not immediately consult with flesh and blood. —Galatians 1:15–16 NASB

My little children, for whom I am again in the anguish of childbirth **until Christ is formed in you!**—Galatians 4:19 ESV

It is no longer I who live, but Christ who lives in me. And the life I now live in the flesh I live by faith in the Son of God, who loved me and gave himself for me.—Galatians 2:20 ESV

And have **put on the new self, which is being renewed in knowledge after the image of its creator**. —Colossians 3:10 ESV

Therefore **be imitators of God**, as beloved children. And walk in love, as Christ loved us and gave himself up for us, a fragrant offering and sacrifice to God. —Ephesians 5:1-2 ESV

And **put on the new self, which in** *the likeness of* **God** has been created in righteousness and holiness of the truth. —Ephesians 4:24 NASB

> It concerns us to know the purpose we seek in life, for then, like archers aiming at a definite mark, we shall be more likely to attain what we want.
>
> —Aristotle

As children of obedience, **not fashioning yourselves to your former lusts** in your ignorance, **but according to the Holy One** who has called you, you also become holy in all conduct; because it has been written, **"Be holy," "because I am holy."** —1 Peter 1:14-16 LITV

As for you, the anointing which you received from Him abides in you, and you have no need for anyone to teach you; but as His anointing teaches you about all

things, and is true and is not a lie, and just as it has taught you, **you abide in Him.**
—1 John 2:27 NASB

Now consider the prayer of Jesus in the garden of Gethsemane:

> **...that they may all be one, just as you, Father, are in me, and I in you**, that
> **they also may be in us**, so that the world may believe that you have sent me. The
> glory that you have given me I have given to them, **that they may be one even as
> we are one, I in them and you in me**, that they may become perfectly one, so
> that the world may know that you sent me and loved them even as you loved me.
> Father, I desire that they also, whom you have given me, may be with me where I
> am, to see my glory that you have given me because you loved me before the
> foundation of the world. O righteous Father, even though the world does not know
> you, I know you, and these know that you have sent me. I made known to them
> your name, and I will continue to make it known, **that the love with which you
> have loved me may be in them, and I in them**." —John 17:21-25 ESV

Questions:
1. Do you see a theme? What is that theme?

2. From these passages, what do you think those first followers would have
seen as the source of this spiritual transformation?
   a) Striving to follow the laws of the New Testament
   b) Striving to follow the examples of the New Testament
   c) An internal feeling
   d) Adopting the mindset, beliefs, values, attitudes and
      priorities of Jesus

> The man
> without
> purpose is
> like a ship
> without a
> rudder.
> **—Nietzsche**

Christianity as a Religion
Now consider the *one reference* that refers to Christianity *as a
religion*[8]:

> **Pure and undefiled religion** in the sight of our God and
> Father is this: to visit orphans and widows in their distress,
> and to keep oneself unstained by the world.
> —James 1:27 NASB

God,
Help me spread Your
Kingdom
in all the earth

In this passage, James describes "following Christ" as a religion, but
not in a manner we would normally equate with religiousness. He reminds them of Jesus' spirit,

---

[8] "Religion" is used only 5 times in the New Testament. James 1:27 is the only reference to Christianity.

where "pure religion" is having compassion on those in need. Their notion of Christianity was not an adherence to a religion (in the sense of following a set of writings or rituals). Their concept and emphasis was always the development of Christ (His likeness) within us.

Question:

3. Many of today's difficulties stem from a poor or unclear definition of what Christianity really is. Today we define Christianity as a religion. But is that how the Apostles *explained* "following Christ" to others? Or did they describe it as growing in His likeness?

Christianity as Christlikeness

Christianity, was by definition, a following of Him. But this "following of Him" creates a different set of difficulties and questions…

> Therefore from now on we recognize no one according to the flesh; even though we have known Christ according to the flesh, yet now we know Him in this way no longer.
>
> —2Corinthians 5:16 NASB

- What did it mean to "follow Christ"?
- Is it following a set of religious practices or rituals that He did?
- Is it striving to do the specific actions He did?
- Is it following a set of spiritual teachings and principles? If so, which ones?
- Is it trying to understand His values, mindset and priorities?

To answer these questions, let us first try to understand a few things regarding the nature of Christ and the Kingdom. Consider *the difference* in how Jesus evaluates the **physical** and **spiritual** sides of Himself:

> Therefore I tell you, every sin and blasphemy will be forgiven people, but the blasphemy against the Spirit will not be forgiven. And **whoever speaks a word against the Son of Man will be forgiven**, **but whoever speaks against the Holy Spirit will not be forgiven**, either in this age or in the age to come. —Matthew 12:31-2 ESV

Jesus essentially divides Himself into 2 parts— His physical human side, and the Spirit that is from God. Now consider our relationship with His spiritual kingdom:

> So that if anyone *is* in Christ, *he* **is a new creation**; the old things have passed away; behold, **all things have become new!**
> —2 Corinthians 5:17 LITV

> A **new heart also will I give you**, and **a new spirit will I put within you**: and I will take away the stony heart out of your flesh, and **I will give you a heart of flesh**. —Ezekiel 36:26 KJV

> For the kingdom of God is not a matter of eating and drinking **but of righteousness and peace and joy in the Holy Spirit**.

—Romans 14:7 ESV

And the *One* sitting on the throne said, Behold! **I make all things new**. —Revelation 21:5 LITV

Paul is constantly reminding his "children," about this new identity they have in Christ. To Paul, *the message*[9] is this new identity. Notice what Paul says to the fleshly church at Corinth:

> **You are our letter**, written in our hearts, known and read by all men; being manifested that **you are a letter of Christ**, cared for by us, **written** not with ink but **with the Spirit of the living God**, not on tablets of stone but **on tablets of human hearts**. —2 Corinthians 3:2–3 NASB

Do you remember how Jesus described those who came out to hear Him?

As I grow in the

Spirit of

Christ

I am the "light of the world"

> **You are the salt of the earth**; but if the salt has become tasteless, how can it be made salty again? It is no longer good for anything, except to be thrown out and trampled under foot by men. **You are the light of the world**. A city set on a hill cannot be hidden; nor does anyone light a lamp and put it under a basket, but on the lampstand, and it gives light to all who are in the house. **Let your light shine before men** in such a way that they may see your good works, and glorify your Father who is in heaven. —Matthew 5:13-16 NASB

Questions:

4. Did the Gospel writers emphasize Jesus' religiousness? Did Paul emphasize a religion or a particular set of rituals? In what manner was Jesus religious?

5. In Ephesians 5:1-2, Paul tells them to *imitate God*. What would that mean to those in the first century?

6. Regarding the crucifixion, what is so amazing about Jesus? Is it His body's ability to take the brutality? Or is it his spirit's motivation and love to allow those beatings to occur?

7. Does Christ allow the abuse because he is weak? Or because he is love and strength, and cares more about us than his own physical life?

---

[9] See Part 3 (Studies #11-20)

One Purpose: God's Likeness in Man
(a.k.a. Christ/Kingdom)

Christ's Relationship with the Law and Scriptures

He came to fulfill the Law (Mt. 5:17)
He is the end(goal) of the Law (Rom.10:4)
The Law is our tutor to lead us to Christ (Ga.3:24)
Scriptures teach us about the mindset
that Christ had (Rom.15:3-5)
Scriptures can make us wise for salvation
through faith in Christ (2Tim.3:15)

Conclusion:
Christ(likeness) is our goal

Christ's Relationship to God

He is the exact representation of God
He is the message/word of God
He is the righteousness of God
He is the wisdom of God
He is the power of God
He is the glory of God
He is the lamb of God
He is the son of God
He is God with us

Conclusion:
Christ is our key to
knowing and relating to God

Forms of Christ

Spirit in Jesus
Spiritual substance that sustained people
in OT (1Cor.10:1-4; 1Pet.1:10-11)
Spirit that is alive in Paul (Gal.2:20)
Spirit that we can grow into
(Gal.4:19; 2Cor.13:5; 2Cor.5:21)
Christ = real substance (Col. 2:16-17)

Conclusion:
Christ = Spirit of God in man

Prophecies of a Spiritual Kingdom

God's Spirit would be poured out (Joel 2:28)
New Covenant would be written on
our hearts (Jer.31:31-33)
All people would know Him (Jer.31:34)
God will be on his throne (2Sam.7:12-17)
Messiah has the keys to David's house (Isa.22:22)

Conclusions:
1. God's Spirit has been poured out
though Christ;
2. the new law is written on our hearts;
3. and everyone would know Him

Christ:
the Likeness of God
(in mankind)

Purpose for Activities & Spiritual Gifts

Communion = remember Him &
examine ourselves (1Cor.11)
Baptism = put to death the old man, and being
born again to a newness of life (Gal.6:4)
Assembly = building each other up in Him;
stimulate one another to love and
good works (Eph.4:15; Heb.10:24-25)
Gifts of the Spirit = for the common good;
edification of the church (1Cor.12,14)

Conclusion:
Build one another up in Him

Followers Relationship with World

We are the light of the world (Mt.5:14)
We are the salt of the earth (Mt.5:13)
we are a letter of Christ (2Cor.3.3)
We give off the aroma of Christ (2Cor.2:14-15)
People glorify God thru our
good works (Mt.5:16)
We are minister of reconciliation (2Cor.5:18)
We preach Christ (spirit of God)
We are the righteousness of God
to others (2Cor.4:21)
We become the likeness of God (Gal.4:19)
We love them like Christ loved us
(Jn.13:34-35)

Conclusion:
We are here to be God's likeness

Christ's Relationship with Followers

He is the light of men (Jn.1:4)
He is the bread of life (Jn. 6:35)
He is God's message to mankind (Jn.1:1)
He authored our faith (Heb.12.2)
Our Lord is the Spirit (Rom.8:9)
Christ is formed within us (Gal.4:19)
We are a letter of Christ (2Cor.3.3)
Be imitators of God (Eph.5:1)
He is our life (Col.3:4)
Put on the likeness of God (Eph.4:24)
We have the mind of Christ (1Cor.2:16)
God now speaks to us through Christ (Heb.1:1-3)
We may become the righteousness of God (2Cor.5:21)
He is the image we are being transformed into (2Cor.3:18)
We are to test ourselves to see if He is in us (2Cor.13:5)
He is the finisher of our faith (Heb.12:2)

Conclusion:
We are to be transforming
into God's likeness

Roles of Apostles and Prophets

Witnesses to Christ (1Pet.5:1)
Have the Spirit of Christ (Rom.15:19)
Ministers of Christ (Rom.15:16)
Minister of reconciliation (2Cor.5.18)
Have authority to build others up in Christ
(not for tearing down) (2Cor.13:10; Gal.4:19)
Determined to know nothing but
Jesus and Him crucified (1Cor.2:2)
Love others like Christ loved them (Jn.13:34-35)
The goal of their instruction is love (1Tim.1:5)
Controlled by the love of Christ (2Cor.5:14)

Conclusion:
They were witnesses and
messengers of Christ's likeness

8. Is it his physical presence that is our Lord? Or is it his spirit of love, strength, and service?

What would Paul say?
The "goal of the church" is the development of Jesus' Spirit within. It is the growth and development of His faith (values, beliefs and priorities…). There is a particular emphasis on Jesus' ability to love His enemies in the most evil of circumstances.

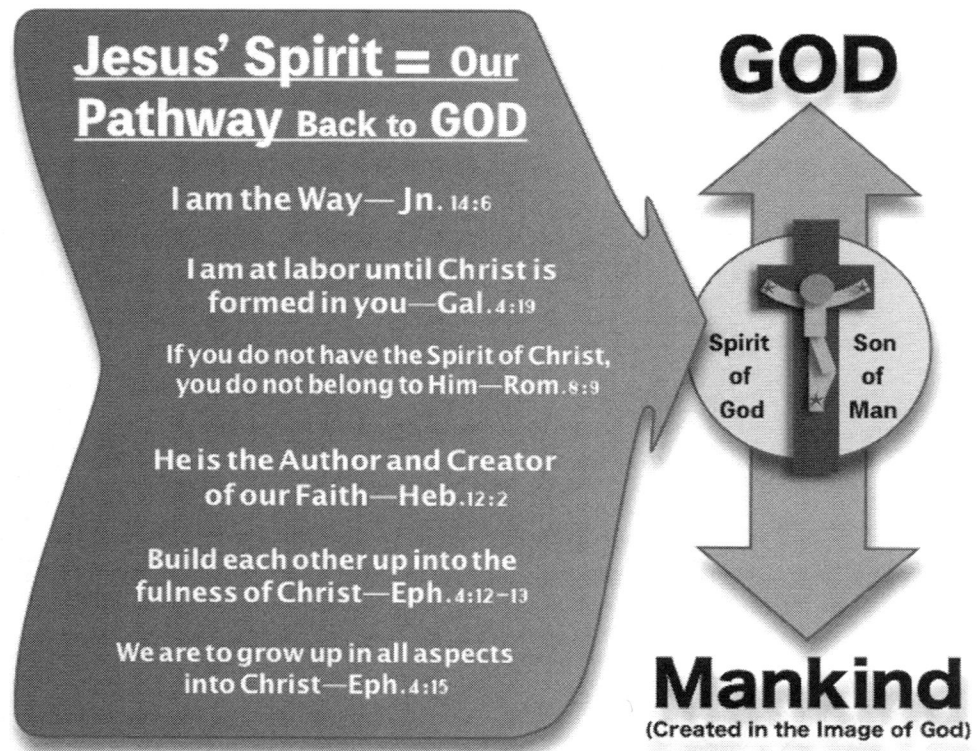

Education is the kindling of a flame, not the filling of a vessel.
—Socrates

Conclusions for Part 1: How Would Paul Explain "Christianity"?

Questions	Answers
What is "perfection"? (highest standard)	Loving your enemies
What is "fulfilling the Law"?	Love
What is "righteousness"?	Christ's Spirit
How do we "avoid judgment"?	Clothed with Christ (love)
What is the goal?	Christ in mankind

The Christ-Spirit is our Pathway and Goal

Paul had a different standard than the Jews (and many of the Christians). His standard was the Spirit of Christ. It was not a checklist of "right and wrong" actions, but rather seems to have been a set of priorities or internal question that comes from the commitment to *the development of Christ's Spiritual likeness*. His internal questions maybe something similar to:

- How can I adopt the mindset, purpose and commitment of Christ?
- How can I increase my understanding of God's infinite love, strength, compassion…?
- What is best for the spiritual welfare of others?
- How can I love as Christ loved me?

Christ(the Spirit in Jesus) was clearly their reference point for everything. Growth in the Christ-Spirit was their goal for everything they taught, and would be the spiritual-likeness that would cover them in the day of judgment.

Paul's "Christianity" = Following Jesus' Spirit

We suffer primarily not from our vices or our weaknesses, but from our illusions.
—Daniel J Boorstin

Part 2: How Would Paul Explain "the Role of the Scriptures"?

Study #6: How Would Paul Explain "Knowledge"?
What exactly is "knowledge"? What facts do we need to know?

Study #7: Why Were the New Testament Letters Written?
What is the purpose for the Bible? Did the writers give us a reason?

Study #8: How Did the Pharisees look at Scripture?
Can we learn from the mistakes of the Pharisees?

Study #9: What is the Embodiment of Knowledge and Truth?
How reliance upon the Law caused the Gentiles to blaspheme God.

Study #10: Is *Following the Bible* the Same as *Following Christ*?
What exactly is the difference? How does God speak to us now?

Conclusion: The Purpose of the Scriptures is the Christ-Spirit in Mankind

The New Testament was written so that we can _____.

a) have a checklist (to make sure we are doing everything "right")

b) pass judgment on others

c) win arguments

d) build each other up in Christ (having the same mind and Spirit that Jesus had)

tools   to lead us to

Part:2   How Would Paul Explain the "Role of the Scriptures"?

Study #6: How Would Paul Explain "Knowledge"?

γνῶσις – gnosis defined: knowledge or recognition

Have you ever heard Christians argue over doctrines? Or what you *must know* (or believe) in order to be saved? I've heard intense discussions between people within and without our churches over these "requirements" of salvation. But are we being consistent with the teachings of the Bible? What does the Bible say about "knowledge" itself?

Is there a specific set of information that we must understand before we can get to Heaven? What did the New Testament writers consider to be "knowledge"? Did they define it as a *knowing of specific facts*? If so, which facts? Were they concerned with knowing the Old Testament or the Law? Did they equate "Christianity" with the knowing and following of a *set of doctrines*? What specific information did they believe was necessary for salvation?

Purpose of Knowledge

Paul uses the term "knowledge" much more frequently than the other New Testament authors. In study #9 we will learn that the Jews had thought that "the Law" had *the embodiment of knowledge and truth*. This thinking led them to committing spiritual adultery and having the Gentiles blaspheme God (Romans 2:17-24). In later chapters Paul reminds them of two of the major purposes of the Law:

> For by the works of the Law no human being will be justified in his sight, since **through the Law comes knowledge of sin**. —Romans 3:20 ESV

> **For Christ is the end (goal) of the law**, for righteousness to everyone that believes. —Romans 10:4 NASB

God, help us to understand how we may use "knowledge" to serve

Your Spirit

Questions:
1. Knowledge of sin comes from where?

2. What was the purpose or goal of the Law?

Accurate Knowledge Used Carelessly

In Corinth, there were many who were arrogant. Notice how Paul describes "knowledge," and the attitude that they should have:

> Now concerning things sacrificed to idols, we know that we all have knowledge. Knowledge makes arrogant, but love edifies. If anyone supposes that he knows anything, he has not yet known as he ought to know; but if anyone loves God, he is known by Him. —1 Corinthians 8:1–3 NASB

Page 58   www.ThinkLikePaul.com

> For if someone sees you, who have knowledge, dining in an idol's temple, will not his conscience, if he is weak, be strengthened to eat things sacrificed to idols? For through your knowledge he who is weak is ruined, the brother for whose sake Christ died. —1 Corinthians 8:10–11 NASB

3. In this example, what attitude did "knowledge" create in the Corinthians?

4. After considering the entire chapter, which is more valuable to Paul?
   a) Their right to eat whatever they want
   b) The developing of a Christlike spirit

5. Which is more important to Paul?
   a) To know God (or think we know God)
   b) To be known by God

Some people had the knowledge that it was acceptable to eat meat sacrificed to idols. While others did not believe it was right to eat meat. Accordingly, Paul addresses those who seem to care more about their rights to eat meat than the spirits of weaker brethren:

> And so, by sinning against the brethren and wounding their conscience when it is weak, you sin against Christ. Therefore, if food causes my brother to stumble, I will never eat meat again, so that I will not cause my brother to stumble. —1 Corinthians 8:12–13 NASB

6. What is Paul's solution to this problem? Why does he choose this solution?

Knowledge as a Gift

> But to each one is given the manifestation of the Spirit **for the common good.** For to one is given the word of wisdom through the Spirit, and to another the word of knowledge according to the same Spirit. —1 Corinthians 12:7–8 NASB

> If I have *the gift of* prophecy, and know all mysteries and all knowledge; and if I have all faith, so as to remove mountains, but do not have love, I am nothing. —1 Corinthians 13:2 NASB

> Love never fails; but if *there are gifts of* prophecy, they will be done away; if *there are* tongues, they will cease; if *there is* knowledge, it will be done away. —1 Corinthians 13:8 NASB

7. The manifestations of the Spirit are for what purpose?
(see also 1 Corinthians 14:1–5, 12)

8. What must knowledge be accompanied with?

9. According to this passage, what is going to happen to knowledge?

Knowledge of Him

> That the God of our Lord Jesus Christ, the Father of glory, may give you a spirit of wisdom and revelation in the **knowledge of him**, having the eyes of your hearts enlightened, [10]that you may know what is the hope to which he has called you, what are the riches of his glorious inheritance in the saints, and what is the immeasurable greatness of his power toward us who believe, according to the working of his great might that he worked in Christ, when he raised him from the dead, and seated him at his right hand in the heavenly places.
> —Ephesians 1:17–20 ESV

In this passage Paul connects several concepts with a "knowledge of Him":

- a spirit of wisdom,
- where the eyes of our hearts are enlightened,
- a hope to which we are called,
- the riches of His glorious inheritance,
- an immeasurable greatness of His power,
- and His great might that He worked in Christ.
- (see also 2Corinthians 2:14-16)

10. This important "knowledge of Him" is probably a reference to:
   a) Knowing a specific set of facts (like Jesus died on the cross for our sins…)
   b) A spiritual understanding of the heart and purpose of God

> And He gave some *as* apostles, and some *as* prophets, and some *as* evangelists, and some *as* pastors and teachers, for the equipping of the saints for the work of service, to the building up of the body of Christ; until we all attain to the unity of the faith, and of the **knowledge of the Son of God**, to a mature man, to the measure of the stature **which belongs to the fullness of Christ**. As a result, we are no longer to be children, tossed here and there by waves and carried about by every wind of doctrine, by the trickery of men, by craftiness in deceitful scheming; but speaking the truth in love, **we are to grow up in all *aspects* into Him** who is the head, *even* Christ, from whom the whole body, being fitted and held together by what every joint supplies, according to the proper working of

---

[10] that, so that, in order that - all denote a purpose.

each individual part, **causes the growth of the body for the building up of itself in love**. —Ephesians 4:11–16 NASB

11. The different roles of the church are for the building up of what? And to the fullness of what?

12. Which aspects of Christ should we "grow up" into?

13. What does this growth cause?

God created the church not to be a religion, but for the work of service, for the building up of the body of Christ until we all attain the unity of faith and the knowledge of the

Son of God

And to know the love of Christ which surpasses knowledge, <u>that</u> you may be filled up to all the fullness of God.—Ephesians 3:19 NASB

to a mature man, to the measure of the stature which belongs to the fullness of Christ.

Love and Knowledge

14. What surpasses knowledge? For what purpose?

15. How can we "be filled up to all the fullness of God"?

True Knowledge

For I want you to know how great a struggle I have on your behalf and for those who are at Laodicea, and for all those who have not personally seen my face, that their hearts may be encouraged, having been knit together in love, and attaining to all the wealth that comes from the full assurance of understanding, resulting in a **true knowledge** of God's mystery, that is, Christ Himself, in whom are hidden all the treasures of wisdom and knowledge. —Colossians 2:1-3 NASB

16.   What is the "true knowledge of God's mystery"?

17. Where are "all the treasures of wisdom and knowledge" hidden?

And this I pray, that your love may abound still more and more in **real knowledge** and all discernment, <u>so that</u> you may approve the things that are excellent, in order to be sincere and blameless until the day of Christ; having been filled with the fruit of righteousness which *comes* through Jesus Christ, to the glory and praise of God. —Philippians 1:9–11 NASB

18. What is the purpose for "real knowledge and all discernment"? We should be knowledgeable and discerning about what?

God, help me understand the Scriptures in the manner in which You intended

"Do You Know God?"

Has anyone ever asked you "Do you know God?" When I was new in the faith somebody asked me this question, and I really didn't know what to say… I mean, I may *think* I know God, but that doesn't mean that I actually know Him. I mean, doesn't most everyone who is religious *thinks* he knows God? … And how do I know this guy asking the question knows God? And while I could not find any passages where anyone asks this question, here's a couple of passages that I thought were interesting:

> But if anyone loves God, he is **known by God**—1Corinthians 8:3 ESV

> But now that you have come to know God, or rather **to be known by God**—Galatians 4:9 ESV

It actually appears that the opposite was more important to Paul: "Does God know you?" In these passages Paul's concern isn't with a cognitive knowledge of Christ, but rather a spiritual, practical knowledge that is *of* Him… and as in all of Paul's writings, he seems to be emphasizing growth in this spiritual likeness.[11]

God, help me clearly focus on developing

the Spirit

of Jesus

for His Spirit is True Knowledge

What would Paul say?
The New Testament divides knowledge into two basic categories:

1. **True Knowledge = the understanding/embodiment of Christ's Spirit (love of God, growth, encouragement, spiritual wisdom…).**

2. **Worldly knowledge = knowledge used without love. (Examples given: for the purposes of binding others, passing judgment on others, or without any concern for their spiritual growth).**

What we are after is the root and not the branches.
The root is the real knowledge; the branches are the surface knowledge.
Real knowledge breeds body feel and personal expression; surface knowledge
breeds mechanical conditioning and imposing limitation and squelches creativity.
—Bruce Lee

---

[11] Note: This study has been abbreviated for the purpose of fitting into this series. For further study consider: 1Cor. 2:2; 12:7–8; 13:2,8; 14:1–5,12; 2Cor. 2:14; 4:5–6; Col. 1:9–12; Phi. 1:4–7

What Exactly is the Role of the Scriptures? (Part 1)

For whatever was written in earlier times was written for our instruction, so that through perseverance and the encouragement of the Scriptures we might have hope. —Romans 15:4

Let's look at the context.

Written for our instruction

so ↓ that

we might have hope

God wants us to have SAME MIND as JESUS

so ↓ that

with 1 accord we may glorify God

↓ Therefore

Accept one another as Christ accepted us

(accept = welcome, receive)

For whatever was written in earlier times was written for our instruction, so that through perseverance and the encouragement of the Scriptures we might have hope. Now may the God who gives perseverance and encouragement grant you to be of the same mind with one another according to Christ Jesus, so that with one accord you may with one voice glorify the God and Father of our Lord Jesus Christ. Therefore, accept one another, just as Christ also accepted us to the glory of God.
—Rom. 15:4-7 NASB

We are supposed to have the same mind as whom?

Does this fit with 1Cor. 2:16?

Are the Scriptures Paul's standard?

OR

Or is his standard the heart and mind of Jesus?

How did they use the Scriptures? How are we using the Scriptures?

Perry Stiltz   Think Like Paul: Searching for the Message that Changed the World

Study #7: Why Were the New Testament Letters Written?

We have passages that declare that Jesus Christ is the Way, the Word, the Alpha and Omega, the righteousness of God, and a host of other things for us. We Christians often proclaim that He is everything, and that we only need Him. But if these things are really true, then why do we need the New Testament? What is its purpose? Why did the authors of the New Testament write their letters? And what function do they serve today?

The relationship between the Law, the Scriptures, and Christ:

> Do not think that I have come to abolish the Law and the Prophets; I have not come to abolish them but **to fulfill them.**—Matthew 5:17 ESV

> Each of us should please our neighbors for their good, to build them up. For even Christ did not please himself but, as it is written: 'The insults of those who insult you have fallen on me.' **For everything that was written in the past was written to teach us**, **so that through the endurance taught in the Scriptures and the encouragement they provide we might have hope. May the God who gives endurance and encouragement give you the same attitude of mind toward each other** <u>that Christ Jesus had</u>, so that with one mind and one voice you may glorify the God and Father of our Lord Jesus Christ. Accept one another, then, just as Christ accepted you, in order to bring praise to God. —Romans 15:2–7 NIV

> And how from infancy you have known the Holy Scriptures, **which are able to make you wise for salvation through faith in Christ Jesus.** All Scripture is God-breathed and is useful for teaching, rebuking, correcting and training in righteousness, **so that the servant of God may be thoroughly equipped for every good work.**[12] —2 Timothy 3:15–17 NIV

> FOR THROUGH THE LAW COMES THE KNOWLEDGE OF SIN.
>
> ROMANS 3:20 NASB

The stated purposes for the New Testament letters:

> **The goal of our instruction is love from a pure heart, a good conscience, and a sincere faith.** —1 Timothy 1:5 NASB

> **I do not write these things to shame you, but to admonish you** as my beloved children. For if you were to have countless tutors in Christ, yet you would not have many fathers; for in Christ Jesus I became your father through the gospel. I exhort you therefore, **be imitators of me** …. —1 Corinthians 4:14–16 NASB

---

[12] For deeper examination of this passage refer to Study #10

I wrote as I did, so that when I came I would not be distressed by those who should have made me rejoice. I had confidence in all of you, that you would all share my joy. For **I wrote you** out of great distress and anguish of heart and with many tears, not to grieve you but **to let you know the depth of my love for you**. —2 Corinthians 2:3–4 NIV

I urge you, therefore, to reaffirm your love for him. **Another reason I wrote you** was **to see if you would stand the test and be obedient in everything**. —2 Corinthians 2:8–9 NIV

I myself am convinced, my brothers and sisters, that you yourselves are full of goodness, filled with knowledge and competent to instruct one another. Yet **I have written you quite boldly on some points to remind you of them again**, because of the grace God gave me to be a minister of Christ Jesus to the Gentiles. He gave me the priestly duty of proclaiming the gospel of God, **so that the Gentiles might become an offering acceptable to God, sanctified by the Holy Spirit**. —Romans 15:14–16 NIV

> What were those first century authors trying to teach?
>
> Were they striving to create a new law or standard?
>
> Or were they striving to teach Christ and what it means to spiritually follow Him?

By referring to this, **when you read you can understand my insight into the mystery of Christ**, which in other generations was not made known to the sons of men, **as it has now been revealed to His holy apostles and prophets in the Spirit**; *to be specific, that the Gentiles are fellow heirs* and fellow members of the body, and fellow partakers of the promise in Christ Jesus through the gospel. —Ephesians 3:4–6 NASB

I am writing these things to you, hoping to come to you before long; but in case I am delayed, *I write so that you will know how one ought to conduct himself in the household of God, which is the church of the living God*, the pillar and support of the truth. By common confession, **great is the mystery of godliness: He who was revealed in the flesh, was vindicated in the Spirit**, seen by angels, proclaimed among the nations, believed on in the world, taken up in glory.—1 Timothy 3:14–16 NASB

Dear friends, this is now my second letter to you. **I have written both of them as reminders to stimulate you to wholesome thinking. I want you to recall the words spoken in the past by the holy prophets and the command given by our Lord and Savior** through your apostles. —2 Peter 3:1–2 NIV

Dear friends, although I was very eager to write to you about the salvation we share, **I felt compelled to write and urge you to contend for the faith that was once for all entrusted to God's holy people.** —Jude 1:3 NIV

John furnishes many reasons for his writings:

It has given me great joy to find some of your children walking in the truth, just as the Father commanded us. And now, dear lady, **I am not writing you a new command but one we have had from the beginning**. I ask that **we love one another**. And this is love: that we walk in obedience to his commands. **As you have heard from the beginning, His command is that you walk in love**. —2 John 1:4–6 NIV

But these have been written **so that you may believe that Jesus is the Christ**, the Son of God; and **that believing you may have life in His name**. —John 20:31 NASB

We write this to make our joy complete. This is the message we have heard from Him and declare to you: God is light; in him there is no darkness at all. —1 John 1:4–5 NIV

My dear children, **I write this to you so that you will not sin**. But if anybody does sin, we have an advocate with the Father—Jesus Christ, the Righteous One. —1 John 2:1 NIV

Dear friends, **I am not writing you a new command but an old one**, which you have had since the beginning. This old command is the message you have heard. Yet I **am writing you a new command; its truth is seen in him and in you**, because the darkness is passing and the true light is already shining. —1 John 2:7–8 NIV

I am writing to you, dear children, **because your sins have been forgiven** on account of his name. **I am writing** to you, fathers, **because you know him** who is from the beginning. **I am writing** to you, young men, **because you have overcome the evil one. I write** to you, dear children, **because you know the Father. I write** to you, fathers, **because you know him** who is from the beginning. **I write** to you, young men, **because you are strong, and the word of God lives in you, and you have overcome the evil one.**—1 John 2:12–14 NIV

I do not write to you because you do not know the truth, but **because you do know it and because no lie comes from the truth.** —1 John 2:21 NIV

I am writing these things to you about those who are trying to lead you astray. As for you, the anointing you received from him remains in you, and you do not need anyone to teach you. But as his anointing teaches you about all things and as that anointing is real, not counterfeit—just as it has taught you, **remain in him**. —1 John 2:26–27 NIV

I write these things to you who believe in the name of the Son of God **so that you may know that you have eternal life**. —1 John 5:13 NIV

Questions:

1. Do you see any themes as to the purpose of these letters? Name them.

2. Do any of the authors claim that their writings comprise a "new law," a "new commandment," or a "new covenant"?

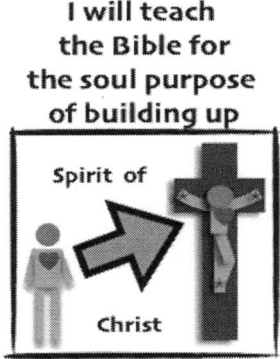

I will teach the Bible for the soul purpose of building up

Spirit of

Christ

within each of us

3. Does it appear that these letters were written to remind them of something that was already taught?

4. Who does Paul want them to imitate?

5. How does Paul want them to treat one another?

6. What do you think "following Christ" meant to Paul or John? In what manner did they follow Christ?

7. Who gets to define "following Christ"? Do we just follow what our pastor teaches? Do we get to define it ourselves? Or should we strive to follow the definition of the first Christians?

Emphasize what the Bible Emphasizes

The first-century emphasis was clearly on Christ. Everything was centered around Him, and everything was in subjection to Him. Consider a situation where even adherence to the law regarding the Sabbath was for the purpose of serving man:

> And it happened that He was passing through the grain fields on the Sabbath, and His disciples began to make their way along while picking the heads of grain. The Pharisees were saying to Him, 'Look, why are they doing what is not lawful on the Sabbath?' And He said to them, 'Have you never read what David did when he was in need and he and his companions became hungry; how he entered the house of God in the time of Abiathar *the* high priest, and ate the consecrated bread, which is not lawful for *anyone* to eat except the priests, and he also gave it to those who were with him?' Jesus said to them, **'The Sabbath was made for man, and not man for the Sabbath.** So the Son of Man is Lord even of the Sabbath.' —Mark 2:23–28 NASB

From this passage, there are two lessons that apply to our study:
   a) The Sabbath and the laws regarding the Sabbath were made to *serve* man.
   b) Christ (the Spirit of God in man) is greater than all things, even the Sabbath.

We are the ones made in God's image. The laws were made *for* us, and more specifically, so that we may know where we have fallen short.

Christianity, from the very beginning, was a belief in Jesus as the Messiah and Son of God. It was not a ritual or a philosophy. It was following His Spirit. It wasn't His actions that made Him so special. It is the Spirit behind the actions that is so infinitely impressive. While Paul followed Jesus' actions (even to the point of suffering and death), his emphasis is always on the Spirit and growing in that Spirit. The Law, the Old Testament, and even Paul's letters are all subservient to the Spirit.

Paul's Instructions Tied to the Purpose of Christ(likeness)

Every Christian teaching/act/tradition is tied to the purpose of growing Christ/Christlikeness (rather than the act for its own sake). Consider these New Testament teachings:

Teaching	Purpose related to growth in Christ/Christlikeness
Spiritual Gifts	To each is given the manifestation of the Spirit **for the common good.** 1Cor. 12:7
	What is *the outcome* then, brethren? When you assemble, each one has a psalm, has a teaching, has a revelation, has a tongue, has an interpretation. **Let all things be done for edification** 1Cor.14:26
Prophecy	But he that prophesieth speaketh unto men *to* **edification, and exhortation, and comfort.** 1Cor. 14:3 KJV
Tongues	So then tongues are **for a sign,** not to those who believe but to unbelievers; but prophecy *is for a sign,* not to unbelievers but to those who believe. 1Cor.14:22
Head coverings	But if one is inclined to be contentious, we have no other practice, nor have the churches of God. 1Cor.11:16 Imitate Paul as he imitates Christ 1Cor.11:1 (ie... Be humble and peaceful like Paul (the opposite of contentious))
Do not submit to rules of religiousness like do not touch, do not eat...	they have appearance of wisdom, but of no value against the flesh Gal. 2:20-23; **substance belongs to Christ** Gal.2:17
Disobeying teachings regarding circumcision	so that **the false brethren would not take away the liberty** that we have in Christ. Gal.2:3-5
Roles of the church: apostles, prophets, evangelist, pastors, teachers	maturity in Christ; **to grow up in all aspects unto Christ** Eph.4:11-15
Assembly	And let us consider how to **stir up one another to love and good works, not neglecting to meet together,** as is the habit of some, but encouraging one another... Heb.10:24-25
Do not go beyond what is written	so that **you do not become arrogant** in behalf of one against another 1Cor.4:3-6 (humility)

Each of these actions are tied to a specific purpose. Paul connects them to a Spirit that God wants us attain. Speaking in tongues or prophecy were to be used for the edification of the church(in Christ). Head coverings were for the contentious women in Corinth, who needed a reminder

What Exactly is the Purpose of the Ecclesia? (church/assembly)

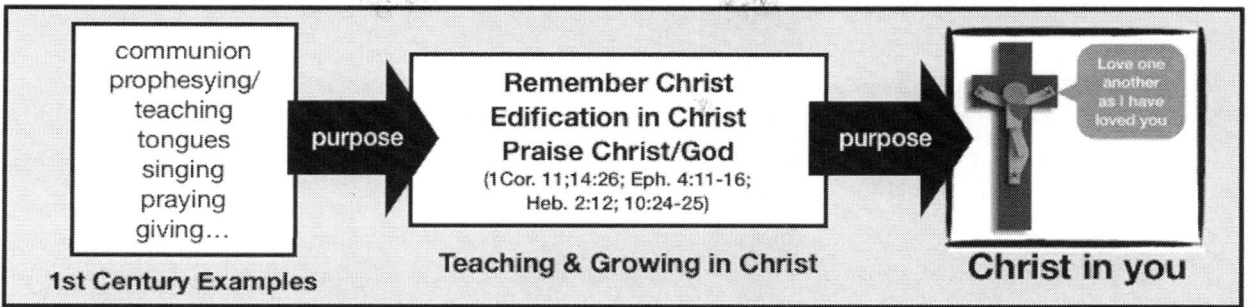

about humility. The different roles of the church were for the purpose of building up one another into Christ. And "not going beyond what is written" was given so that they would not become arrogant against one another.

The Christ-Spirit has always been about more Christ-Spirit. It is His Spirit that we should be striving to spread, and our actions should be in service to the development of this Spirit within.

God, may we use the assembly to stimulate one another unto

Thinking About Our Thinking

As we continue our studies, let's think about our approach to the Bible:

1. Do we see their letters as the first recipients saw them?
2. What is *our* purpose for the Bible? Is our purpose the same as the writers?
3. Consider how you have been taught to look at the New Testament? As a law book? A covenant? A book of history, or a book of fairy tales? Or a list of actions (or patterns) for us to replicate?
4. If we look inside our own hearts, what exactly has been our goals or motivations for our Bible studies?

What would Paul say?

The intent of those letters were to teach and encourage the Christ-Spirit in people. They were a reminder of Him and His faith, and were not written for the purposes of starting a new written standard or religious system.

Christ is the Alpha and Omega. Our solutions are in this Spirit. The Scriptures are centered on Him and are consistently striving to remind and encourage growth in His Spirit.

How Did the Pharisees Look at Scripture?

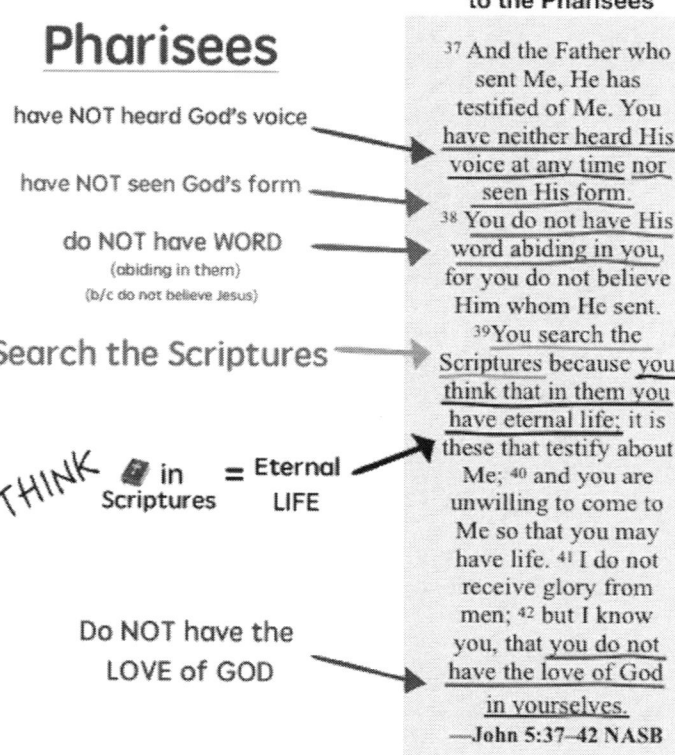

Pharisees

have NOT heard God's voice

have NOT seen God's form

do NOT have WORD
(abiding in them)
(b/c do not believe Jesus)

Search the Scriptures

THINK 📖 in Scriptures = Eternal LIFE

Do NOT have the LOVE of GOD

Jesus speaking to the Pharisees

37 And the Father who sent Me, He has testified of Me. You have neither heard His voice at any time nor seen His form. 38 You do not have His word abiding in you, for you do not believe Him whom He sent. 39 You search the Scriptures because you think that in them you have eternal life; it is these that testify about Me; 40 and you are unwilling to come to Me so that you may have life. 41 I do not receive glory from men; 42 but I know you, that you do not have the love of God in yourselves.
—John 5:37–42 NASB

Did Jesus equate the "word" with the Scriptures?

Where did the Pharisees think they could receive eternal life?

What were the Pharisees missing?

In Conclusion, "Eternal Life" is probably best found in···

Scriptures?
or
having the Spirit of Jesus?

From this context, what could "the Word" be a reference to?
The Scriptures? The Spirit of God/Christ?

Perry Stiltz   Think Like Paul: Searching for the Message that Changed the World

**Christ is the culmination of the law so that there may be righteousness for everyone who believes.
—Romans 10:4 NIV**

Study #8: How Did the Pharisees look at Scripture?

Many of the Pharisees opposed Jesus. Their arrogance didn't allow them to understand who He was, or what He was about. At the core of their self-righteousness was an ignorance regarding the role of the Scriptures. Let us examine an encounter where Jesus differentiates between *Scriptural knowledge* and *God's Word*:

> And the Father who sent Me, He has testified of Me. You have neither heard His voice at any time nor seen His form. You do not have His word abiding in you, for you do not believe Him whom He sent. You search the Scriptures because you think that in them you have eternal life; it is these that testify about Me; and you are unwilling to come to Me so that you may have life. I do not receive glory from men; but I know you, that you do not have the love of God in yourselves.
> —John 5:37–42 NASB

Answer the following questions and notice how Jesus describes these "experts":

1. What/Who were they searching for?

2. What/Who did they not hear?

3. What/Who did they not see?

4. What did they think they had in the Scriptures?

5. What/Who were they unwilling to come to?

6. Where did they need to go to have life?

7. What did they *not* have?

8. Where did the Pharisees receive their glory?

9. Do you think the Pharisees were studious?

10. Were they confident about their teachings?

11. What were they missing?

12. From this context, what might Jesus be referring to as God's "voice" or "form"?

13. What could this "word" be referring to?

Think Like Paul:

What exactly is "the word" Jesus is referring to?
Is it the Scriptures?
Or is it something spiritual?

Consider how Paul describes the Lord and our relationship with Him:

> Now the Lord is the Spirit, and where the Spirit of the Lord is, there is liberty. But we all, with unveiled face, beholding as in a mirror the glory of the Lord, are being **transformed into the same image** from glory to glory, just as from the Lord, the Spirit. —2 Corinthians 3:17–18 NASB

Knowing Scriptures ≠ Knowing the Word

14. What image are we being transformed into?

Consider the following:

> Therefore **be imitators of God**, as beloved children; and walk in love, just as Christ also loved you and gave Himself up for us, an offering and a sacrifice to God as a fragrant aroma. —Ephesians 5:1–2 NASB

> But the people of Israel, who pursued the law as the way of righteousness, have not attained their goal. —Romans 9:31 NIV

15. Should we pursue the law, the Spirit, or something else?

16. Is "imitating God" and "developing the Spirit of Christ" the same as trying to follow the Bible as a rule book?

17. What do you think was the approach of the Pharisees referred to in John 5?

18. Did they have a relationship with the spiritual Father? Or was their relationship with the Law?

God! Help me to understand the difference between the Scriptures and your Word

so that I may come to a true knowledge of your Spirit

What would Jesus say?

Even though the Pharisees knew the Scriptures, Jesus says that they did not have God's "word" abiding in them. They had replaced God with the Scriptures (and their thoughts about the Scriptures). This reliance upon their own thinking caused them to not recognize God or the Messiah. The Scriptures were not given to be idolized. They were given to point us to the Christ-Spirit, so that we may recognize God and may come into a relationship with Him.

Pharisees thought that "in the Scriptures" they could find eternal life

The Embodiment of Knowledge and Truth?

Jewish Christians in Rome

1. Passing judgment on others

2. do NOT understand the kindness, patience, and tolerance of God

3. do NOT understand that God's Kindness *leads people to* Repentance

4. Stubborn, unrepentant hearts (storing up wrath from God)

5. RELY UPON the LAW

6. think they are so wise

7. confident about their teachings

8. think "LAW = Embodiment of KNOWLEDGE and TRUTH"

9. Are THIEVES, ADULTERERS, and IDOLATERS

because ↓ of you

the Gentiles BLASPHEMED GOD

Romans 2:1-5 NASB
Therefore you have no excuse, everyone of you who passes judgment, for in that which you judge another, you condemn yourself; for you who judge practice the same things. And we know that the judgment of God rightly falls upon those who practice such things. But do you suppose this, O man, when you pass judgment on those who practice such things and do the same yourself, that you will escape the judgment of God? Or do you think lightly of the riches of His kindness and tolerance and patience, not knowing that the kindness of God leads you to repentance. But because of your stubbornness and unrepentant heart you are storing up wrath for yourself in the day of wrath and revelation of the righteous judgment of God.

Romans 2:17–24 NASB
But if you bear the name "Jew" and rely upon the Law and boast in God, and know His will and approve the things that are essential, being instructed out of the Law, and are confident that you yourself are a guide to the blind, a light to those who are in darkness, a corrector of the foolish, a teacher of the immature, having in the Law the embodiment of knowledge and of the truth, you, therefore, who teach another, do you not teach yourself? You who preach that one shall not steal, do you steal? You who say that one should not commit adultery, do you commit adultery? You who abhor idols, do you rob temples? You who boast in the Law, through your breaking the Law, do you dishonor God? For "THE NAME OF GOD IS BLASPHEMED AMONG THE GENTILES BECAUSE OF YOU," just as it is written.

Rom. 2:28-29 NASB
For he is not a Jew who is one outwardly, nor is circumcision that which is outward in the flesh. But he is a Jew who is one inwardly; and circumcision is that which is of the heart, by the Spirit, not by the letter; and his praise is not from men, but from God.

What matters most to Paul?

Obedience to the Spirit in Jesus?

or

Obedience to the Law/ Scriptures?

If the "embodiment of Knowledge and Truth" is NOT in the LAW··· then where is it? What are we supposed to rely upon? The Scriptures? Or the Spirit in Jesus?

Perry Stiltz   Think Like Paul: Searching for the Message that Changed the World

For the love of Christ controls us, because we have concluded this:
that one has died for all, therefore all have died; and he died for all,
that those who live might no longer live for themselves but for him
who for their sake died and was raised.
—2Corinthians 5:14-15 ESV

Study #9: What is the Embodiment of Knowledge and Truth?

> …and if you are sure that you yourself are a guide to the blind, a light to those who are in darkness, an instructor of the foolish, a teacher of children, **having in the law the embodiment of knowledge and truth**… —Romans 2:19-20 ESV

Before we analyze this, let us understand the chapter as a whole. In the first five verses Paul describes several unchristlike attitudes of these "experts":

> Therefore you have no excuse, every one of you who **passes judgment**, for in that which **you judge another**, you condemn yourself; for you who judge practice the same things. And we know that the judgment of God rightly falls upon those who practice such things. But do you suppose this, O man, when you pass judgment on those who practice such things and do the same *yourself*, that you will escape the judgment of God? **Or do you think lightly of the riches of His kindness and tolerance and patience, not knowing that the kindness of God leads you to repentance?** But because of **your stubbornness** and **unrepentant heart** you are storing up wrath for yourself in the day of wrath and revelation of the righteous judgment of God. —Romans 2:1-5 NASB

Questions:

1. What were some of the problems in Rome?
    a) Passing judgment on others
    b) Being too kind to the Gentiles
    c) Being stubborn
    d) Having an unrepentant heart

God, develop Your Kindness **within me so that others may be led to You**

2. What leads people to repentance?
    a) Judging them
    b) Condemning them
    c) Scripture
    d) Following the law
    e) Recognizing God's kindness

Then a few verses later he describes the difference between the "doers" and the "hearers":

> For all who have sinned without the Law will also perish without the Law, and all who have sinned under the Law will be judged by the Law; for *it is* not the hearers of the Law *who* are just before God, but the doers of the Law will be justified. For when Gentiles who do not have the Law do instinctively the things of the Law, these, not having the Law, are a law to themselves, in that they show the work of the Law written in their hearts, their conscience bearing witness and their thoughts alternately accusing or else defending them, on the day when,

according to my gospel, God will judge the secrets of men through Christ Jesus.
—Romans 2:12–16 NASB

3. Who are accounted "just" before God?
   a) Hearers
   b) Doers

4. The hearers refer to:
   a) The Jews who know the law, but didn't do it
   b) The gentiles who do the law

5. From the passage, give three descriptions for those who are "a law to themselves":

   a)

   b)

   c)

6. Where does God want His law written?

7. How will man be judged?

God, help me understand the Spirit of Your Son

so that I may know Your Standard

Paul then mocks the mentality that within the law we can "have the embodiment of knowledge and truth." He accuses the Jews of theft and adultery, and then calls them blasphemers.

> But if you bear the name "Jew" and **rely upon the Law** and boast in God, and know His will and approve the things that are essential, being **instructed out of the Law**, and are confident that you yourself are a guide to the blind, a light to those who are in darkness, a corrector of the foolish, a teacher of the immature, **having in the Law the embodiment of knowledge and of the truth**, you, therefore, who teach another, **do you not teach yourself?** You who preach that one shall not steal, **do you steal?** You who say that one should not commit adultery, **do you commit adultery?** You who abhor idols, **do you rob temples? You who boast in the Law**, through your breaking the Law, **do you dishonor God?** For **"THE NAME OF GOD IS BLASPHEMED AMONG THE GENTILES BECAUSE OF YOU,"** just as it is written. —Romans 2:17–24 NASB

The Jews were familiar with the Old Testament prophets who equated idolatry with adultery and stealing from God.

My people consult their wooden idol, and their diviner's wand informs them; For a spirit of harlotry has led them astray, And they have played the harlot, departing from their God. —Hosea 4:12 NASB

Paul's accusations were made to those who *thought* they were practicing authentic faith. They *thought* they had the proper ceremonies and ordinances. But Paul calls them thieves and adulterers. Their emphasis on law and their thinking that "within the law is righteousness" was minimizing the Spirit, and thus taking away from the relationship God wanted to have with them.

Questions:

According to Romans 2:

8. What did the Jewish Romans rely upon?

9. What did the Jews think they had within the law?

10. What did they cause the Gentiles to do?

I have no agenda, except for

within each of us

Consider what Paul writes next:

For circumcision indeed is of value if you obey the law, but if you break the law, your circumcision becomes uncircumcision. So, if a man who is uncircumcised keeps the precepts of the law, will not his uncircumcision be regarded as circumcision? Then he who is physically uncircumcised but keeps the law will condemn you who have the written code and circumcision but break the law. For no one is a Jew who is merely one outwardly, nor is circumcision outward and physical. But a Jew is one inwardly, and circumcision is a matter of the heart, by the Spirit, not by the letter. His praise is not from man but from God.—Romans 2:25–29 ESV

Now let us review the chapter as a whole, and consider the mentality Paul states or implies that the Jewish Christians had:
  - passed judgment on Gentiles,
  - not known that kindness leads people to repentance,
  - were stubborn and unrepentant,
  - relied upon the law and boasted in God,
  - thought they knew God's will,
  - thought they were guides to the blind
  - thought the law was the embodiment of knowledge and truth

Which had caused:
  - them to spiritually rob God's temple, commit adultery, and dishonor God
  - the Gentiles to blaspheme God
  - themselves to be judged by the Gentiles (who kept God's spiritual law)

Questions:

11. From this context, what was their approach to the Scriptures?

12. What is Paul's solution to those who relied upon the Law? (2:29)

13. What would Paul want for us?
    a) To develop the Spirit of Christ
    b) To look at his letters as the New Law or Covenant

14. Do you think Paul would be angry if he could return today and found us regarding his letters as a "Christian Torah"? Why or why not?

> What kind of letter would you write
>
> ...if you were trying to help a church develop the spirit Jesus had?
>
> ...if you writing to a divided, boastful, arrogant, and fleshly church that had little or no love for one another?
>
> (see 1 & 2 Corinthians)

What would Paul say?

The Jewish Christians in Rome believed that they had the "embodiment of truth and knowledge" within the Law. Paul calls them thieves, idolaters, and adulterers because they had accepted Christ as the Messiah and equated "following Him" with the adherence to the Law. Their approach of keeping (and binding) the Law/ Scriptures had become a stumbling block to themselves and the Gentiles.

Paul rebukes these self-righteousness jewish Christians by telling them that the Gentiles (who don't know the Law, but somehow had God's law in their hearts) would judge them. Paul seems to be supremely focused on teaching these Christians the spiritual nature of Christianity, particularly love, kindness, humility, and liberty.

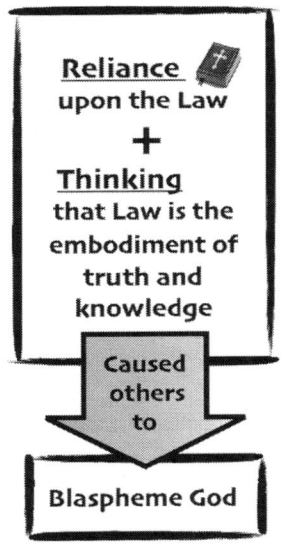

Jesus = Embodiment of Knowledge and Truth

God... in these last days has spoken to us in His Son.
—Hebrews 1:2 NASB

What Exactly is the Role of the Scriptures? (Part 2)

All Scripture is inspired by God and profitable for teaching, for reproof, for correction, for training in righteousness. —2 Timothy 3:16 NASB

Let's look at the context.

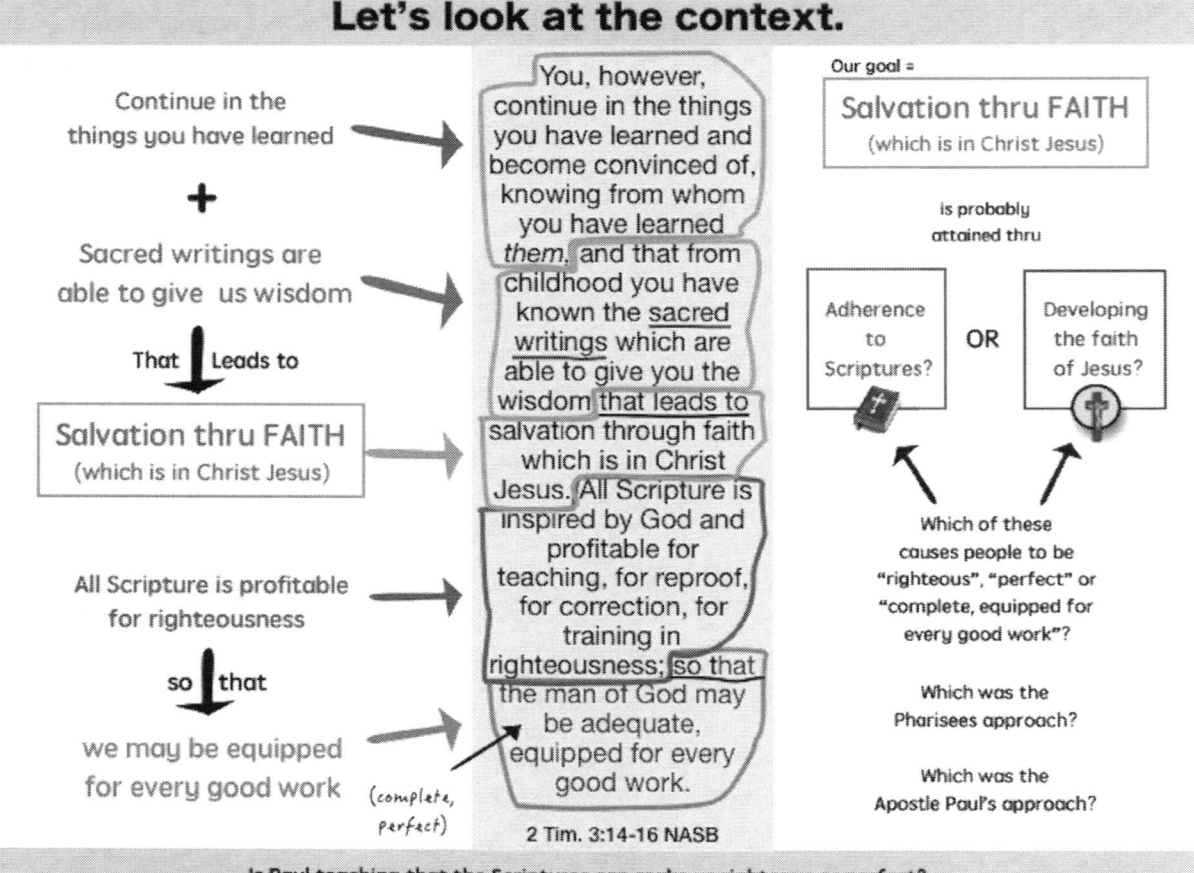

Is Paul teaching that the Scriptures can make us righteous or perfect?
Or is he encouraging them to use the Scriptures to grow in wisdom,
which is able to lead them to the faith and spirit that Jesus had?

Perry Stiltz   Think Like Paul: Searching for the Message that Changed the World

Study #10: Is *Following the Bible* the Same as *Following Christ*?

What about 2 Timothy chapter 3?
Let's examine some of the differences between the
Scriptures and Christ:

> But as for you, continue in what you have
> learned and have firmly believed, knowing
> from whom you learned it and how from
> childhood you have been acquainted with the
> **sacred writings, which are able to make you wise
> for salvation through faith in Christ Jesus. All Scripture is
> breathed out by God** and profitable for teaching, for reproof, for correction, and **for
> training in righteousness, that the man of God may be complete, equipped for every
> good work.** —2Timothy 3:14-17 ESV

(thought bubble) What about 2Tim. 3:14-17?!? How do the Scriptures train us in righteousness? How are we "made complete" and "equipped for every good work"?

Questions:

1. According to the context, are the Scriptures inspired(breathed out) by God?

2. Which "sacred writings" or "Scriptures" is Paul probably referring to?

3. Does this context equate the Scriptures with the "Word of God"?

4. Consider the manner in which "all Scripture" can "train a man for righteousness." What does Paul likely mean?[13]
   a) By informing him of a series of actions that are correct and righteous.
   b) By helping him become more like the Spirit of God/ Christ.
   c) By helping him understand God's spiritual principles.
   d) both (b) and (c)

> **What exactly is a "good work"?**
> "Now the God of peace, that brought again from the dead our Lord Jesus, that great shepherd of the sheep, through the blood of the **everlasting covenant, make you perfect** in **every good work** to do his will, working in you that which is **wellpleasing in his sight, through Jesus Christ**; to whom be glory for ever and ever. Amen."
> —Hebrews 13:20-21 KJV
>
> Notice 4 things Paul associates with a "good work":
> 1. Eternal covenant (Study #22)
> 2. We can be made "perfect" (Study #1)
> 3. It is well pleasing to God
> 4. It happens through Christ.

5. How could the Scriptures make a man "complete" and "equipped for every good work"?
   a) By informing him of a series of actions that are correct and righteous.
   b) By helping him become more like the Spirit of Christ.
   c) By helping him understand God's spiritual principles.
   d) both (b) and (c)

---

[13] Study #4 "What is righteousness?"

6. Could a "good work" be a reference to acting with the Spirit of Christ? What exactly makes an action "good" or "righteous"? (Study #4)

So we have the **prophetic word** *made* more sure, to which you do well to pay attention as to a lamp shining in a dark place, until the day dawns and the **morning star arises in your hearts**. But know this first of all, that **no prophecy of Scripture is *a matter* of one's own interpretation, for no prophecy was ever made by an act of human will, but men moved by the Holy Spirit spoke from God**. —2Peter 1:17-21 NASB

6. What/Who is the morning star?

Now notice some of the ways the writers describe Christ:

For other **foundation** can no man lay than that is laid, **which is Jesus Christ**. —Corinthians 3:11 KJV

But of him are ye in Christ Jesus, who of God is made unto us wisdom, and **righteousness**, and sanctification, and redemption. —1 Corinthians 1:30 KJV

Him hath God exalted with his right hand *to be* a Prince and a Savior, for to give repentance to Israel, and **forgiveness of sins**. —Acts 5:31 KJV

Jesus saith unto him, **I am the way, the truth, and the life**: no man cometh unto the Father, but by me. —John 14:6 KJV

…seeing that His divine power has granted to us **everything pertaining to life and godliness, through the true knowledge of Him** who called us by His own glory and excellence. —2 Peter 1:3 NASB

And he *was* clothed with a vesture dipped in blood: and **his name is called The Word of God**. —Revelation 19:13 KJV

Questions:
7. According to the Jesus "the way, the truth, and the life" are in:
   a) The Scriptures
   b) Jesus Christ

8. According to the the Apostle John, the "Word of God" is:
    a) The Scriptures
    b) Christ

I have everything pertaining to life and godliness in a true knowledge of the Spirit of Jesus

9. According to the Apostle Paul, "our foundation" is:
    a) The Scriptures
    b) Christ

10. According to the Apostle Paul, "righteousness" is in:
    a) The Scriptures
    b) Christ

11. According to the Luke, forgiveness is in:
    a) The Scriptures
    b) Christ

12. According to the Apostle Peter, everything pertaining to life and godliness comes through:
    a) The Scriptures
    b) Knowledge of Christ

Now let's consider how we are to "be led":

> For as many as are **led by the Spirit of God**, they are the sons of God.
> —Romans 8:14 KJV

13. According to the Apostle Paul, we should be led by:
    a) The Scriptures
    b) The Spirit of God

Now let's contemplate how Christ may be different than Paul's writings…

Paul's Opinion…

Do you remember study #7? The purposes of the New Testament letters were *not* to create a new standard, but rather to remind them of the Spirit of Christ. This is consistent with what Paul declares as "his opinion," or which is "not a command" from the Lord. For example, consider some of Paul's comments on different marital situations in 1 Corinthians 7:

> But to the rest **I say, not the Lord,** that if any brother has a wife…
> —1 Corinthians 7:12 NASB

> But concerning the betrothed, **I have no command from the Lord, but I give my judgment** as one who is trustworthy. —1 Corinthians 7:25 ESV

But if her husband dies, she is free to be married to whom she wishes, only in the Lord. **Yet in my judgment** she is happier if she remains as she is. And I think that I too have the Spirit of God. —1 Corinthians 7:40 ESV

Paul's letters put a clear emphasis on Christ and having a Christlike spirit. When we say that his writings are "commands from the Lord," we create a logical contradiction when we encounter these verses. But Paul, who is focused on Christ (including growth into Him), explains the purpose of his opinions in that same context:

I say this for your own benefit, not to lay any restraint upon you, but **to promote good order** and **to secure your undivided devotion to the Lord**. —1 Corinthians 7:35 ESV

Paul is squarely focused on the Spirit, which is the Lord.

A Key Difference

The Spirit of Jesus *is* the message. It is not just about what He says or what He does. It is about His heart. It is about His nature. It is about His purpose, intentions, thoughts, and beliefs. It is about where His words and actions come from.

Consider these passages regarding Christ and the Law:

But **the end of the commandment** is **love** out of a pure heart and a good conscience, and faith not pretended, —1 Timothy 1:5 LITV

For the whole law is fulfilled in one word: "**You shall love your neighbor as yourself.**" —Galatians 5:14 ESV

But now apart from the law **the righteousness of God has been manifested**, being witnessed by the Law and the Prophets. — Romans 3:21 NASB

But by His doing **you are in Christ Jesus, who became to us wisdom from God, and righteousness and sanctification, and redemption.**—1 Corinthians 1:30 NASB

> Until we all attain to the unity of the faith, and of the **knowledge of the Son of God**, to a mature man, to the measure of the stature which belongs to the **fullness of Christ**. —Ephesians 4:13 NASB

Clearly Christ is the center of everything! And clearly the inspired writers have wisdom and instruction for different churches. But notice some notions that are *not* in the Bible:

• The goal of our instruction is obedience to our letters.
• Righteousness comes from a strict adherence to our letters.
• The New Covenant is following a collection of writings.
• Jesus proclaiming that there would be a new written standard.

The New Testament writers could have written any of these... but they didn't. The letter to the Hebrews declares something different:

> **God**, after He spoke long ago to the Fathers in the prophets in many portions and in many ways, in these last days **has spoken to us through His Son.**—Hebrews 1:1–2 NASB

The New Testament authors wrote for the purpose of developing and spreading Christ (likeness) within the recipients. If their main concern was growing into the Spirit of Christ, then shouldn't that be our main concern? If they wrote their letters *for the purpose* of spreading the Spirit of Christ, then shouldn't that be our purpose?

Questions:

14. Which of the following were *emphasized* in Paul's letters?

_____ understanding the character of Christ

_____ the following of certain traditions

_____ the following of certain rules

_____ the building up of each other in Christ

_____ the preparing ourselves for persecution

_____ being guided by unfamiliar or mysterious spirits

_____ the following of specific actions within church worship

15. How would you think churches, who had not known the letters of Paul, Peter or John, have "followed Christ"?

God, develop

Your

Spirit

within me so that I may be complete and ready for **every good work**

What would Paul say?
Christ's Spirit makes us complete and ready for every good work. When Paul was writing his letters he was singularly focused on helping people grow to be more like Christ. His letters were guided by his love for them, and his desire for their growth. He wasn't striving to create a new standard or a holy book. He was simply striving to teach Christ.

But speaking the truth in love, we are to grow up in all aspects into Him who is the head, even Christ. —Ephesians 4:15 NASB

Conclusion for Part 2: How Would Paul Explain the "Role of the Scriptures"?

Questions	Answers
What is "True Knowledge"?	Knowing Christ's Spirit
How did the Pharisees consider the Scriptures?	They thought that within the Scriptures they had eternal life.
Did the Pharisees have the "word"?	No. Jesus said they did not have the word abiding in them.
1. What is the purpose for the OT? 2. The Law? 3. The Scriptures?	1. Lead us to Christ. 2. To inform us where we have fallen short. 3. So that we may have the same mind as Christ.
Why did the NT authors write their letters?	To teach Christ and build people up in Him, and express their love for them (recipients).
Where can we find the embodiment of knowledge and truth?	Jesus. (the Law is NOT the embodiment of truth and knowledge)

Authority of the Scriptures

Paul's letters were a reminder to the churches of his love for them. His letters were instructions and spiritual wisdom for their different questions and struggles. He wrote to remind them of the Christ-Spirit that sacrificed Himself for mankind. These letters were spread to serve the church's purpose of *growth in Christ's Spirit*. For Paul, the mysteriously strong and loving Spirit of Jesus was both God's Message and God's Way. He did not see his letters as some new written standard, but rather as a reminder of the One who is the standard.

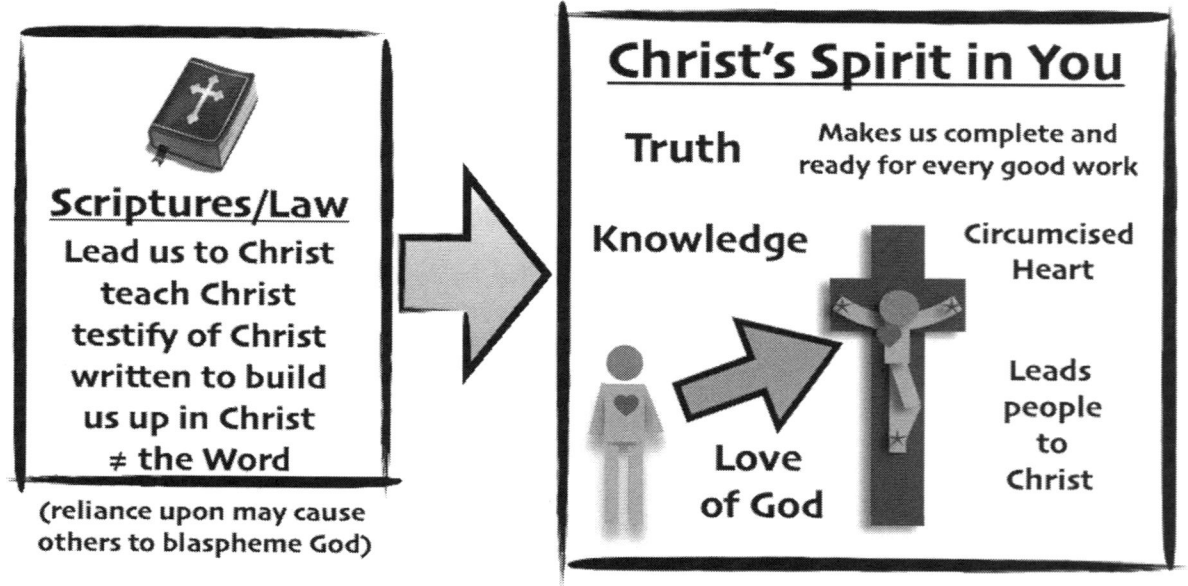

The Christ-Spirit vs. Everything Else

Christ *is* the Spirit of God. For Paul everything else was subservient to the development of this "Christ" within. He was here to teach and build up *this* Spirit. He was not commissioned to write a new "Word of God," for he knew that Christ was God's message.[14] He was not creating some new standard of right and wrong, for he believed that Christ was the goal of the Law. He didn't set out to create a new written source for "knowledge and Truth." He only set out to live and preach "knowledge and Truth" through the building up of the Christ-Spirit within himself and others. He did not want reliance upon the Scriptures, but rather wanted the Scriptures to be used as a tool for the growth and development of the Spirit (love, endurance, faith, and everything we find in Christ).

CHRIST
True Knowledge,
Wisdom of God,
Righteousness of God,
Our Foundation,
Word of God,
the Way,
the Truth,
and the Life.

The NT authors point us toward HIS GREATNESS

God now speaks to us through

His Son

Paul had authority to build people up— not tear people down, and **he wrote his letters for the expressed purpose of encouraging the Spirit to grow within.** He committed his life to this goal. Paul saw himself as a servant for the sake of Christ. He was striving to help people be the light in a dark world.

All of his instructions (about marriage, or head coverings, spiritual gifts, or whatever) were given to build them up in Christ, for the Christ-Spirit was everything to Paul.

> ...in accordance with the authority which the Lord gave me for building up and not for tearing down.
>
> —2 Corinthians 13:10 NASB

Purpose for the Scriptures = the Christ-Spirit in Mankind

**The shortest and surest way of arriving
at real knowledge is to unlearn the lessons
we have been taught, to mount the first principles,
and take nobody's word about them.
—Henry Bolingbroke**

---

14 This will become more obvious in Part 3.

Questions	Answers
What does Paul preach? What is his "Word of God"?	the Spirit of Christ or "Christ in you" (Studies #11-20)
Where is Paul's focus?	"I determined to know nothing, except Jesus and Him crucified." 1Cor. 2:2
What is the purpose of the Old Testament?	"the Law has become our tutor to lead us to Christ." Gal. 3:24
What does Jesus say about the Pharisees who "search the scriptures" and "think that in them they have eternal life"?	"You have neither heard His voice at any time nor seen His form. You do not have His word abiding in you, for you do not believe Him whom He sent... you do not have the love of God in yourselves." John 5:37-42 (Study #8)
What leads people to repentance?	Kindness of God. Rom. 2:4 (Study #9)
What does Paul say about Christians who "rely upon the Law"?	They are thieves, adulterers and cause the Gentiles to blaspheme God. Rom.2 (Study #9)
What is Paul's solution for those who "rely upon the Law"?	Their hearts need to be circumcised by the Spirit, not by the letter. Rom. 2:29 (Study #9)
What is Paul's goal for the recipients of his letters?	That the recipients be complete in Christ. Col.1:28 "I am at labor until Christ is formed in you." Gal. 4:19 (Study #5)
Why does Paul give his instructions?	"the goal of our instructions is love..." 1Tim.1:5 So that they may imitate Paul as he imitates Christ. 1Cor. 4:14; 11:1 To let them know his love for them. 2Cor. 2:3-4 To remind them of points he had taught them before. Rom 15:14-16 So that they may know how to act in assembly. 1Tim.3:14-16 To stimulate them to wholesome thinking, and the command given by the Lord. 2Pet.3:1-2 (Study #7)
How does God now speaks to us?	"God now speaks to us through His Son." Heb. 1:1-2
Where does his faith come from?	Christ authored and perfected the faith. Heb. 12:2
What is "real knowledge"?	Spirit of Christ (Study #6)
Whose mindset should we have?	For WHO HAS KNOWN THE MIND OF THE LORD, THAT HE WILL INSTRUCT HIM? But we have the mind of Christ. 1Cor. 2:16

Questions	Answers
What specifically did Paul want the church to grow up to be?	"we are to grow up in all aspects into Him who is the head, even Christ." Eph. 4:15 (Study #5)
What does Paul believe is the proper use of the Scriptures? (Studies #7 and #10)	Building people up to be more like the Spirit found in Jesus: "For everything that was written in the past was written to teach us, so that **through the endurance** taught in the **Scriptures** and the encouragement they provide we might have hope. May the God who gives endurance and encouragement give you **the same attitude of mind toward each other that Christ Jesus had.**" Rom.15:4-5 (Study #7) The "**sacred writings are able to make you wise for salvation through faith in Christ Jesus.** All Scripture is breathed out by God and profitable for teaching, for reproof, for correction, and for training in righteousness, that **the man of God may be complete, equipped for every good work.**" 2Tim.3:15-17 (see below for explanation of a "good work") (Study #10)
What does Paul have authority to do?	"the authority which the Lord gave me for **building up and not for tearing down.**" 2Cor. 13:10
Does Paul equate his own writings with the "sacred writings" or scripture?	Unspecified (though the principle of "using scriptures for the purpose of growing into Christ," he would certainly apply to his own letters)
How did they describe Christ?	Alpha and Omega...(Love of God, word of God, righteousness of God, wisdom of God, power of God, Head of the church, Foundation, Spiritual Building, Emmanuel, Rock, High priest, prophet, Messenger/Apostle, the Way, the Truth, and the Life, Perfect, Almighty, Prince of peace, Lord, Savior, Messiah, Redeemer, Mediator, Judge, Good Shepherd, Hope of Glory, Light of the World, Bread of Life, Lion of Judah, Son of David, Son of God, Son of man, Goal of the Law, Author and finisher of our faith, exact representation of God...)
Does Jesus ever refer to a new written standard? Do we have any record of Him commissioning people to create a new set of rules or traditions?	No record of Jesus making a statement like that. He says that "nobody comes to the Father but through Me."
Does the Old Testament describe the New Covenant as something that would be written down?	Yes. Jeremiah describes it as something that would be written on the hearts of men. Jeremiah 31:31 (Study #22)

Part 3: What Exactly Was Paul's "Word of God"?

Study #11: How Did the Apostle John Define "the Word"?
The message that became human

Study #12: How Did the Apostle Peter Define "the Word"?
Does Peter use the "word" in a similar manner?

Study #13: How Did the Apostle Paul Define "the Word"?
The Christ-in-you message

Study #14: What are the Powers of the Word?
The Word of God is living and active…

Study #15: What is the "Sword of the Spirit"?
The sword is not the Bible?!?

Study #16: What is the "Washing of Water by the Word"?
How the Christ-Spirit cleanses others (Ephesians 4)

Study #17: What is "Sanctified by the Word of God"?
Sanctified by a Christlike Spirit (1 Timothy 4)

Study #18: What is "Adulterating the Word of God"?
Manifestation of truth vs. Adulterating the Word (2 Corinthians 4)

Study #19: What is "Reviling the Word of God"?
How a non-Christlike spirit reviles the Message (Titus 2)

Study #20: Instructions to Those Receiving the Word of God
Considering the multiple "Word of God" phrases in 1Thessalonians 2

Conclusion: God's Message is Christ's Spirit

Did Paul Know that He Wrote the "Word of God"?

We know from our previous studies that the New Testament authors were striving to build people up to be more like Christ…. But what about this "Word of God"? What exactly is it? What would make sense for those in the first century?

When Paul sat down to address the church in Corinth, did he think to himself "I am writing *the* word of God"? Did those in Corinth think he was writing *the* word of God? Or is that a construct that came years or centuries later?

The Apostle John described the word as Christ, while Peter refers to the Word's existence at Creation—but does Paul think of this word in the same manner? What are the attributes of this word? Is it God? Is it a body of knowledge or a set of facts? Is it a spiritual being? Does it have unique abilities or powers? What exactly is it?

The Dilemma

My dilemma originated in a college course in Singapore. We were studying the fourth chapter of Hebrews, and we came across one of our favorite memory verses on the 'word of God':

> For the word of God is living and active and sharper than any two-edged sword, and piercing as far as the division of soul and spirit, of both joints and marrow, and able to judge the thoughts and intentions of the heart. —Hebrews 4:12 NASB

Time and Location

Consider the timing and placement of those first letters. What exactly were they following in those first couple of decades?

Letter	Year Written Estimated	Years After Christ's Physical Life (30-33 A.D.)
Earliest Letters of New Testament		
James	50	17-20 yrs
1 & 2 Thess.	52-53	19-23 yrs
Galatians	55	22-25 yrs
1 & 2 Cor.	57	24-27 yrs
Romans	57-58	24-27 yrs
Phil., Col., Phi., Eph.	62-63	29-33 yrs

Today, we typically use this verse to emphasize the importance of Bible study and the Bible's power to change our hearts. But here in this class, something didn't seem right, and the more I thought about it, the more my mind filled up with a series of questions:

Is this "word of God" a reference to his own letter?
What is the "word of God" in *this* context?
Does defining the "word" as the Bible really fit with the context of this passage?
What would the recipients have thought is this "word of God"?

To put it in other words, my dilemma started from contemplating two very simple realities:
1. Before the New Testament letters were written, there were **no** New Testament letters.
2. The New Testament writers quite frequently wrote about the Word (or Word of God).

Each of these is simple and obvious. But when we combine these statements, *an important question arises*: **What were the New Testament writers referring to when they wrote about "the word of God"?**

The "word of God" phrase obviously meant something to the first-century Christians. And the New Testament letters either didn't exist yet or were in the process of being written. So what, specifically, did this phrase mean *to them*?

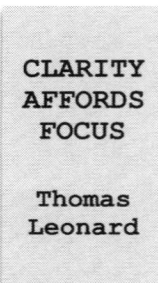

CLARITY
AFFORDS
FOCUS

Thomas
Leonard

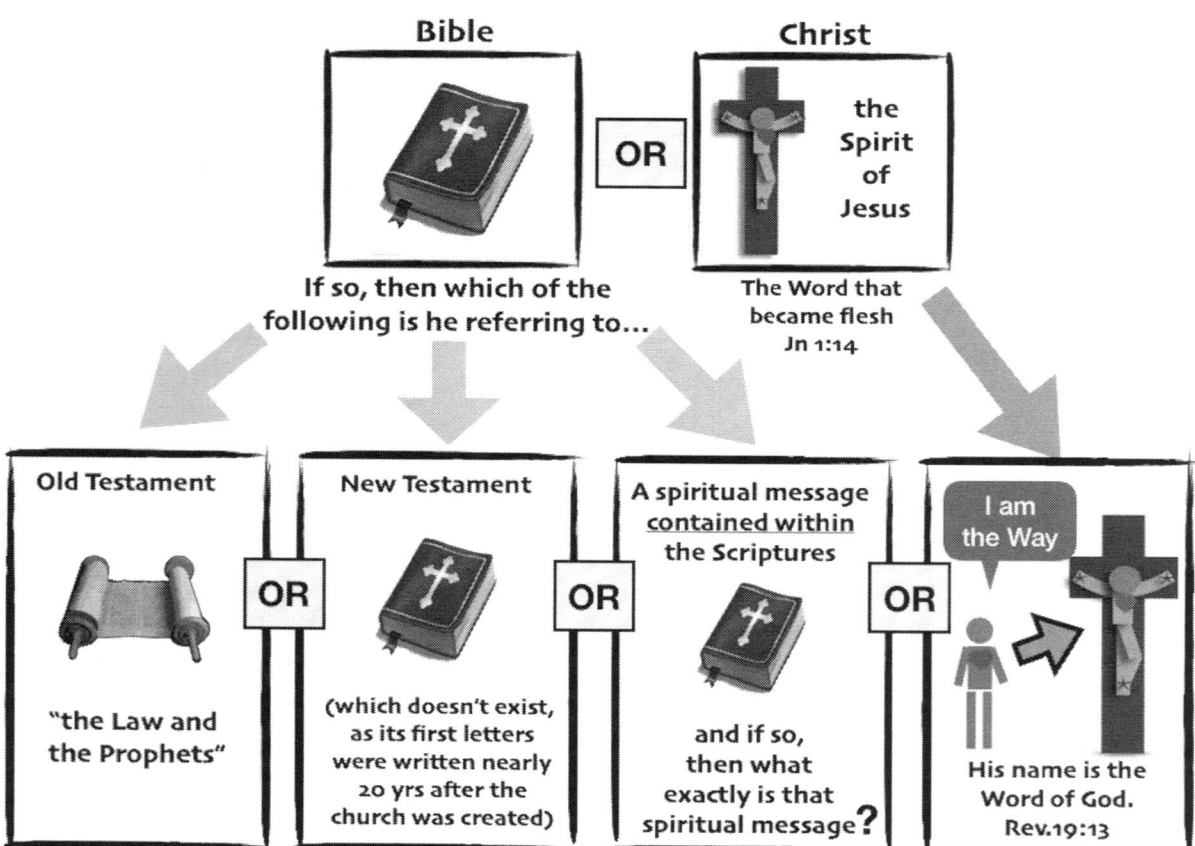

What would the Apostle Paul say is "the Word of God"?

Which of these makes the most sense for any given passage?

Potential Definitions for the "Word" or "Word of God"

While there are many ways we may define terms like *word*, *faith*, or *love*, the author *usually* intends it only one way. The five most common and probable interpretations(today) for the "word" or "word of God" are:

1. The Word of God = Christ/Spirit[15]
2. The Word of God = the Bible (old and/or new testaments)
3. The Word of God = a message within the Bible[16] (factual or spiritual)
4. The Word of God = a message of God (unspecified)
5. The Word of God = verbal expression of God (unspecified)

> There is no greater impediment to the advancement of knowledge than the ambiguity of words.
>
> —Thomas Reid

Each of these should be given an examination and may need to be considered for any given biblical context. We want to be precise with the language, and vague definitions are not going to help us understand their perspective (and probably wouldn't have helped the first Christians either). Understanding *their* specific and intended meanings should be our greatest concern.

Also, while there are some inherent difficulties with each of these, typically only one or two of them would truly fit for any given context. And whichever definition we use should make sense in regard to:

- Their current time and location
- Their current difficulties (especially spiritual)
- What they had heard about Christ and the life he led
- Their knowledge (or lack thereof) of other New Testament letters
- The purpose of their letters.

Since the last two definitions (a message of God and a verbal expression) do not give us a clear or specific message, we will focus on the first 3, in the hope of ascertaining what God's word actually is. Some of the questions we need to ask begin with—

Is the word of God…

(1) A spiritual entity?
(2) A body of information?
(3) God or a part of God?
(4) The New Testament?
(5) Genesis through Revelation?
(6) A message contained within the Bible?
(7) And if so, what is that message?

> A QUESTION NOT ASKED IS A DOOR NOT OPENED.
>
> MARILEE ADAMS

---

[15] a variation of this is "Christ in you" (Study #13)

[16] Ultimately we will find that this "Word" is both the *Christ-Spirit* and the *embodiment of God's spiritual precepts* (which is what the Scriptures were leading us toward).

The flowchart FC#1 Questions and difficulties that arise from equating the Bible with the Word of God.

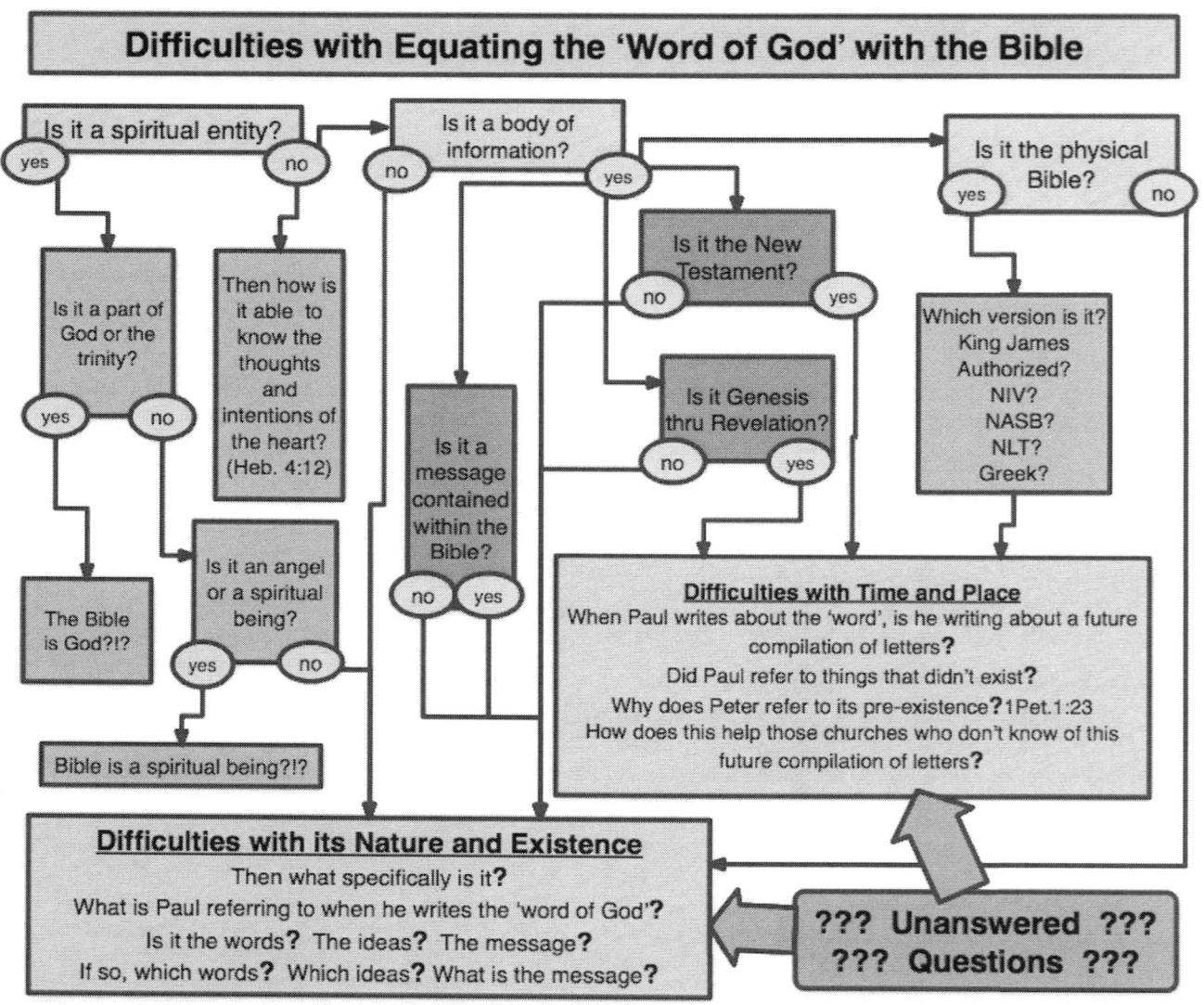

Before we Start Looking at the "Word"
The New Testament refers to the "word of God" 45 times. These studies will cover the most descriptive and informative passages regarding the *word of God*. Some of the passages may give us little insight into the definition of the "word of God," while others offer clues. Some will contrast it with selfish and ungrateful attitudes, while other passages associate it more clearly with God and His love. But examining each passage in context is the only way we can understand the writer's intended meaning. (There are more "Word" passages in the conclusions)

Ultimately, the conclusion will be easy to understand. In fact it will be much easier than what most of us have been taught. But in order to get there we will have to take a critical look at some of our current teachings. For many, especially those of us who have been trained, this study may be challenging and heavy, as it will question some of our core paradigms. My desire is to stay true to the truth of the New Testament and the Spirit we find in Christ. And my intention is to serve you, so that we all may grow, and effectively teach others about this infinitely good Creator.

> **"Message of Bob" Limitation**
> The most basic definition for the *word of God* is "message of God." This, of course, is a literal answer. But it essentially tells us that "God *has* a message." It's like saying "the *message of Bob*". That phrase tells us nothing in regard to its contents (Can you imagine someone coming up to you and telling you that your mother has a message for you, but doesn't tell you what the message is???). What good would a "message of God" be, if we don't know its contents? How could we possibly teach the "word of God," if we don't know what that phrase means?

The Logos vs. Rhema Consideration
There are 2 Greek words that are translated into English as 'word', logos and rhema. While there is some discussion regarding the nature and usage of these words. Here are some things to consider:

1. The Septuagint (the Hebrew Bible translated into Greek) translates both of these terms from the same Hebrew word 'dabar'.
2. Luke equates logos with rhema: "While Peter was still saying these things (rhema), the Holy Spirit fell on all who heard the word (logos)." Acts 10:44
3. Peter uses logos (1Pet.1:23) and rhema (1Pet.1:25) in the same context to seemingly refer to the same subject.
4. Both logos (word) and rhema(saying) contain the notion of 'a message'.
5. They are both frequently translated into English as 'word'.

While there are subtle differences in the usage of these terms, their core meanings are defined and explained by our English words: "word" or "message." And for the purposes of this study, this will be sufficient. And as you will see both "logos" and "rhema" will be used to represent the Spirit of Jesus.

(For a deeper study of the Greek "logos" and "rhema" terms, there are a variety of good resources available on the internet. Here is one of the more thorough studies: https://annointing.files.wordpress.com/2013/01/rhema-vs-logos-a-scholars-perspective.pdf)

Capitalization:
The original Greek did not have uppercase and lowercase letters. Since the English language makes these distinctions, translators have had an extra burden of trying to determine whether or not terms like "spirit" or "word" are references to deity and therefore should be capitalized. And since God did not introduce Christ in a dual case alphabet like English, and therefore doesn't regard it to be crucial, I likewise don't consider it essential to understanding the passage. (Personally, I would rather read them as the first Christians read them, with all the letters in the same case.)

Punctuation:
The original Greek did not have punctuation. So translators have also had to determine this aspect of translation. Our different style of writing has, at times, aided in our misunderstanding of certain passages. To better understand the flow of thought, I have given a couple of passages that are better understood without the punctuation(studies #13, 14, and 19).

A Powerful Message

What if "preaching the word" was not a reference to the Bible, but simply meant "preaching Christ's Spirit"?

What if the "sword of the Spirit, which is the word of God" was not a reference to Paul's own letter, but rather was a reference to the Spirit of Jesus? How would we wield that sword?

What if the "pure milk of the word" was not a reference to the Scriptures but was speaking of the heart and motivation of Jesus Himself? How would we strengthen the weak and immature? How would we nourish ourselves with the "milk of the word"?

When any real progress is made,
we unlearn and learn anew
what we thought we knew before.
—Henry David Thoreau

The Word Causes Followers to be One with...

The night before He goes to the cross,

Jesus Prays that:

1. Disciples have His joy,
2. Disciples are kept from evil,
3. Disciples are sanctified in the truth (= God's word)

> Sanctified = made holy

so | that

4. Disciples and future believers are ONE with Christ (& God)

so | that

5. the world may **know Christ**, & know that God **loved** the world (just as God loved Jesus)

Jesus Prays to God
(John 17:13-26 NASB)

But now I come to You; and these things I speak in the world so that they may have My joy made full in themselves. I have given them **Your word**; and the world has hated them, because they are not of the world, even as I am not of the world. I do not ask You to take them out of the world, but to keep them from the evil *one*. They are not of the world, even as I am not of the world. **Sanctify them in the truth; Your word is truth.** As You sent Me into the world, I also have sent them into the world. For their sakes I sanctify Myself, that they themselves also may be sanctified in truth. I do not ask on behalf of these alone, but for those also who believe in Me through their **word**; that they may all be one; even as You, Father, *are* in Me and I in You, that they also may be in Us, so that the world may believe that You sent Me. The glory which You have given Me I have given to them, that they may be one, just as We are one; I in them and You in Me, that they may be perfected in unity, so that the world may know that You sent Me, and loved them, even as You have loved Me.

What causes people to come to "know Christ"?
What is Jesus likely referring to as God's Word?

Think Like Paul: Searching for the Message that Changed the World

Study #11: How Did the Apostle John Define the Word?

> And the Word became flesh and dwelt among us, and we have seen his glory, glory as of the only Son from the Father, full of grace and truth. —John 1:14 ESV

You have probably heard about this "word" that became "flesh." But have you really thought about what that means? … I mean how can a word be a person? Seriously!! …Well, let's see if we can get a grasp of what John means. Here are two other related passages where John explicitly declares that Christ is the Word:

> In the beginning was the Word, and the Word was with God, and the Word was God. —John 1:1 ESV

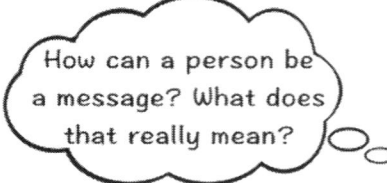

> He is clothed with a robe dipped in blood, and His name is called The Word of God. —Revelation 19:13 NASB

These are different concepts than the other descriptions of Jesus. This is more than being a prophet, a priest, or a king. This is different than stating, "He has the words of life," or "He is the Son of God." Those are true, but John equates Jesus with logos (the message of God).

Jesus = the Message

Let's think about what this means…

A word or message is usually a communication from one person to another. It could be in an explicit verbal request like "Go to the store and buy some milk," or it may come in a different kind of auditory expression like laughter, crying, a knock, an alarm, or screeching tires. And of course it may also come in a written form like the Bible, a menu, or this book. But a message may also come in a much more subtle way, such as a wink, a smile, a raised eyebrow, or even silence.

> For it became Him, for whom are all things, and by whom are all things, in bringing many sons unto glory, to make the captain of their salvation perfect through sufferings.
> –Hebrews 2:10 KJV

But how can a message be a person? And what would the message of Christ be saying to mankind? I mean, if Christ is God's message, then what is God saying? What is He telling us to do? Or be? What is the life of Jesus saying about God? … Or man? … Or what it means to be righteous?

Let's first consider what is known about the life of Jesus:

Questions:

1.   What are Jesus' main accomplishments?

2.   What are His core teachings?

> For we have not an high priest which cannot be touched with the feeling of our infirmities; but was in all points tempted like as we are, yet without sin.
> —Hebrews 4:15 KJV

3.   What is His greatest achievement?

4.   Would you say that Jesus embodied the spiritual principles that the Scriptures taught?

5.   What happened to Him? How was He treated?

6.   How did He react to that treatment?

7.   Why do you think Jesus reacted to the torture in the way that He did?

8.   In order for Jesus to endure what He did, what kinds of thoughts do you think He had to contemplate or meditate upon?

Now let's consider how He is God's message:

9.   If Jesus, the man with the Spirit of God, *is* the actual message of God, then what does that say about God? What are His attributes?

10.   What does God care most about?

11.   How much does God value man?

12.   What does His life and death say about those whom you have considered enemies?

13.   In light of this *message*, how should we think of others?

Behold, the days are coming, declares the LORD, when I will make a **new covenant** with the house of Israel and the house of Judah, not like the covenant that I made with their fathers on the day when I took them by the hand to bring them out of the land of Egypt, my covenant that they broke, though I was their husband, declares the LORD. For this is the covenant that I will make with the house of Israel after those days, declares the

LORD: I will put my law within them, and I will write it on their hearts. And I will be their God, and they shall be my people. And no longer shall each one teach his neighbor and each his brother, saying, 'Know the LORD,' for they shall all know me, from the least of them to the greatest, declares the LORD. For I will forgive their iniquity, and I will remember their sin no more. —Jeremiah 31:31-34 ESV

14.   Consider Jeremiah's description above, and explain how a new covenant may fit with John's description of the "word"?

How would John explain this today?
John refers to Christ as the word/message of God. This is a real-life human who embodies God's spiritual principles. This is a message that is beyond thought and language. This is a message of being-ness.

You yourselves are our letter of recommendation, written on our hearts, to be known and read by all. And you show that you are a letter from Christ delivered by us, written not with ink but with the Spirit of the living God, not on tablets of stone but on tablets of human hearts. Such is the confidence that we have through Christ toward God.
—2 Corinthians 3:2-4 ESV

The "Word" that "Was Preached to You"

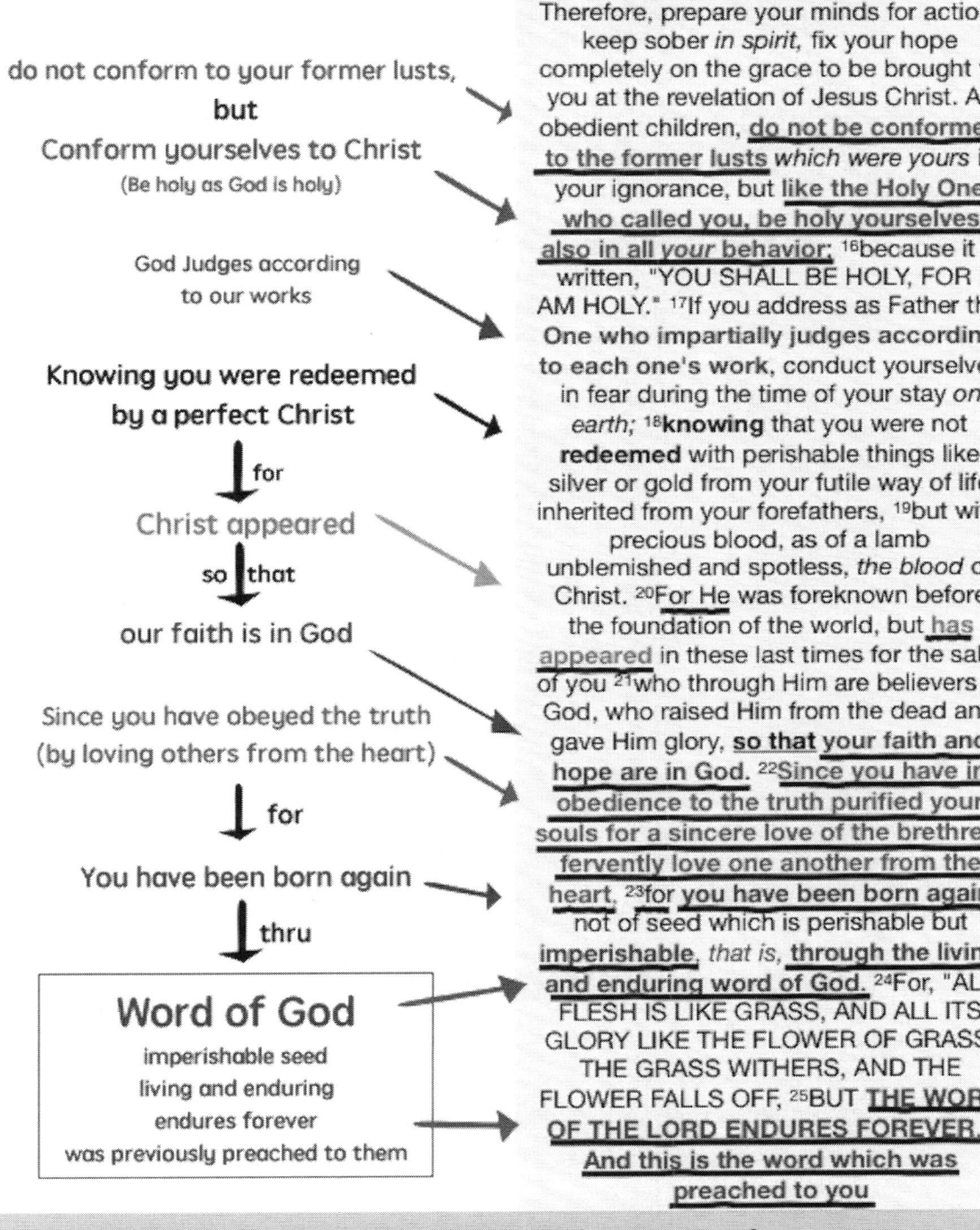

do not conform to your former lusts,
but
Conform yourselves to Christ
(Be holy as God is holy)

God Judges according
to our works

**Knowing you were redeemed
by a perfect Christ**

↓ for

Christ appeared

so ↓ that

our faith is in God

Since you have obeyed the truth
(by loving others from the heart)

↓ for

You have been born again

↓ thru

Word of God
imperishable seed
living and enduring
endures forever
was previously preached to them

1Peter 1:13-25 NASB
Therefore, prepare your minds for action, keep sober *in spirit,* fix your hope completely on the grace to be brought to you at the revelation of Jesus Christ. As obedient children, do not be conformed to the former lusts *which were yours* in your ignorance, but like the Holy One who called you, be holy yourselves also in all *your* behavior; 16because it is written, "YOU SHALL BE HOLY, FOR I AM HOLY." 17If you address as Father the One who impartially judges according to each one's work, conduct yourselves in fear during the time of your stay *on earth;* 18**knowing** that you were not **redeemed** with perishable things like silver or gold from your futile way of life inherited from your forefathers, 19but with precious blood, as of a lamb unblemished and spotless, *the blood* of Christ. 20For He was foreknown before the foundation of the world, but has appeared in these last times for the sake of you 21who through Him are believers in God, who raised Him from the dead and gave Him glory, **so that** your faith and hope are in God. 22Since you have in obedience to the truth purified your souls for a sincere love of the brethren, fervently love one another from the heart. 23for you have been born again not of seed which is perishable but imperishable, *that is,* through the living and enduring word of God. 24For, "ALL FLESH IS LIKE GRASS, AND ALL ITS GLORY LIKE THE FLOWER OF GRASS. THE GRASS WITHERS, AND THE FLOWER FALLS OFF, 25BUT THE WORD OF THE LORD ENDURES FOREVER." And this is the word which was preached to you

What exactly is the "Word of God" that Peter is referring to?

What Exactly is the "Pure Milk of the Word"?

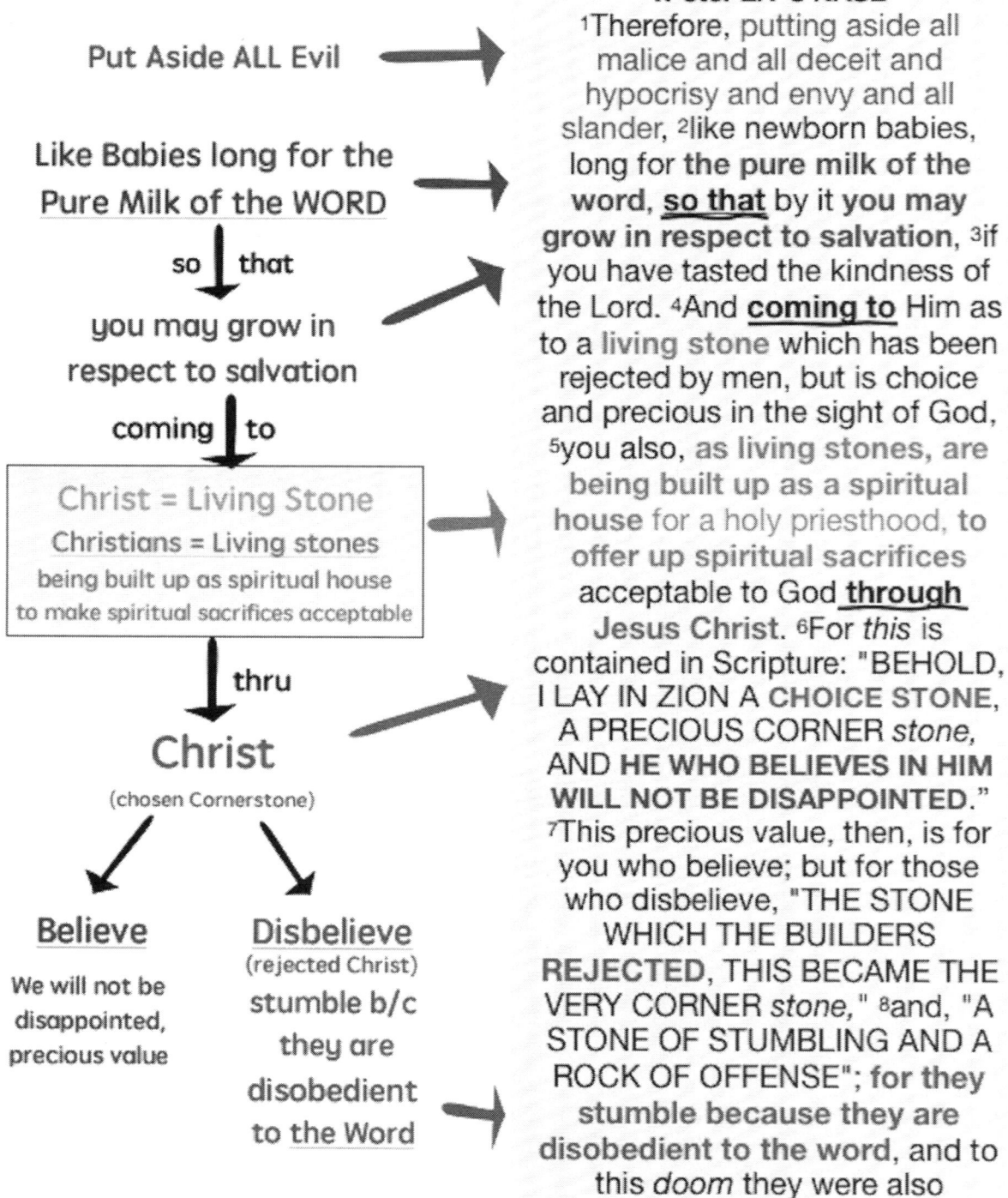

Put Aside ALL Evil ➡

Like Babies long for the Pure Milk of the WORD ➡

so ↓ that

you may grow in respect to salvation ➡

coming ↓ to

Christ = Living Stone
Christians = Living stones
being built up as spiritual house
to make spiritual sacrifices acceptable ➡

↓ thru

Christ
(chosen Cornerstone) ➡

↙   ↘

Believe
We will not be disappointed, precious value

Disbelieve
(rejected Christ)
stumble b/c they are disobedient to the Word ➡

1Peter 2:1-8 NASB
¹Therefore, putting aside all malice and all deceit and hypocrisy and envy and all slander, ²like newborn babies, long for **the pure milk of the word**, **so that** by it **you may grow in respect to salvation**, ³if you have tasted the kindness of the Lord. ⁴And **coming to** Him as to a living stone which has been rejected by men, but is choice and precious in the sight of God, ⁵you also, as living stones, are being built up as a spiritual house for a holy priesthood, to offer up spiritual sacrifices acceptable to God **through** Jesus Christ. ⁶For *this* is contained in Scripture: "BEHOLD, I LAY IN ZION A **CHOICE STONE**, A PRECIOUS CORNER *stone,* AND **HE WHO BELIEVES IN HIM WILL NOT BE DISAPPOINTED.**" ⁷This precious value, then, is for you who believe; but for those who disbelieve, "THE STONE WHICH THE BUILDERS REJECTED, THIS BECAME THE VERY CORNER *stone,*" ⁸and, "A STONE OF STUMBLING AND A ROCK OF OFFENSE"; for they stumble because they are disobedient to the word, and to this *doom* they were also appointed.

What is the "Word" that fits into these contexts?
The Scriptures? The Spirit of Christ? Or something else?

Study #12: How Did the Apostle Peter Define the Word?

Peter uses the terminology in a couple of different ways. We will start with the clearer usage.

A.   The Earth was Formed by the Word of God. (2 Peter 3:5)

> For they deliberately overlook this fact, that the heavens existed long ago, and **the earth was formed out of water and through water by the word of God**, and that by means of these the world that then existed was deluged with water and perished. But, by the same word, the heavens and earth that now exist are stored up for fire, being kept until the day of judgment and destruction of the ungodly.
> —2 Peter 3:5-7 ESV

Question

1.   What are the likely or possible meanings for this "word of God" in this context?
   e)   the Bible
   f)   Christ/Spirit of God
   g)   a message within the Bible
   h)   a verbal expression of God

> All things were made by Him; and without Him was not any thing made ...
> —John 1:3 KJV

Now Let's Consider 1 Peter: (See Passage Diagrams)

Notice the language of internal transformation Peter associates with the obedience to the truth: a purification of souls, sincere love of the brethren, fervent love for one another from the heart, being born of an imperishable seed, putting aside of all malice, hypocrisy, envy, and slander, growing with respect to salvation, tasting of the kindness of the Lord, being built up into a spiritual house, and an entrusting oneself to God.

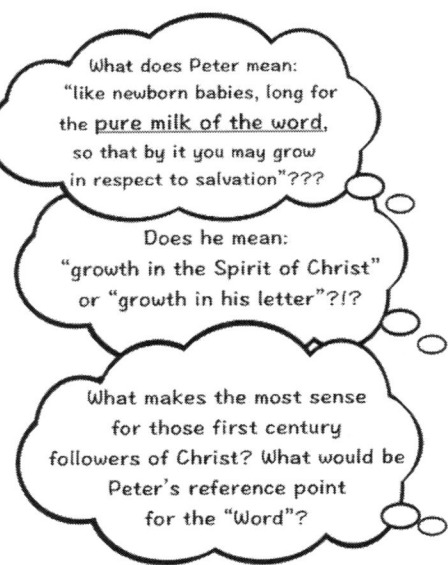

What does Peter mean: "like newborn babies, long for the pure milk of the word, so that by it you may grow in respect to salvation"???

Does he mean: "growth in the Spirit of Christ" or "growth in his letter"?!?

What makes the most sense for those first century followers of Christ? What would be Peter's reference point for the "Word"?

Questions (Some may have more than one answer.)

2.   How many of these notions fit with the idea that we are to put on the Spirit of Christ?

3.   How many references are there to:
   a.   The Bible?
   b.   Paul's letters?
   c.   Peter's Letters?
   d.   Any New Testament letters?
   e.   The Old Testament Scriptures?

4. According to 1 Peter 1:25, when was the word preached? In this context, can the "word" be the letter Peter is currently writing?

5. According to the context, which of the following best describes the essence or nature of the Word of God?
   a. It is a book.
   b. It is a message contained within a book.
   c. It is a particular set of facts or information.
   d. It is alive.
   e. It is spirit.
   f. It is God.
   g. It is characteristics of Christ/God.

I will cling to the imperishable

Spirit of Jesus

for that message abides forever

6. Contextually, this word is connected to:

   a. Bible study
   b. Love
   c. Spirit
   d. Scriptures
   e. Attitudes
   f. Growth
   g. Malice and slander

7. In this context, does Peter consider the "word" as John did—Christ?

8. If "tasting the goodness and love of God," is a reference to the "seed," then how would you spread this "seed"?

9. So if John and Peter explicitly declare that the "word of God" is Christ/God, then is it possible that other "word of God" passages are a reference to this Christ/God spirit?

God, nourish my soul with the pure milk of

Your Word

so that I may be built up into Your Son's likeness

How would Peter explain this today?
Peter uses the "word" in a couple of different passages. In 2 Peter 3:5, he refers to the existence of the word during Creation. In first Peter, he describes it as **living, enduring**, and as **an imperishable seed**. He refers to the "milk of the word" as something that **nourishes us**, and builds us up, **into being more like Christ**. He also refers to it as something that had previously been taught.

After considering the context of Peter's letter,
what should we consider to be "the Word that was preached"?
What does he mean by "pure milk of the Word"?

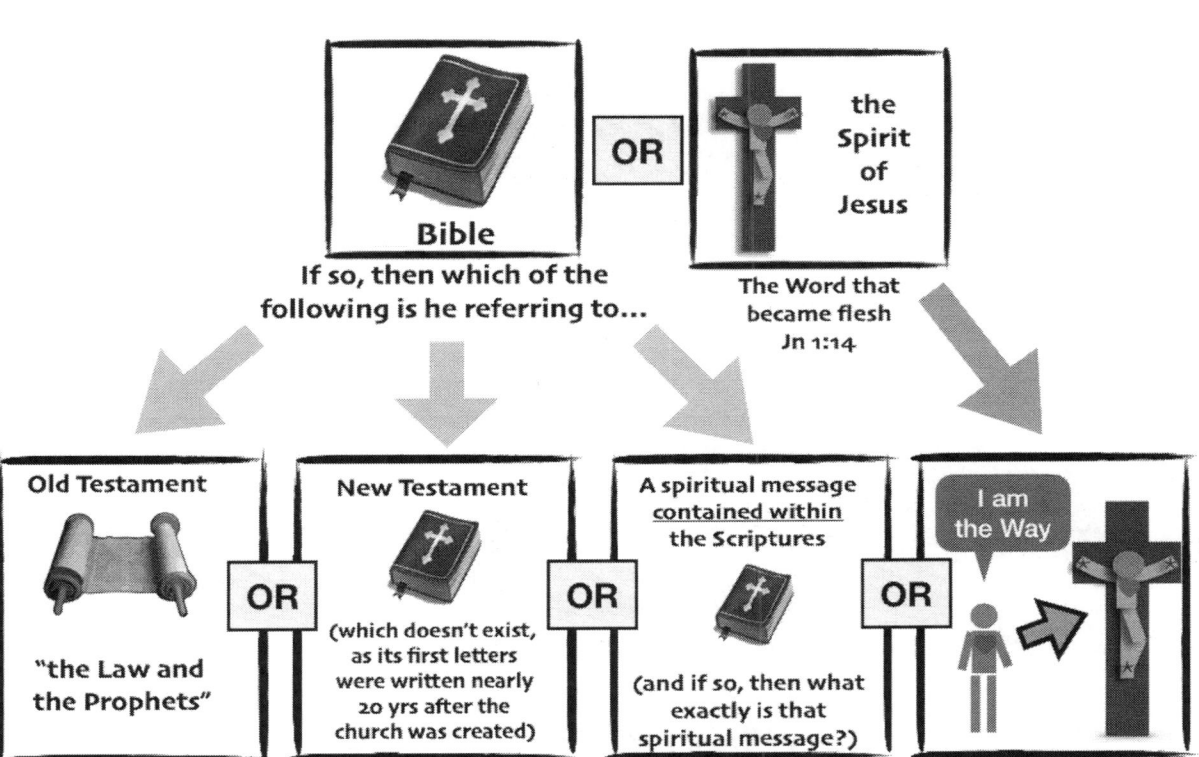

Which of these makes sense within the contexts of
"conforming ourselves to Christ" and
"being built up into a spiritual house" as Christ was?
If Peter is referring to the Bible, is he also referring to his own letter?
Which parts of the Bible would he be referring to?
Or do you think he is referring to Christ (God's Spirit in man)?
Which of these makes sense within the context of this letter?
Or the perspective of Peter? Or the perspective of those first century believers?
Which of these can best help us understand God?
Which is most edifying and nourishing?

What Exactly is the Word of God?   (Colossians 1:25-29)

Of *this church* I was made a minister according to the stewardship
from God bestowed on me for your benefit, so that I might fully carry
out the *preaching of* the word of God, — Col.1:25

Let's look at the context.

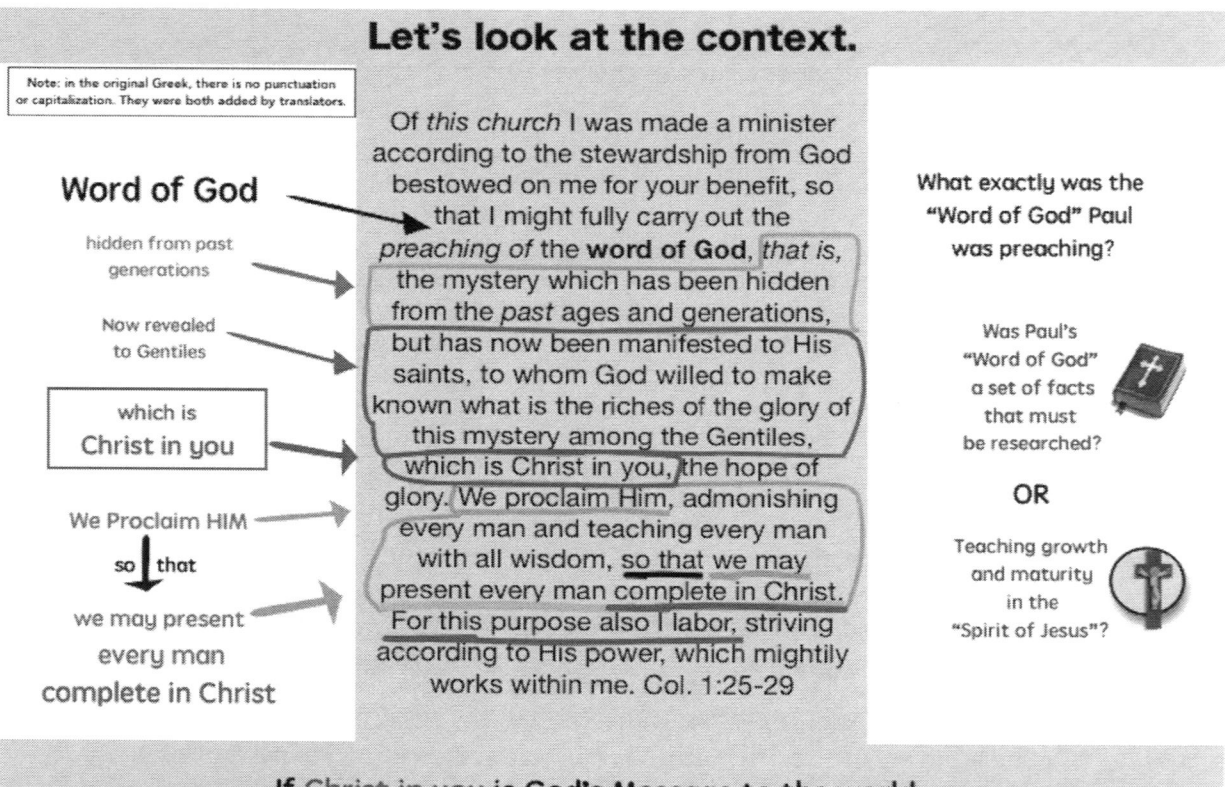

Note: in the original Greek, there is no punctuation or capitalization. They were both added by translators.

Word of God

hidden from past generations

Now revealed to Gentiles

which is
Christ in you

We Proclaim HIM

so ↓ that

we may present
every man
complete in Christ

Of *this church* I was made a minister according to the stewardship from God bestowed on me for your benefit, so that I might fully carry out the *preaching of* the **word of God**, *that is,* the mystery which has been hidden from the *past* ages and generations, but has now been manifested to His saints, to whom God willed to make known what is the riches of the glory of this mystery among the Gentiles, which is Christ in you, the hope of glory. We proclaim Him, admonishing every man and teaching every man with all wisdom, so that we may present every man complete in Christ. For this purpose also I labor, striving according to His power, which mightily works within me. Col. 1:25-29

What exactly was the "Word of God" Paul was preaching?

Was Paul's "Word of God" a set of facts that must be researched?

OR

Teaching growth and maturity in the "Spirit of Jesus"?

If Christ in you is God's Message to the world···
Then what is our message?

Perry Stiltz   Think Like Paul: Searching for the Message that Changed the World

Study #13: How Did the Apostle Paul Define the Word?

While the author of Hebrews doesn't place his name on his letter, the earliest traditions claim that the author was Paul. Though there may be some discussion about who the writer was, let's consider one of his clearer thoughts regarding the Word of God[17]:

> Through faith we understand that **the worlds were framed by the word of God**, so that things which are seen were not made of things which do appear.
> —Hebrews 11:3 KJV

This verse is strikingly similar to the way Peter uses it in our previous study. And while there may be some discussion as to the nature of this "word," it is clear that this is not a reference to scripture or the Bible, as it clearly exists at Creation. So whether or not the author is Paul, it is clear that the Spirit who wrote the letter believed the "word" to be God/Christ or the spoken words of God.

Let's consider another passage of Paul's:

> Of this church I was made a minister according to the stewardship from God bestowed on me for your benefit, **so that I might fully carry out the preaching of the Bible***, that is, the mystery which has been hidden from the past ages and generations, but **has now been manifested to His saints**, to whom God willed to make known what is the riches of the glory of this mystery among the Gentiles, **which is Christ in you, the hope of glory. We proclaim Him**, admonishing every man and teaching every man with all wisdom, **so that we may present every man complete in Christ**.—Colossians 1:25–29 NASB (*Note: "**Bible**" has been substituted for the phrase "word of God.")

1.   Does this modified passage make sense to you?

2.   Do you think Paul came to preach the Bible?

This passage would make no sense to Paul or the recipients, if this is a reference to the New Testament. It makes even less sense if it is a message contained within the Bible.

Now review the original passage: (I've taken out capitalization and punctuation to help us see what those first recipients would have seen)

> of this church I was made a minister according to the stewardship from god bestowed on me for your benefit **so that I might fully carry out the preaching of the word of god** that is the mystery which has been hidden from the past ages

---

[17] (Hebrews 4:12 will be considered in study #14)

and generations but has now been **manifested to his saints** to whom god willed to make known what is the riches of the glory of this mystery among the gentiles **which is christ in you the hope of glory we proclaim him** admonishing every man and teaching every man with all wisdom **so that we may present every man complete in christ** —Colossians 1:25–29 NASB

4. How did Paul describe this 'word of God'? (select all that apply)
    a) mystery hidden from past ages and generations
    b) has now been manifested to His saints
    c) had been mysterious to the gentiles
    d) makes known the riches of God's glory
    e) Christ in you
    f) the hope of glory
    g) the letter he is writing
    h) the letters of other writers
    i) the Law or Old Testament

5. Why does Paul teach this "word of God'? What is his purpose? (v.28-29)

6. If the "word of God" is a metonymy[18] for the "Spirit of God," does the following passage make more sense or less sense, from Paul's perspective?

> Of this church I was made a minister according to the stewardship from God bestowed on me for your benefit, **so that I might fully carry out the preaching of the _Spirit of God_,*** that is, the mystery which has been hidden from the past ages and generations, but has now been **manifested to His saints**, to whom God willed to make known what is the riches of the glory of this mystery among the Gentiles, **which is Christ in you, the hope of glory**. We proclaim Him, admonishing every man and teaching every man with all wisdom, so that we may present every man complete in Christ. For this purpose also I labor, striving according to His power, which mightily works within me. —Colossians 1:25–29 NASB (*Note: "Spirit of God" has been substituted for the phrase "word of God.")

7. Is this reading more mysterious or more coherent?

8. After Paul declares 'which is Christ in you, the hope of glory," what does Paul proclaim in the next verses?

9. Why does he proclaim it?

10. Is this consistent with the notion that we are to follow Jesus?

---

[18] Metonymy: the substitution of the name of an attribute or adjunct for that of the thing meant, for example *suit* for *business executive, or* "England decides to keep check on immigration" where England refers to the government.

11. According to this context, which of the following best defines this "word of God"?

   a) His letters
   b) Peter's letters
   c) John's letters
   d) James's letter
   e) Jude's letter
   f) Matthew's gospel
   g) Mark's gospel
   h) The Old Testament
   i) A message hidden within the Bible
   j) A message *contained* within the Bible
   k) Christ-in-you (spirit)
   l) The hope of glory

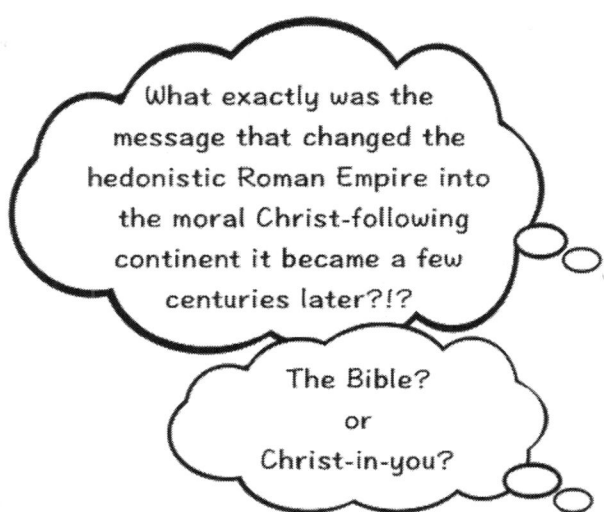

Word of God
- Hidden from past generations
- Now made manifest
- Christ in you
- Hope of glory
- What Paul proclaims

How would Paul explain this today?
In Hebrews, Paul refers to the word's existence at Creation. In Colossians, **Paul explicitly refers to the "word of God" as "Christ in you."**

God, help me understand how

within me is your message to humanity

**The natural person does not accept the things of the Spirit of God, for they are folly to him, and he is not able to understand them because they are spiritually discerned. The spiritual person judges all things, but is himself to be judged by no one.
—1 Corinthians 2:14–15 ESV**

What Exactly is the Word of God? (Hebrew 4:12)

For the word of God is living and active and sharper than any two-edged sword, and piercing as far as the division of soul and spirit, of both joints and marrow, and able to judge the thoughts and intentions of the heart. —Hebrews 4:12 NASB

Let's look at the context.

Living and Active

Able to Judge the Thoughts and Intentions of the Heart

Can see ALL THINGS

"Therefore··· JESUS CHRIST"

Note: in the original Greek, there is no punctuation or capitalization. They were both added by translators.

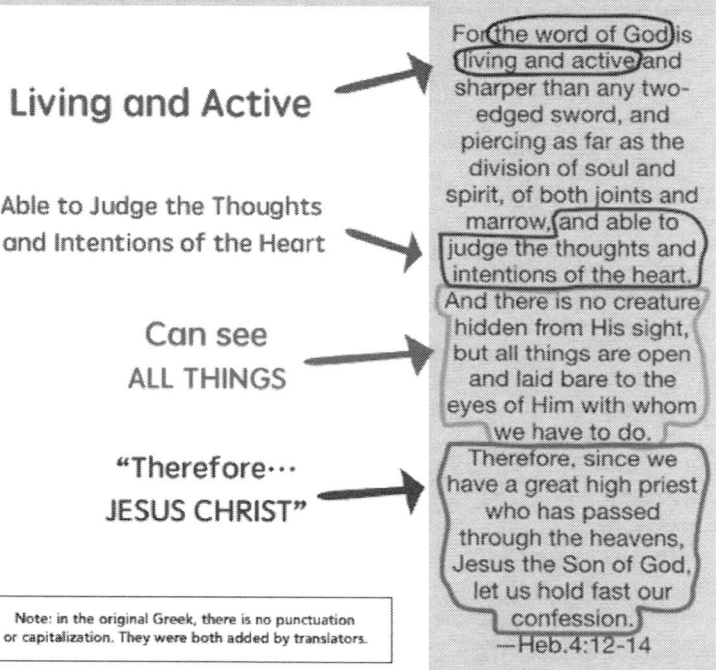

For the word of God is living and active and sharper than any two-edged sword, and piercing as far as the division of soul and spirit, of both joints and marrow, and able to judge the thoughts and intentions of the heart. And there is no creature hidden from His sight, but all things are open and laid bare to the eyes of Him with whom we have to do. Therefore, since we have a great high priest who has passed through the heavens, Jesus the Son of God, let us hold fast our confession.
—Heb.4:12-14

If you were living in the first century,

and you received this letter from one of Jesus' apostles,

and you did not have a New Testament···

Then what would you think is the "Word of God"?

Would you think "this letter is THE word of God"?

OR

Would you remember that the "Word became flesh"?

If Christ's Spirit is God's Message to humanity, then what should be our message?

Perry Stiltz   Think Like Paul: Searching for the Message that Changed the World

Study #14: What Are the Powers of the Word?

Now comes our favorite "word of God" passage! This is the passage that caused me to ask some serious questions. I mean, like "What is he *really* talking about?" "Is this "word of God" a body of information?" "Is it a spiritual entity?" "What exactly is it?" and "What would make sense for those in the first century?" …Well, let's take a look:

> For the **Word of God** is living and active and sharper than any two-edged sword,
> and piercing as far as the division of soul and spirit, of both joints and marrow,
> and able to judge the thoughts and intentions of the heart. —Hebrews 4:12 NASB

In Context:
Now let's consider the larger context without the translator's insertion of capitalization and punctuation:

> for the **word of god** is living and active and sharper than any two-edged sword
> and piercing as far as the division of soul and spirit of both joints and marrow
> and able to judge the thoughts and intentions of the heart and there is no creature
> hidden from his sight but[19] all things are open and laid bare to the eyes of him
> with whom we have to do therefore since we have a great high priest who
> has passed through the heavens jesus the son of god let us hold fast our confession
> for we do not have a high priest who cannot sympathize with our weaknesses but
> one who has been tempted in all things as we are yet without sin therefore let
> us draw near with confidence to the throne of grace so that we may receive mercy
> and find grace to help in time of need —Hebrews 4:12–16 NASB

From this context list the descriptions of the "word of God":

1.

2.

3.

4.

5.

6.

7.

What can "judge the thoughts and intentions of my heart"?

If I was sitting there in the first century reading this letter, would I think that this "Word of God" is a reference to his own letter?

Can his letter can do that? What specifically is he referring to?

---

[19] The Greek word for "but" is δέ, which may also be translated as "and" or "also."

Questions

> What if the NT authors were simply using the "word" as a metonym to refer back to the Spirit of Christ?

1.   Are these characteristics spiritual in nature?

2.   Are these characteristics similar to those that belong to God/Christ?

3.   Are there any references to the writings of the apostles or prophets?

4.   This verse has been used to describe some mystical powers of the Bible. Do you think Paul intended his letters to be mystical? Or did he write them to teach them about Christ and what it means to "follow Him"?

5.   Do you think Paul intended people to quote his letters as the "word of God"?

6.   The writer of Hebrews is probably using the phrase "word of God" to refer to:
      a. His own letter
      b. The gospel—death, burial, and resurrection (1 Cor. 15:1–4)
      c. The New Testament
      d. The Bible as a whole (Genesis through Revelation)
      e. A secret (or hidden) message *contained* within the Bible
      f. The Spirit of God/Christ

7.   Do you think Paul wrote to encourage a spiritual likeness of Christ? Or was he more interested in them following his letter?

In Your Spirit

we overcome the world

> For **Christ is the end (goal)** of the law for righteousness to everyone who believes. —Romans 10:4 ESV

> But the **goal of our instruction** is love from a pure heart and a good conscience and a sincere faith.—1 Timothy 1:5 NASB

The Old and New Testaments both point us to Christ. Christ (or Christlikeness) has always been the goal.

Many of us have been taught that Hebrews 4:12 is a reference to the Bible, and have never had any real reason to doubt this statement. But what if this verse isn't referring to the Bible (or a message within the Bible)? What if this "word of God" is used in the same manner as we have already discovered(the Spirit of God/Christ)?

Let's consider this passage with Paul's definition[20], replacing the "word of God" with the "Spirit of Christ" as follows:

> For the <u>Spirit of Christ</u> is living and active and sharper than any two-edged sword, and piercing as far as the division of soul and spirit, of both joints and marrow, and able to judge the thoughts and intentions of the heart. —Hebrews 4:12 NASB ("Spirit of Christ" has replaced "word of God")

8.   Would defining the "word of God" as "spirit of Christ" make sense in this passage?

9.   Does the context suggest that he is referring to his own written letters? Or does this sound like he is referring to Christ/God?

What would Paul say?
This Word of God has powers/abilities like God Himself (particularly its ability to "judge the thoughts and intentions of the heart"). **The context supports a spiritual being/likeness like Christ, rather than the idea he is referencing his own letters as "the word."**

Which of these notions of the "Word" is most powerful?

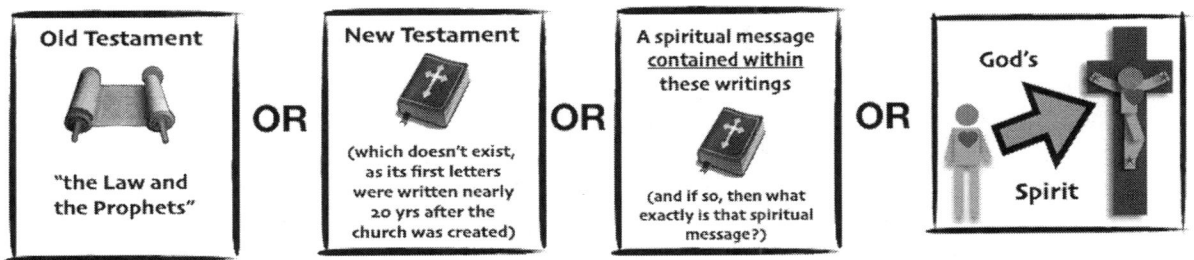

Which of these makes the most sense for Hebrews 4?

The Bible makes it clear that self-righteousness is the premier enemy of the Gospel...
Thankfully, while our self-righteousness reaches far, God's grace reaches farther.
—Tullian Tchividjian

---

[20] From Col.1:25-28 (Study #13)

Study #15: What is the "Sword of the Spirit"?

> And take the helmet of salvation, and **the sword of the Spirit, which is the word of God.** —Ephesians 6:17 ESV

In this context, what *exactly* is Paul referring to as the "word of God"? And what is the "sword of the Spirit"? Let's start with first considering how Paul uses "spirit" in this letter:

> That the God of our Lord Jesus Christ, the Father of glory, **may give to you a spirit of wisdom and revelation in *the* full knowledge of Him.** —Ephesians 1:17 LITV

> For we are His workmanship, **created in Christ Jesus for good works,** which God prepared beforehand, that we should walk in them. —Ephesians 2:10 ESV

> That He would grant you, according to the riches of His glory, to be strengthened with power through **His Spirit in the inner man; <u>so that</u> Christ may dwell in your heart through faith,** that you, being rooted and grounded in love, may be able to comprehend with the all the saints what is the breadth and length and height and depth, **and to know the love of Christ which surpasses knowledge, that you may be filled up to all the fullness of God.** —Ephesians 3:16–19 NASB

In determining the purpose of the different roles of the church (apostles, prophets, evangelists, teachers etc.), Paul stated:

> …for the equipping of the saints for the work of service, to the building up of the body of Christ; until we all attain the unity of the faith, and of the **true knowledge of the Son of God,** to a **mature(or perfect) man, to the measure of the stature which belongs to the fullness of Christ.** —Ephesians 4:12–13 NASB

God, may I walk in love

Just as You have loved me

> But speaking the truth in love, **we are to grow up in all aspects into Him,** who is the head, Christ, from whom the whole body, being fitted and held together by that which every joint supplies, according to the proper working of each individual part, causes the **growth of the body for the building up of itself in love.** —Ephesians 4:15–16 NASB

> And be kind to one another, tender hearted, forgiving each other, just as God in Christ also has forgiven you. Therefore **be imitators of God,** as beloved children; and **walk in love, just as Christ also loved you, and gave Himself up for us.** —Ephesians 4:32–5:2 NASB

Questions

1.   What kind of spirit does Paul pray for? (1:17)

2.   Why were we created? (2:10)

3.   What do we need to be "filled up to the fullness of God"? (3:19)

4.   From this letter, list three descriptions that our spirits should grow up into:

      a.

      b.

      c.

5.   How do we imitate God? (5:1) What would that mean to those in the first century?

Now let's go back to our context of "the sword of the spirit, which is the word of God," and consider these questions:

6.   Is the phrase "word of God" a reference to the letter he is in the process of writing—the Ephesian letter

7.   Does it appear to be a reference to the Old Testament?

8.   Could it be a reference to his past letters? …or maybe his future letters?

9.   Does it make sense that the "word of God" is a reference to a hidden message contained within Paul's writings?

An Ephesians Perspective

Now let's consider some facts of the time period:
-   The Ephesians letter is believed to have been written AD 60–62, which makes it around thirty years after Jesus walked the earth.
-   Paul makes no reference to the four Gospels of Matthew, Mark, Luke, or John.
-   Paul makes no reference to other New Testament writings.
-   Paul defines the "word of God" as "Christ in you" in Colossians. (study #13)
-   John states that Jesus is the "word of God." (study #11)

What does Paul refer to when he writes the "sword of the spirit, which is the word of God"?
Is this a reference to the Old Testament, the New Testament, or something else? Let's consider some of our possible definitions:

i.   The word of God = Christ-Spirit (the embodiment of God's spiritual principles)

ii.   The word of God = the Bible (OT and NT)

iii.   The word of God = a message within the Bible (OT and NT)

10. Which of the following notions are likely to be the viewpoint of the first century Ephesians?

I)   The sword of the Spirit (of Christ) = message of God

II) The sword of the Spirit = the word of God = the New Testament (which did not exist)

III) The sword of the Spirit = the word of God = a message contained within the New Testament (which did not exist)

Options (II) and (III) require and are dependent upon a new collection of writings (which are unknown at the time of this writing). But (I) is in alignment with Paul's and John's assertion that the "Spirit of Christ" = "word of God," and is consistent with the context of the Ephesian letter.

In Romans, Paul equates putting on the armor of God to putting on Jesus:

> Do this, knowing the time, that it is already the hour for you to awaken from sleep; for now salvation is nearer to us than when we believed. The night is almost gone, and the day is at hand. Let us therefore lay aside the deeds of darkness and **put on the armor of light**. Let us behave properly as in the day, not in carousing and drunkenness, not in sexual promiscuity and sensuality, not in strife and jealousy. But **put on the Lord Jesus Christ**, and make no provision for the flesh in regard to its lusts. —Romans 13:11–14 NASB

11. If the "armor of light" *is* Jesus Christ, then could the sword of the spirit also be Christ?

I will put on the armor of light which is the

Spirit of

Jesus

12. If the sword is a Christlike spirit, how would you wield it? How would we thwart our spiritual enemies?

Consider the chart on the following page, and the difficulties and the unanswered questions of equating the "Word of God" with the Bible.

Then consider the flow and emphasis of the Ephesian letter. What makes more sense? Is Paul referring to a collection of letters that don't currently exist? or is he emphasizing the Spirit of Christ as he is in the rest of the letter?

A spirit (or Spirit) of God is one that acts to serve from a pure heart, who blesses the righteous and the unrighteous, and will sacrifice self for others. He is one who even loves those who hate him, and is willing to commit himself to their welfare. He acts humbly but with resolve and perseveres faithfully. He commits himself to love in spite of the way he has been treated.

How else would the first-century Christians have seen Jesus? Would they have looked at Him as the creator and author of a new series of laws to follow? And if so, what laws? Or would they have thought of Him as the author and finisher of a spiritual faith?

What would Paul say?
Contextually, there is no reason to conclude that Paul is referring to his own letter(s) as the word of God. Both, the flow of letter, and the immediate context emphasizes spiritual qualities. They would have understood the *Word of God* to be the *sword of the Spirit* (just as it says). To put it in other words:

The Spirit of Christ (in man) = God's weapon

God, please give me a spirit of wisdom and revelation in a full knowledge of Your Son

For He is our weapon for advancing against the enemy

**Without context, a piece of information is just a dot.
It floats in your brain with a lot of other dots and doesn't mean a thing.
Knowledge is information-in-context… connecting the dots.
—Michael Ventura**

FC#2 What is the Sword of the Spirit?

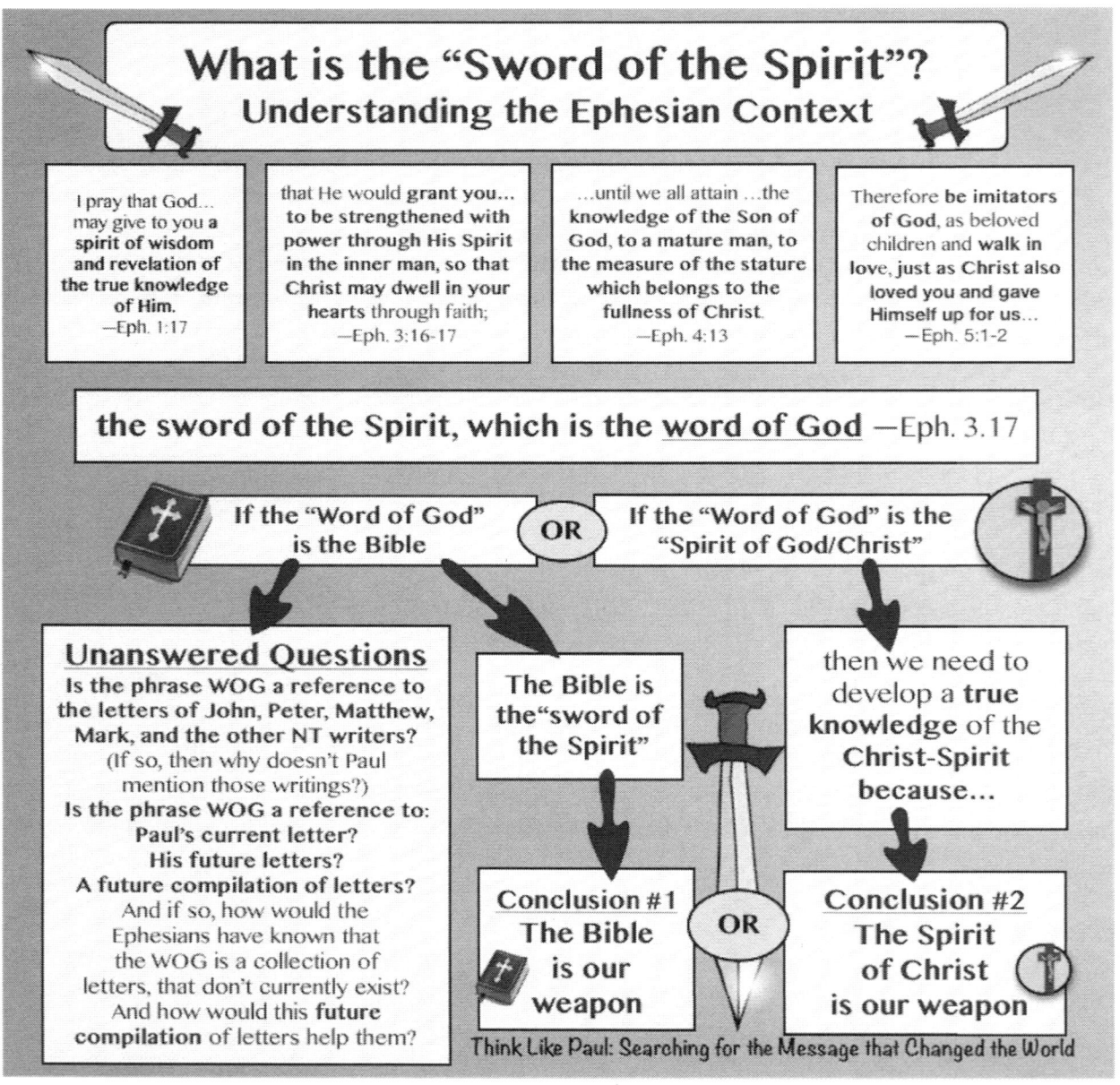

After considering the context of Paul's letter to the Ephesians,
what specifically is Paul referring to when he writes about
"the sword of the Spirit, which is the word of God"?

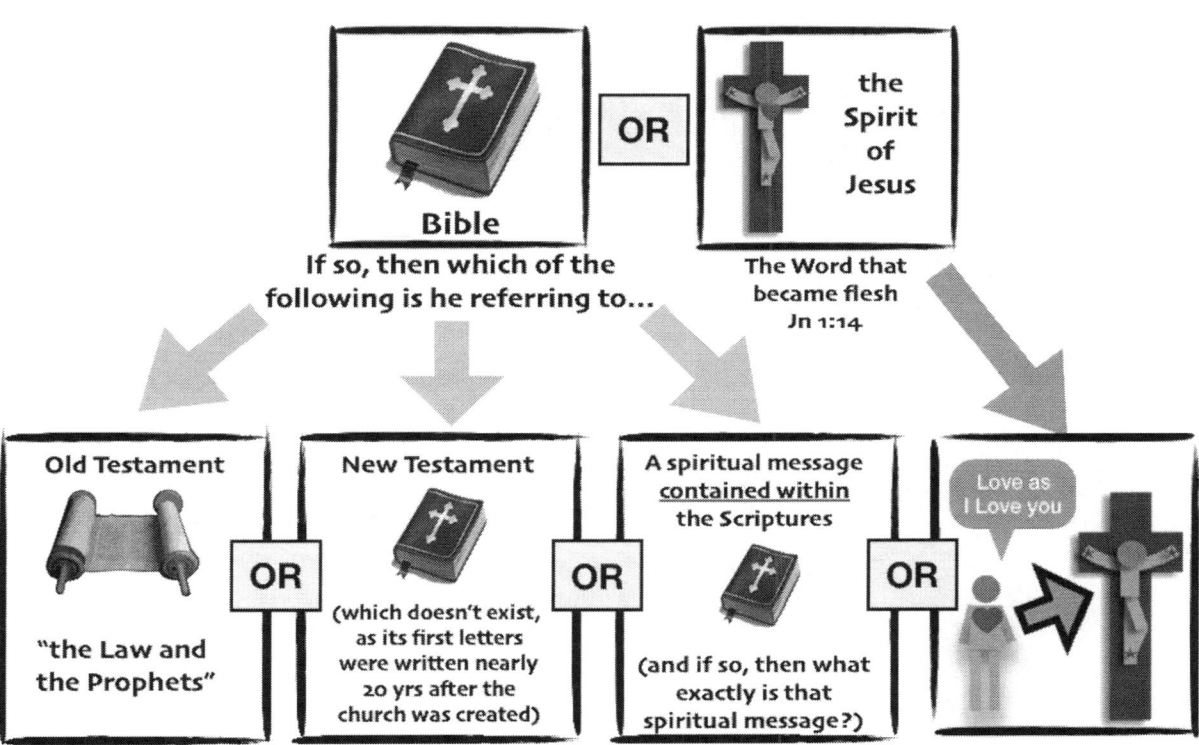

Which of these makes sense within the context of this letter?
Or the perspective of Paul? Or the perspective of those first century believers?
Which of these can best help us understand God?
Which is most edifying and nourishing?

What Exactly Is "the Word" in James 1?
Is "the word" a reference to the Scriptures? Or the "Spirit (of Christ)"?

James 1:21-25 NASB
Therefore, putting aside all filthiness and *all* that remains of wickedness, in humility receive the word (Scriptures) implanted, which is able to save your souls. But prove yourselves doers of the word (Scriptures), and not merely hearers who delude themselves. For if anyone is a hearer of the word (Scriptures) and not a doer, he is like a man who looks at his natural face in a mirror; for *once* he has looked at himself and gone away, he has immediately forgotten what kind of person he was. But one who looks intently at the perfect law, the *law* of liberty, and abides by it, not having become a forgetful hearer but an effectual doer, this man will be blessed in what he does.

If the letter of James is the *first* of the NT letters to be written, as most scholars believe, then what is the word that James is referring to?

Is he referring to Scriptures?
And if so, which Scriptures? Is it the Old Testament? Or the New Testament? (which doesn't exist at the time of this writing)

OR

Is he simply referring to the "Spirit of Christ"?

What exactly is this "word" that James is referring to?

Which makes the most sense for those first followers?

Which one best fits with verses 26 and 27?

Or the rest of the letter?

James 1:21-25 NASB
Therefore, putting aside all filthiness and *all* that remains of wickedness, in humility receive the word (Spirit of Christ) implanted, which is able to save your souls. But prove yourselves doers of the word (Spirit), and not merely hearers who delude themselves. For if anyone is a hearer of the word (Spirit) and not a doer, he is like a man who looks at his natural face in a mirror; for *once* he has looked at himself and gone away, he has immediately forgotten what kind of person he was. But one who looks intently at the perfect law, the *law* of liberty, and abides by it, not having become a forgetful hearer but an effectual doer, this man will be blessed in what he does.

Could the "the perfect law, the Law of liberty" be a reference to Christ's new commandment to "love one another as I have loved you"? (Jn.13:35)
Does that fit with this context? What else would fit for this "perfect law of liberty"?

Perry Stiltz   Think Like Paul: Searching for the Message that Changed the World

Study #16: What is "Washing of Water by the Word"?

Let's consider another passage from Paul's letter to the
Ephesians:

> So that He might sanctify her, **having cleansed her
> by the washing of water with the word**....
> —Ephesians 5:26 NASB

If the "Spirit of Christ" is our weapon, what exactly is the "Spirit of Christ"?

What exactly would the "Spirit of Christ" have meant to those in the first century?

Here we have an unusual word picture of a washing with water
and *the word*. In this passage Paul uses the "word"(rhema) and associates it to a very
specific action that Christ took in regard to the church. Here it is in context:

> Husbands, love your wives, just as Christ also loved the church and gave Himself
> up for her, so that He might sanctify her, **having cleansed her by the washing of
> water with the word**, that He might present to Himself the church in all her
> glory, having no spot or wrinkle or any such thing; but that she would be holy and
> blameless. So husbands ought also to love their own wives as their own bodies.
> He who loves his own wife loves himself; for no one ever hated his own flesh, but
> nourishes and cherishes it, just as Christ also *does* the church, because we are
> members of His body. FOR THIS REASON A MAN SHALL LEAVE HIS
> FATHER AND MOTHER AND SHALL BE JOINED TO HIS WIFE, AND
> THE TWO SHALL BECOME ONE FLESH. This mystery is great; but
> I am speaking with reference to Christ and the church.
> Nevertheless, each individual among you also is to love his own
> wife even as himself, and the wife must *see to it* that she respects
> her husband. —Ephesians 5:25–33 NASB

May I love others as

Christ

loved the church

Paul compares it with Christ and the church, and suggest that if we can
wash people with the word, we can sanctify and cleanse them. And
defining the "word" as the Bible or Christ does not make this passage any easier. (What would it
mean to wash people with the Bible or Christ?) Is Paul talking about something mystical and
mysterious? Can we surmise what Paul is trying to convey?

Notice what is mentioned with this "washing with the word":
  (1)   Husbands should love their wives.
  (2)   Christ loves the church so much that he gave his life for her.
  (3)   Christ's desire for the church is to sanctify her, and present her in all her glory,
        spotless, holy and blameless.
  (4)   A man ought to love his own wife as Christ loved the church.
  (5)   A man should consider his wife and himself as one body.

Questions

1.   In this context the "washing of water with the word" is probably a reference to the spiritual cleansing that comes from:
    d)   reading your Bible
    e)   repeating Bible verses to your spouse
    f)   water immersion
    g)   loving others as Christ loved the church

2.   Does it appear that there were some marital struggles within the church in Ephesus? If so, what might they be?

3.   What is Paul's solution?

4.   For whom did Christ give his life for? Jews or Gentiles? Good or bad? Friends or enemies? Or all?

5.   What do you think the life and death of Christ meant to them?

6.   Does this context fit with the idea that the Word is the Bible? Or do these concepts relate better to the word as a reference to the spirit of love that we see in Christ?

What would Paul say?

For Paul, "Christ-in-you" *is the* message. In this particular context, it was a message of a love that was stronger than death (or the fear of death). This is why he refers twice to Christ giving His life for His bride, the church. **The word (or message) Paul is striving to teach is the spirit we see in Christ, particularly the love that would be needed to sacrifice oneself.**

Paul wants them to make decisions based upon a love like Christ's, rather than a law or a book of rules. In this context Paul mentions that husbands need to love their wives three times. He compares this with Christ giving His life for the church. The "word" is a reference to the Spirit that led Jesus to the cross.

As I immerse myself into the

Spirit of Jesus

God's Word can cleanse others as they are able to see God's love for them (within me)

If your want to upgrade your circle of influence, it begins with upgrading yourself.
—Hal Elrod

Study #17: What is "Sanctified by the Word of God"?

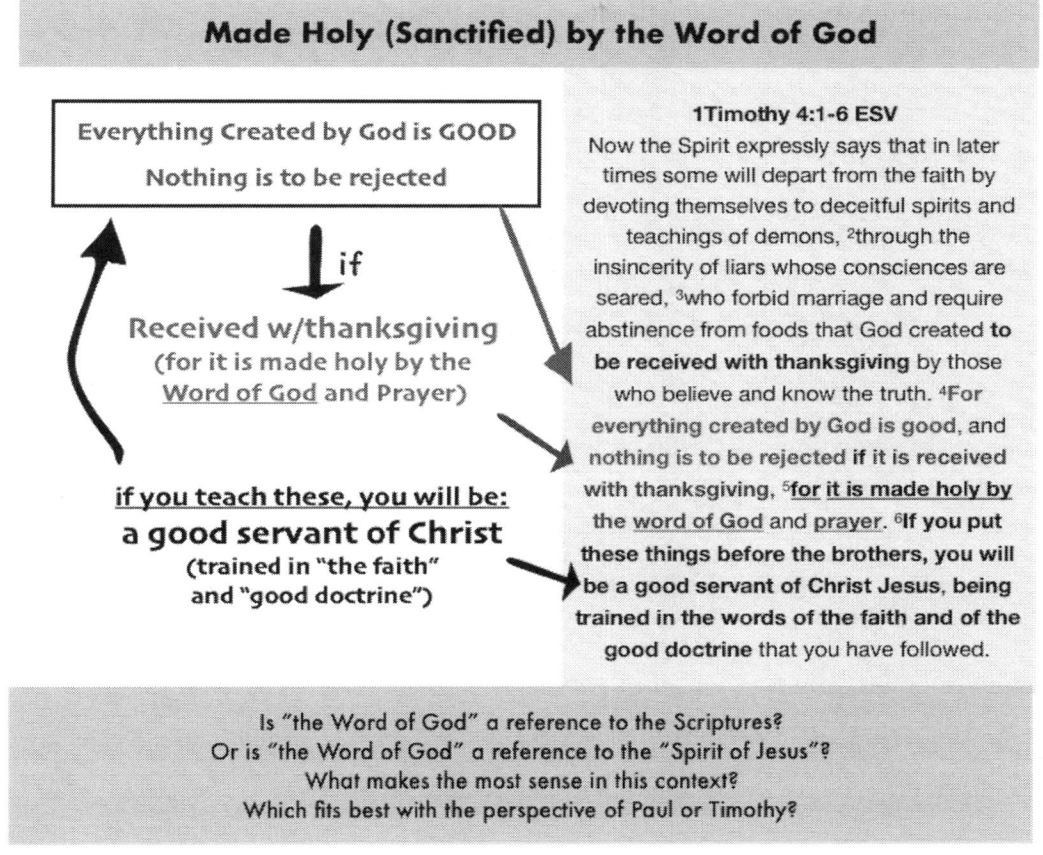

Made Holy (Sanctified) by the Word of God

Everything Created by God is GOOD

Nothing is to be rejected

↓ if

Received w/thanksgiving
(for it is made holy by the
Word of God and Prayer)

if you teach these, you will be:
a good servant of Christ
(trained in "the faith"
and "good doctrine")

1Timothy 4:1-6 ESV
Now the Spirit expressly says that in later times some will depart from the faith by devoting themselves to deceitful spirits and teachings of demons, ²through the insincerity of liars whose consciences are seared, ³who forbid marriage and require abstinence from foods that God created **to be received with thanksgiving** by those who believe and know the truth. ⁴For everything created by God is good, and nothing is to be rejected **if it is received with thanksgiving, ⁵for it is made holy by** the word of God and prayer. ⁶If you put **these things before the brothers, you will be a good servant of Christ Jesus, being trained in the words of the faith and of the good doctrine** that you have followed.

Is "the Word of God" a reference to the Scriptures?
Or is "the Word of God" a reference to the "Spirit of Jesus"?
What makes the most sense in this context?
Which fits best with the perspective of Paul or Timothy?

Consider the context of this *"word of God"* in Paul's first letter to Timothy:

Questions
According to this passage:

1.   What is good?

2.   What makes it good?

3.   In pointing out "these things," you will be a good servant of _____.

4.   What are "these things"? Let's look at the context and consider what he might mean:
    a.   Honesty (the opposite of deceitful)
    b.   Sincerity (the opposite of hypocrisy)
    c.   Truthfulness
    d.   Thankfulness for all he has received

5.   In this context, the word of God refers to:
     a.   The Bible
     b.   The Spirit of Christ (or a Christlike spirit)
     c.   Jesus (the man)

> For why should my liberty be determined by someone else's conscience? **If I partake with thankfulness**, why am I denounced because of that for which I give thanks? So whether you eat or drink, or whatever you do, do all to the glory of God.
>
> 1 Cor.10:29-31 ESV

6.   Could "the word of God," be a reference to the spirit that we put on?

7.   What could you be thankful for today? What would happen to your quality of life (emotion/spirit) if you lived in gratitude?

8.   Are there people in your life who would benefit from your gratitude? Who else would benefit from your thankfulness?

9.   In order to have this gratitude, what would you need to stop complaining about?

10. In order to be grateful for everything, what would you have to believe about:

     a.   God

     b.   Life

     c.   Death

     d.   Pain and suffering

     To the pure, all things are pure, but to those who are defiled and unbelieving, nothing is pure, but both their mind and their conscience are defiled. —Titus 1:15 NASB

James also indicates that our conscience affects whether or not something is wrong.

     So whoever knows the right thing to do and fails to do it, for him it is sin.
     —James 4:17 ESV

But even more revealing is what Jesus told the Pharisees:

While Jesus was speaking, a Pharisee asked him to dine with him, so he went in and reclined at table. The Pharisee was astonished to see that he did not first wash before dinner. And the Lord said to him, "Now you Pharisees cleanse the outside of the cup and of the dish, but inside you are full of greed and wickedness. You fools! Did not he who made the outside make the inside also? **But give as alms those things that are within, and behold, everything is clean for you**. —Luke 11:37–41 ESV

12.   What is clean for you? For everything to be "clean for you," what has to happen?

13.   If alms are a gift from the heart, what does he mean?

Maybe he means what he says ... or maybe he is just emphasizing what is important. Either way, it is clear that he wants us to give that which is from within. God wants us to be of His Spirit, not just givers, not just people who do things because we are told, but people who love others and give that which is spiritual to them.

14.   What strengths did Jesus have?

15.   Do you ask with expectancy, faith, and confidence? With the notions of His love and power in your heart?

God, help me live in a state of gratitude, for with the

heart & mind

of Christ

all things are clean for me

16.   What would happen if we started dwelling upon His great Spirit, and how that Spirit dwells in us?

What would Paul say?
The word of God (a Christlike spirit) can sanctify. This passage connects this Christlike spirit with an attitude of thanksgiving.

The greatest obstacle to discovery is not ignorance—
it is the illusion of knowledge.
—Daniel J. Boorstin

Study #18: What is "Adulterating the Word of God"?

> But we have renounced the things hidden because of shame, not walking in craftiness or **adulterating the word of God**, but by the manifestation of truth commending ourselves to every man's conscience in the sight of God. —2 Corinthians 4:2 NASB

This chapter is connected to the previous chapter with a "therefore." So let's first consider a few of the main points of chapter three[21]:

a) Paul describes this "New Covenant" as the Spirit of God written on our hearts.
b) The Spirit of God(on their hearts) is known and read by all men.
c) Their new ministry is described as a life giving Spirit.
d) The old ministry is described as one of condemnation and death.

Now, let's go back to our immediate context of chapter 4:

> Therefore, since we have this ministry, as we received mercy, we do not lose heart, but we have renounced the things hidden because of shame, not walking in craftiness or adulterating the **word of God**, but by the manifestation of truth commending ourselves to every man's conscience in the sight of God. And even if our gospel is veiled, it is veiled to those who are perishing, in whose case the god of this world has blinded the minds of the unbelieving so that they might not see the light of the gospel of the glory of Christ, who is the image of God. For what **we proclaim** is not ourselves, but **Jesus Christ as Lord**, with **ourselves as your servants for Jesus' sake**. —2 Corinthians 4:1-5 ESV

Notice the two messages Paul proclaims in that final sentence:
(1)   Jesus is Lord
(2)   Himself (Paul) as a bond servant (of the Corinthians) for the sake of Jesus

Now notice that Paul contrasted "adulterating the word of God" with "the manifestation of truth commending ourselves to every man's conscience."

I am your servant for the sake of growing you into the love & strength of Christ Himself

Questions:
1.   Considering the context of these two chapters, this "manifestation of truth" is likely a reference to:
  a.   Scripture
  b.   The Bible
  c.   Christ's Spirit in themselves

2.   Is Paul's message consistent with Christ's commandment?

---

[21] For more descriptions of these two covenants refer to Study #22 and homework #17

(John 13:34)

3.   Does it appear that Paul is trying to establish a new teaching, or to remind them of Christ?

4.   In this context, is there any reason to believe that the word of God, the truth, or the gospel are references to his letter, a set of letters, or the Scriptures?

He explains it further in the next verse:

> For God, who said, "Let light shine out of darkness," **has shone in our hearts to give the light of the knowledge** of the glory of God **in the face of Jesus Christ.**
> —2 Corinthians 4:6 ESV

5.   Does the definition "Christ in you" make more sense in 2 Corinthians 4?

6.   How would you try to fulfill Christ's commandment?

What would Paul say?
The context clearly refers to the Spirit of Christ/God. **Adulterating the word of God seems to be the defiling of the Christ-spirit that has shone in our hearts.** We are changed because God Himself has shone into our dark hearts.

God, may I not adulterate the "Spirit of Christ in me" (a.k.a. word of God) with deceit or craftiness, but rather may the Manifestation of Truth be evident within me

It is Christ himself, not the Bible,
who is the true Word of God.
The Bible, read in the right spirit,
and with the guidance of good teachers,
will bring us to Him.
— C.S. Lewis

After considering the context of Paul's letter to the Corinthians, what specifically is Paul referring to when he writes about "adulterating the word of God"?

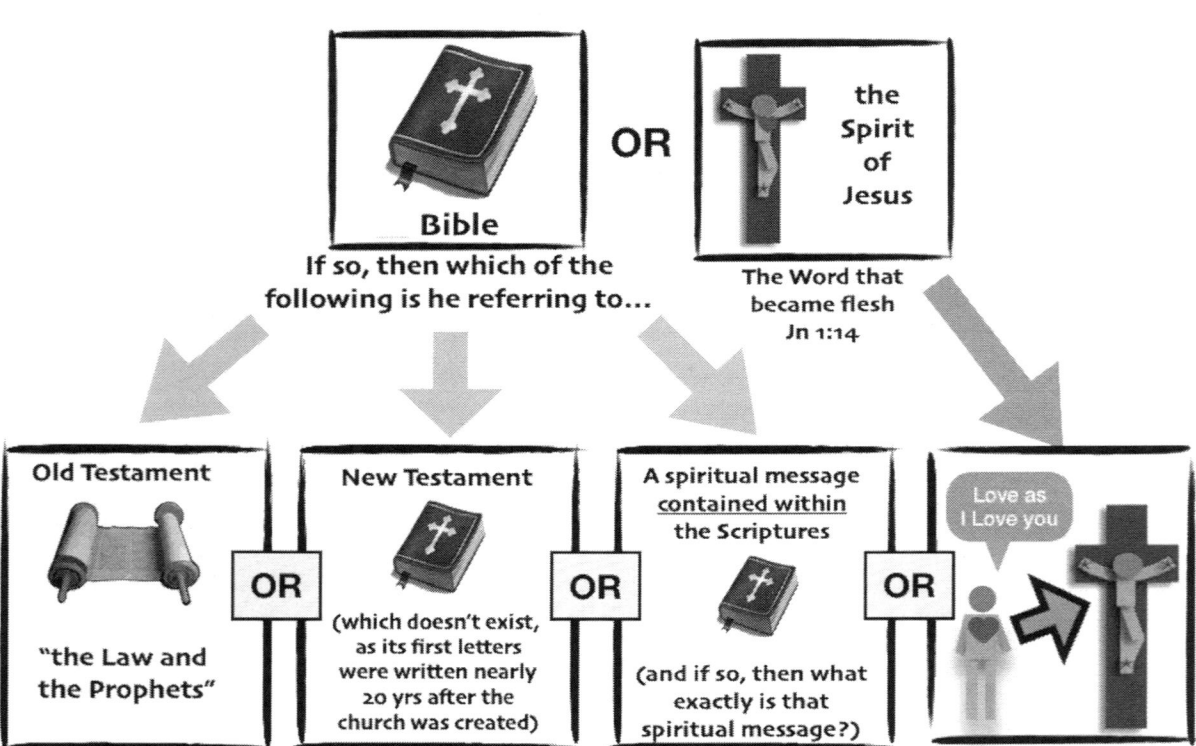

Do you think he meant "adulterating the Bible/Scriptures"?

If so, which parts of the Bible would he be referring to?

Or do you think he is referring to Christ (God's Spirit in man)?

Which of these makes sense within the context of this letter?

Or the perspective of Paul? Or the perspective of those first century believers?

Which of these can best help us understand God?

Which is most edifying and nourishing?

What Exactly is "the Word" in Jesus Parable of the Sower?

Is the "Word" the Spirit of God? Or the Scriptures? Or something else?

Mark 4:11-20 NASB
("word" replaced by "Spirit")

And He was saying to them, "To you has been given the mystery of the kingdom of God, but those who are outside get everything in parables, so that WHILE SEEING, THEY MAY SEE AND NOT PERCEIVE, AND WHILE HEARING, THEY MAY HEAR AND NOT UNDERSTAND, OTHERWISE THEY MIGHT RETURN AND BE FORGIVEN." And He *said to them, "Do you not understand this parable? How will you understand all the parables? "The sower sows the Spirit of God/Christ. These are the ones who are beside the road where the Spirit is sown; and when they hear, immediately Satan comes and takes away the Spirit which has been sown in them. "In a similar way these are the ones on whom seed was sown on the rocky *places*, who, when they hear the Spirit, immediately receive it with joy; and they have no *firm* root in themselves, but are *only* temporary; then, when affliction or persecution arises because of the Spirit, immediately they fall away."And others are the ones on whom seed was sown among the thorns; these are the ones who have heard the Spirit, but the worries of the world, and the deceitfulness of riches, and the desires for other things enter in and choke the Spirit, and it becomes unfruitful. "And those are the ones on whom seed was sown on the good soil; and they hear the word and accept it and bear fruit, thirty, sixty, and a hundredfold."

Mark 4:11-20 NASB
("word" replaced by "Scriptures")

And He was saying to them, "To you has been given the mystery of the kingdom of God, but those who are outside get everything in parables, so that WHILE SEEING, THEY MAY SEE AND NOT PERCEIVE, AND WHILE HEARING, THEY MAY HEAR AND NOT UNDERSTAND, OTHERWISE THEY MIGHT RETURN AND BE FORGIVEN." And He *said to them, "Do you not understand this parable? How will you understand all the parables? "The sower sows the Scriptures. "These are the ones who are beside the road where the Scriptures is sown; and when they hear, immediately Satan comes and takes away the Scriptures which has been sown in them. "In a similar way these are the ones on whom seed was sown on the rocky *places*, who, when they hear the Scriptures, immediately receive it with joy; and they have no *firm* root in themselves, but are *only* temporary; then, when affliction or persecution arises because of the Scriptures, immediately they fall away."And others are the ones on whom seed was sown among the thorns; these are the ones who have heard the Scriptures, but the worries of the world, and the deceitfulness of riches, and the desires for other things enter in and choke the Scriptures and it becomes unfruitful. "And those are the ones on whom seed was sown on the good soil; and they hear the word and accept it and bear fruit, thirty, sixty, and a hundredfold."

What is the message that God is sowing?
What was evidenced in the person of Jesus? Or the lives of the disciples?

Perry Stiltz   Think Like Paul: Searching for the Message that Changed the World

Study #19: What is "Reviling the Word of God"?

What is "reviling the word of God"? What does that mean?

> But as for you, teach what accords with sound doctrine. Older men are to be sober-minded, dignified, self-controlled, sound in faith, in love, and in steadfastness. Older women likewise are to be reverent in behavior, not slanderers or slaves to much wine. They are to teach what is good, and so train the young women to love their husbands and children, to be self-controlled, pure, working at home, kind, and submissive to their own husbands, that the **word of God may not be reviled**. —Titus 2:1–5 ESV

Remember, the original greek manuscripts did not have capitalization or punctuation. Let's reconsider this entire passage without punctuation or capitalization, and replace the "word of God" with Paul's definition of "Christ in you" (from study #13):[22]

> but as for you teach what accords with sound doctrine older men are to be sober-minded dignified self-controlled sound in faith in love and in steadfastness older women likewise are to be reverent in behavior not slanderers or slaves to much wine they are to teach what is good, and so train the young women to love their husbands and children to be self-controlled pure working at home kind and submissive to their own husbands that the **christ in you** may not be reviled likewise urge the younger men to be self-controlled show yourself in all respects to be a model of good works and in your teaching show integrity dignity and sound speech that cannot be condemned so that an opponent may be put to shame having nothing evil to say about us slaves are to be submissive to their own masters in everything; they are to be well-pleasing not argumentative not pilfering but showing all good faith so that in everything they may adorn the doctrine of god our savior —Titus 2:1–10 ESV (*Note: "Spirit of Christ in you" has been substituted for "word of God.")

> I came that they may have life and have it abundantly.
>
> John 10:10 ESV

Questions:

1. Is this more coherent?

2. From this passage, list the character traits Paul wanted them to attain:

---

[22] If the "word of God" is the Bible, then that passage is nonsensical. How would my actions and selfish spirit bring reproach to a book, or its message? But, if the "word of God" refers to the Spirit of Christ living within us, then it makes complete sense.

3.   Was Paul trying to teach adherence to his letters? Or to a spirit?

4.   Since the "word of God" is the "Spirit of Christ in you," then how would you teach this notion?

God, help me put aside the spirit of arrogance, selfishness, hatred, and indifference, so that your Word of God **can abide in me**

5.   Considering the context, how do we revile the word of God?

What would Paul say?
The "word of God" is a reference to the Spirit of Christ living within us. So **when our spirits are arrogant, selfish, ungrateful, or unloving, we bring reproach to the Spirit of Christ(a.k.a. the Word of God) that resides within us.**

Two "Words of God"?!?!?!?
Suppose you were Timothy, Philemon, or a member of the Corinthian church…And you had been taught that **Christ is the Word** (message) of God…And you just received a letter from Paul, the man who had taught you the good news… Would you have thought that "Paul's letter is **also** the Word of God"? Would defining His letter as the "Word of God" make things easier or more confusing?

Educating the mind without educating the heart is no education at all.
—Aristotle

Study #20: Instructions to Those Receiving the Word of God

For this reason we also constantly thank God that when you received the **word of God** which you **heard from us**, you accepted it not as the word of men, but for what it really is, the **word of God**, which also performs its work in you who believe.
—1 Thessalonians 2:13 NASB

Here Paul describes the Word of God as something that the Thessalonians "heard" from Paul. So let us first consider this in its context, and see what we can ascertain:

Did those in the first century find these writings difficult and problematic?

Or have we made them difficult because we are not defining their terminology the way they did?

For you recall, brethren, our labor and hardship, how working night and day so as not to be a burden to any of you, we proclaimed to you the gospel of God. You are witnesses, and so is God, how devoutly and uprightly and blamelessly we behaved toward you believers; just as you know how we were exhorting and encouraging and imploring each one of you as a father would his own children, so that you would **walk in a manner worthy of the God** who calls you into His own kingdom and glory. For this reason we also constantly thank God that when you received the **word of God** which you **heard** from us, you accepted it not as the word of men, but for what it really is, **the word of God**, which also performs its work in you who believe. For you, brethren, **became imitators of the churches** of God **in Christ Jesus** that are in Judea. —1 Thessalonians 2:9–14 NASB

I will no longer withhold forgiveness and love from others, as my Lord

did not withhold them from me

This passage brings difficulty, because the phrase "word of God" appears to be used in two different ways. So, let us first consider their situation and what is *explicitly* stated:

(1)   Paul had worked hard so as not to be burdensome to them.
(2)   Paul had already proclaimed the gospel to them.
(3)   The Thessalonians were witnesses to how well Paul treated them.
(4)   Paul reminded them of how he had encouraged them to walk in a manner worthy of God.
(5)   They had both *received* and *heard* the "word of God" from Paul.
(6)   They accepted it as the word of God.
(7)   The word of God performs its work in those who believe.

Additional considerations:
- (a)   Word of God = Message of God
- (b)   The preceding points 1 through 4 all deal with Paul's spirit of care for the brethren.
- (c)   After Paul mentions that he encouraged them to walk in a manner worthy of God, He thanks God that they had indeed received the word of God.
- (d)   In Acts 10:44–11:1, while hearing the message of Christ, the house of Cornelius received the Holy Spirit.
- (e)   There is no reference or mention of any of Paul's previous letters being *the* word of God.

Questions:

Answer from the context of 1 Thessalonians 2.

Lord, may the word of God = Spirit of Christ work in me, such that I may walk in a manner worthy of God

1.   Did they possess the word of God prior to this letter?

2.   Where does this word of God work?

3.   How many references did Paul make to his letters? Or to other letters of the New Testament?

4.   Who taught them the word of God?

5.   Does this word of God seem to be a spiritual entity?

6.   Does it seem to be a body of information?
(If so, what do you think is that information?)

Now reread this passage and consider this "word of God" to be a metonym for Christ's commandment:

> For you recall, brethren, our labor and hardship, how working night and day so as not to be a burden to any of you, we proclaimed to you the gospel of God. You are witnesses, and so is God, how devoutly and uprightly and blamelessly we behaved toward you believers; just as you know how we were exhorting and encouraging and imploring each one of you as a father would his own children, so that you would **walk in a manner worthy of the God** who calls you into His own kingdom and glory. For this reason we also constantly thank God that when you received the **word of God** which you **heard** from us, you accepted it not as the word of men, but for what it really is, **the word of God**, which also performs its

work in you who believe. For you, brethren, **became imitators of the churches**
of God **in Christ Jesus** that are in Judea. —1 Thessalonians 2:9–14 NASB

7.   If the "word of God" was a metonym for Christ's commandment, would this passage make less or more sense?

8.   If Paul considered the "New Commandment" to be God's message to humanity, what kind of letter would he write to you? Or your church? How well are you following this commandment?

God, help me
understand your
commandment to
"love one another as
You have loved us,"

for it is by this
Spirit that all men
will know that we
are Your disciples

What would Paul say?
While the simplest definition may be at play here: "the message of God," it is also possible, if not probable, that this "word of God" is a reference to Christ's spirit (and/or His commandment[23]). The context directs the reader toward the spiritual walk of Jesus, and thus seems to be a perfect fit for his "love one another as I have loved you" commandment.[24]

**You will either step forward into growth,
or you will step backward into safety.
—Abraham Maslow**

---

[23] In *Study #22* and *Final Thoughts* this "New Commandment" is explored in relation to how it may fit with the "New Covenant".

[24] In Acts 10:44–11:1, there is the connection between "hearing the word of God" and "receiving the Holy Spirit." This may suggest that "hearing of the word of God" could also be a metaphor for an "open-hearted understanding of Christ's Spirit/commandment."

A Future Compilation of Letters?

From the Thessalonians' perspective, there was no New Testament Bible. The Bible would simply be a "future compilation of letters" from their perspective.

First Thessalonians declares that the readers had already received the word of God, and assumes they already know what the "word of God" is. The "word of God" existed prior to Paul's sending of this letter, and any notion that the "word of God" is a reference to some future compilation of letters is speculation and unsupported by the context.

> **Give a man a truth and he will think for a day. Teach a man to reason and he will think for a lifetime.**
>
> **—Phil Plait**

Furthermore, how would those in Thessalonica have known about this "future compilation of letters"? Where, in this letter, is this "future compilation of letters" described? When would it be revealed? And how would it have helped their current situation?

Since they obviously did not refer to the New Testament as *the* word of God, then why do we refer to it as *the* word of God? Do we have the authority to change their definitions?

**People don't want to hear the truth because
they don't want their illusions destroyed.
—Friedrich Nietzsche**

Conclusions for Part 3:

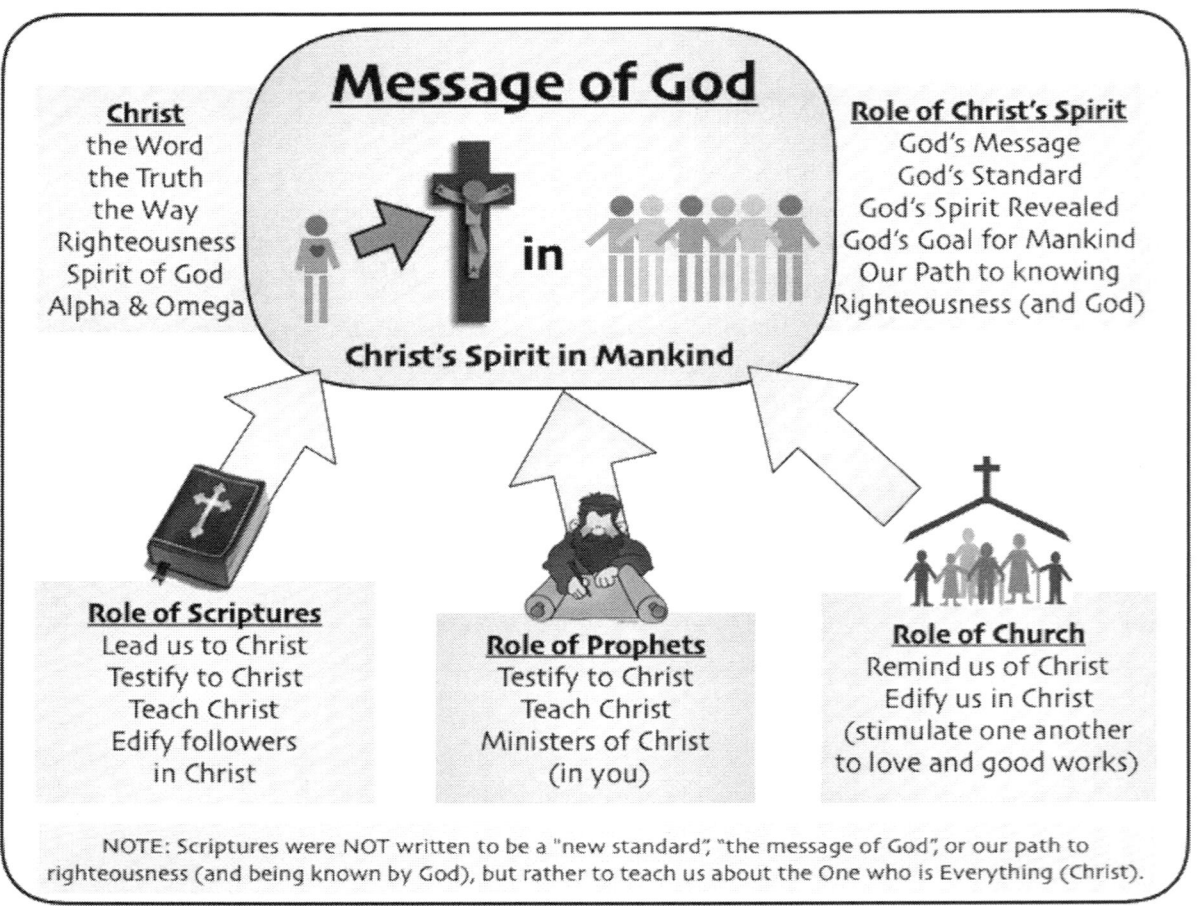

The Ultimate Message

Throughout history God has used many different methods for informing humanity. He has used prophets, dreams, laws, scripture, animals, nature, creation, and our own experiences to teach us.

But His *ultimate* message, Christ (the embodiment of God's spiritual teachings), is the one message that should tell us everything we need to know. In other words, the Creator revealed His own Spirit through a man who is mocked, beaten, and humiliated… and then nailed to a cross.

So, as He is God's message, it seems safe to say that it is in this Spirit of Christ that we learn…

(1)   All we need to know about God.
(2)   All we need to know about ourselves.
(3)   All we need to know about having a relationship with God.
(4)   All we need to know about how to treat others.
(5)   All we need to know about suffering and tribulations.
(6)   All we need to know about love, courage, strength, peace, forgiveness, humility, self control…
(7)   All we need to know, period.

> But speaking the truth in love, **we are to grow up in all aspects into Him** who is the head, even Christ.
> —Ephesians 4:15 NASB

What would Paul Say?
Everything points to one thing—Christ. God's message is Christ (or Christ in you). Paul is controlled by the Spirit of Christ, and sees Christ as man's pathway back to God. His emphasis is not in his letters, but rather is the Spirit of Christ, which explains his mission of building up of others in Christ. …Here is a visual representation explaining the hierarchal differences between the pharisees' mindset and the Apostle Paul's mindset:

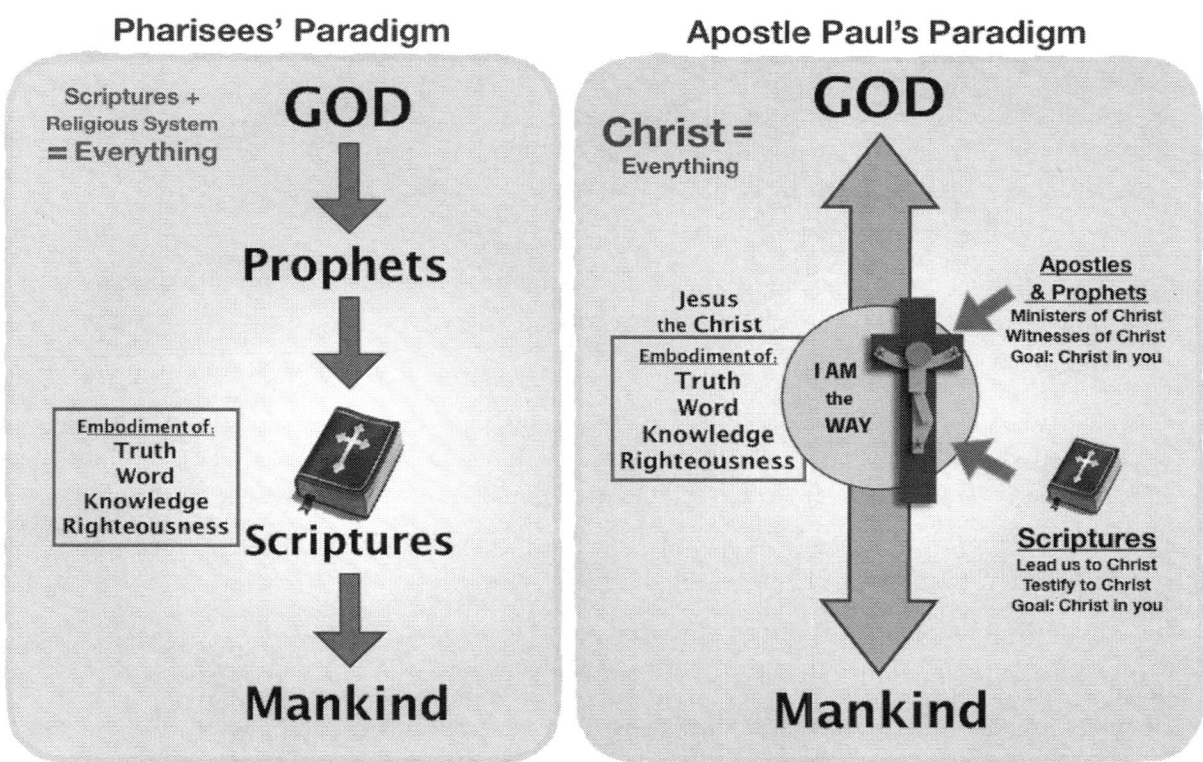

Think Like Paul: Searching for the Message that Changed the World
by Perry Stiltz

Does it Really Matter?

What are the practical differences between these 2 paradigms? Is our faith different than Paul's faith? If so, what are the differences? After mulling this over for years, I think I've come up with some useful distinctions and their possible ramifications. Here are a few of them:

1. It creates an unclear, confusing, and inconsistent view of what God's message actually is. Is it the Bible? Is it Christ? Is it Spirit? Is it a spiritual message? Is it the knowledge of certain facts? What exactly is His message? This unclear message has caused many to define Christianity in their own manner.

2. "Following Christ" is confused with a following of rules and rituals, or the experiencing of a subjective experience, rather than the internalizing of God's spiritual principles.

3. The Bible tends to become our standard, rather than Christ.

4. "Being led by the Holy Spirit" is more confusing and uncertain. When we do not understand the Spirit of Christ, we don't understand the Holy Spirit that God has poured out onto humanity. (Studies #21-25)

5. The Bible as the word of God is a distorting of the first century reality, as they specifically called Christ "the Word" (and they did not have the collection of documents we now call the Bible).

6. We may rely upon our knowledge (or perceived knowledge) of the Scriptures more than Christ. This encourages the keeping of the Bible as a law book, which directs attention away from understanding the Christ-Spirit— the image of the One we are supposed to be transforming into. (Studies #5-10)

> "It is done! I am the Alpha and the Omega, the beginning and the end. To the thirsty I will give from the spring of the water of life without payment."
> —Revelation 21:6 ESV

7. The Bible is considered our source for righteousness, which puts it in the same sphere as God. And we forget that the Bible is a *product* of the Spirit, and speaks to *His* greatness, not its own. (study # 4)

8. The role of the spirit of Jesus, is greatly reduced and sometimes is made practically irrelevant. We can talk around Christ and never really discuss what causes His righteousness (His Spirit, or how He makes decisions). Also Christ as the "author and finisher of our faith" (Heb. 12:2) is not really understood as we place decreased emphasis on understanding His spirit/faith.

9. Judgment of others is often permitted in the guise of comparing each other to the Bible (our perceived standard), rather than the Spirit we see in Jesus (our real standard).

10. Our perceptions of examples and patterns (within the Scriptures) can becomes our standard for right and wrong, rather than Christ.

11. It has given many Christians an inappropriate view of the Bible. It is reminiscent of the Pharisaic Jews, whose clinging to the Law kept them from knowing Christ, and whom Paul calls idolaters and adulterers. (Studies #8 and 9)

12. It also suggest that the passages are magical. While memorizing Bible verses are helpful, they do not usually contain the power or purpose of Christ himself. The "magic" is in Christ. It is understanding the spirit (mindset, beliefs, and purpose) of the One who is righteousness itself. (Studies #14, 19, 21 and 22)

13. The Bible as a rule book often leads to a legalistic rigidity which is frequently uninviting to those outside of Christ (which may also cause them to blaspheme God…(Study #9))

14. If the Bible is the message of God, there is typically little emphasis on our identity. But if the message of God is Christ-in-you, then the development of this Christ identity is foundational to everything else.

For I could wish that I myself were accursed, separated from Christ for the sake of my brethren, my kinsmen according to the flesh, who are Israelites, to whom belongs the adoption as sons ….

Romans 9:3–4
NASB

Discussion Questions:

1. If you had to put into words what God's message is, what would you say? What is the best way to "preach the word"?

2. How can we grow in the Spirit of Christ? What can we specifically do or practice?

3. So if the Word is Christ, how well do we know that Word? Are we willing to sacrifice our need for respect? Are we willing to be humiliated if it serves another? Are we willing to be tortured and love the torturer? Are we willing to sacrifice all that is physical, including life itself, for the sake of love? For the sake of service to another? Most of us would give up life for the personal gain of Heaven. But have we completely devoted ourselves to "love" in the manner that Jesus and Paul have? How can we more fully commit ourselves to the Spirit we find in Jesus and Paul?

Our Challenge

These studies have been a challenge for me on many levels. But the biggest challenge did not come from the text, but rather from my own *ingrained definition*— the Bible is *the* Word of God —a statement that our churches have repeated countless times. I've had to continuously remind myself of the 1st century perspective: the Word of God is the Christ-Spirit (God's spiritual principles embodied in man).

And although considering the Word as the Spirit of Christ (within us) makes the passages clearer and more powerful, it will remain so only if we represent it that way internally. It is our internal concepts of the "word" that matter, not our verbiage. So, at least in part, the answer to our challenge is simply in reminding ourselves of *their metaphor* of "the word". And the more we realize and emphasize that Spirit, the more we will understand the Scriptures, and who we are supposed to be.

Pay bad people with your goodness;
fight their hatred with your kindness.
Even if you do not achieve victory over other people,
you will conquer yourself.
—Leo Tolstoy

What is *the Word*?

Today's Paradigm Word = Scriptures		Paul's Paradigm Word = Spirit of Christ
Scriptures are living and active and can judge the intentions of the heart	"the word of God is living and active…" (Heb:4:12)	Spirit of Christ/God is living and active and can judge the intentions of the heart
the Bible is our weapon against the enemy	"the sword of the Spirit, which is the word of God" (Eph.6:17)	the Spirit of Jesus (in you) is our weapon against the enemy
preach the Bible	"Preach the word" (2 Tim. 4:2)	preach Christ (the Spirit of Jesus in you)
the Bible will nourish us	"pure milk of the word" (1Pet.2:2)	the Spirit we find in Jesus (going to the cross) will nourish us
faith comes from reading/hearing the Bible	"Faith comes by hearing, and hearing by the word of God" (Rom. 10:17)	faith comes from hearing/understanding the Spirit of Christ (in you)
????	"Washing of water by the word" (Eph.5:26)	loving your wife (and others), as Christ loved the church, can change their hearts
accurately handling the Bible	"accurately handling the word of truth" (2Tim. 2:15)	accurately handling the Spirit of Christ (in you)
????	"for it is sanctified by means of the word of God and prayer" (1Tim.4:5)	having the 'Spirit of Christ (in you)' during prayer sanctifies things
????	"adulterating the word of God" (2Cor.4:2)	deceit and craftiness adulterates the Spirit of Christ (in you)
the seed is the Scriptures	"the seed is the word of God" (Lk. 8:11)	the seed is the Spirit of God
the Pharisees made void the Scriptures	"you have made void the word of God" (Mt. 15:6)	the Pharisees made void the Spirit of God
message of God (unspecific)	"the word of God continued to increase" (Acts 6:7)	Spirit of Christ (message of God)
message of God (unspecific)	"the word of the Lord has sounded forth from you" (1Thes.1:8)	Spirit of Christ (message of God)

Think Like Paul: Searching for the Message that Changed the World   Perry Stiltz

More *Word* Passages

Mt. 15:6	you have made void the word of God	the Pharisees made void the Spirit of God (in them)
Lk. 8:11 (Mt.13-18-23; Lk.4:14-20)	the seed is the word of God	the seed is the Spirit of God
John 1:1	In the beginning was the Word, and the Word was with God, and the Word was God.	Word = Christ
John 1:14	And the Word became flesh, and dwelt among us	Word = Christ
Acts 6:4,7	devote ourselves... to the ministry of the word; the word of God continued to increase	Spirit of Christ (message of God)
Acts 13:5	to proclaim the word of God	Spirit of Christ (message of God)
Rom. 10:17	Faith comes by hearing, and hearing by the word of God	faith comes from hearing/ understanding the Spirit of Christ (in you)
Gal. 6:6	who is taught the word is to share all good things	Spirit of Christ (message of God)
Col. 3:16	Let the word of Christ richly dwell within you	let the message of Christ richly dwell within you
2Tim. 2:15	accurately handling the word of truth	accurately handling the Spirit of Christ (in you)
2Tim. 4:2	Preach the word	preach Christ (the Spirit of Jesus in you)
1Pet. 1:23	for you have been born again not of seed which is perishable but imperishable, that is, through the living and enduring word of God.	They were "born through" the living and enduring Word of God
1Pet. 1:27	but the word of the Lord remains forever, and this word is the good news that was preached to you.	"remains forever" "good news" "previously preached"
1Pet. 2:2	pure milk of the word	the Spirit we find in Jesus (going to the cross) will nourish us
1Pet. 2:8	a stone of stumbling and a rock of offence —who are stumbling at the word.	They stumbled over Jesus (as the message)
Rev. 19:13	He is clothed in a robe dipped in blood, and the name by which he is called is The Word of God.	Word = Christ

Think Like Paul: Searching for the Message that Changed the World   Perry Stiltz

Part 4: How Would Paul Explain the "New Covenant"?

Study #21: How Specifically did Paul "Follow Christ"?
Does Paul have the same priorities as Jesus? If so, what are they?

Study #22: What Exactly is the "New Covenant"?
What is a Covenant? How did they describe this New Covenant?

Study #23: A Covenant Unto Death?!?
Considering their preoccupation with death.

Study #21: How Specifically did Paul "Follow Christ"?

> But speaking the truth in love, **we are to grow up in all**
> **aspects into Him** who is the head, *even* Christ.
> —Ephesians 4:15 NASB

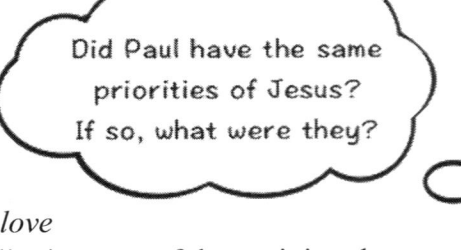

We are clearly supposed to "grow up" to be more like
Christ. But what does that really mean? Is that "*love*" in the
generic and unspecific sense that is tossed around today?
Some say that "love" is an action. If so, then what action(s)? If *love*
is the answer, then what kind of love is it? Do we have any qualitative way of determining the
Spirit of Christ? Can we look at the life of Jesus and determine what some of His priorities are?
Can we see the priorities in Paul? Do they match the priorities of Jesus?

Priorities of Jesus
Jesus clearly put the needs of humanity above himself. The cross represents a love for us that is
greater than life itself. He was compassionate with those who needed compassion, and critical
with those who needed humility. Ultimately, it appears that everything we know about Him
points us toward one overriding goal. He wanted people to understand the spiritual kingdom of
God, so that mankind can have a relationship with his spiritual Father.

> For the son of man is come to seek and to save that which was lost.
> —Luke 19:10 KJV

Jesus had rights that He never used. He could have demanded respect and honor from the
Pharisees… But He gives no order. He had the right to defend Himself before Pilate… But He
chose to remain silent. He had the authority to call down 12,000 angels to stop the torture… But
no plea is uttered. Jesus, like the Father, chose love. He chose love over rights. He chose Spirit
over flesh. He chose humility over respect. He chose humanity over life itself… And He
demonstrated all of this with nails and a cross. His priorities were not in anything earthly. His
priority was in revealing and exemplifying God's Spirit…. the image we were designed to be.

Priorities of Paul
Was Paul's priorities in alignment with Jesus' priorities? What was most important to Paul? What
was he most concerned about? Did he value certain principles more than others? Did the Spirit
work the same way in him, as it did in Jesus?

In Corinth there was jealousy, strife and immaturity within the church. In Paul's letters to them
he seems to be responding to doubts and questions regarding his apostleship. In the following
passages consider Paul's responses to their doubts and criticisms, particularly, what he is willing
to sacrifice, and why he is willing to make that sacrifice:

Let a man regard us in this manner, as servants of Christ and stewards of the mysteries of God. In this case, moreover, it is required of stewards that one be found trustworthy. But to me **it is a very small thing that I may be examined by you, or by *any* human court**; in fact, **I do not even examine myself.** For I am conscious of nothing against myself, yet I am not by this acquitted; but the one who examines me is the Lord. —1 Corinthians 4:1–4 NASB

God!
Help me to put aside the desire for approval, and center myself on doing what is best for others

Just as you have done for me

Already you have all you want! Already you have become rich! Without us you have become kings! And would that you did reign, so that we might share the rule with you! For I think that God has exhibited us apostles as last of all, like men **sentenced to death**, because **we have become a spectacle to the world**, to angels, and to men. **We are fools for Christ's sake**, but you are wise in Christ. We are weak, but you are strong. You are held in honor, but we in disrepute. To the present hour we hunger and thirst, we are poorly dressed and buffeted and homeless, and we labor, working with our own hands. When reviled, we bless; when persecuted, we endure; when slandered, we entreat. We have become, and are still, **like the scum of the world**, the refuse of all things. —1 Corinthians 4:8–13 ESV

For through your knowledge he who is weak is ruined, the brother for whose sake Christ died. And so, by sinning against the brethren and wounding their conscience when it is weak, you sin against Christ. Therefore, **if food causes my brother to stumble, I will never eat meat again, <u>so that</u> I will not cause my brother to stumble**. —1 Corinthians 8:11–13 NASB

> "If food causes my brother to stumble, I will never eat meat again, so that I will not cause my brother to stumble."
> 1Cor.8:13 NASB

Now we pray to God that you do no wrong; **not** that we ourselves may appear approved, but **<u>that</u> you may do what is right, even though we may appear unapproved**. —2 Corinthians 13:7 NASB

God!
Help me to value others as You

have valued me

If we sowed spiritual things in you, is it too much if we reap material things from you? If others share the right over you, do we not more? Nevertheless, **we did not use this right, but we endure all things <u>so that</u> we will cause no hindrance to the gospel of Christ.** —1 Corinthians 9:11–12 NASB

just as I also please all men in all things, **not seeking my own profit but the profit of the many, <u>so that</u> they may be saved**. —1 Corinthians 10:33 NASB

I will most gladly spend and be expended for your souls —2 Corinthians 12:15 NASB

1. How does Paul respond to those who are persecuting him? Is this similar to the way Jesus responded to persecution?

2. What things is Paul willing to endure? What sacrifices is he willing to make for the Corinthians? Or the gospel?

3. What is Paul's goal for the sacrifices he makes?

4. What does Paul care more about?

   a) being paid
   b) looking good
   c) being respected
   d) appearing righteous
   e) following a set of rules
   f) following a set of traditions
   g) developing the same kind of love that had
   h) that they would come to better understand the Spirit in Christ

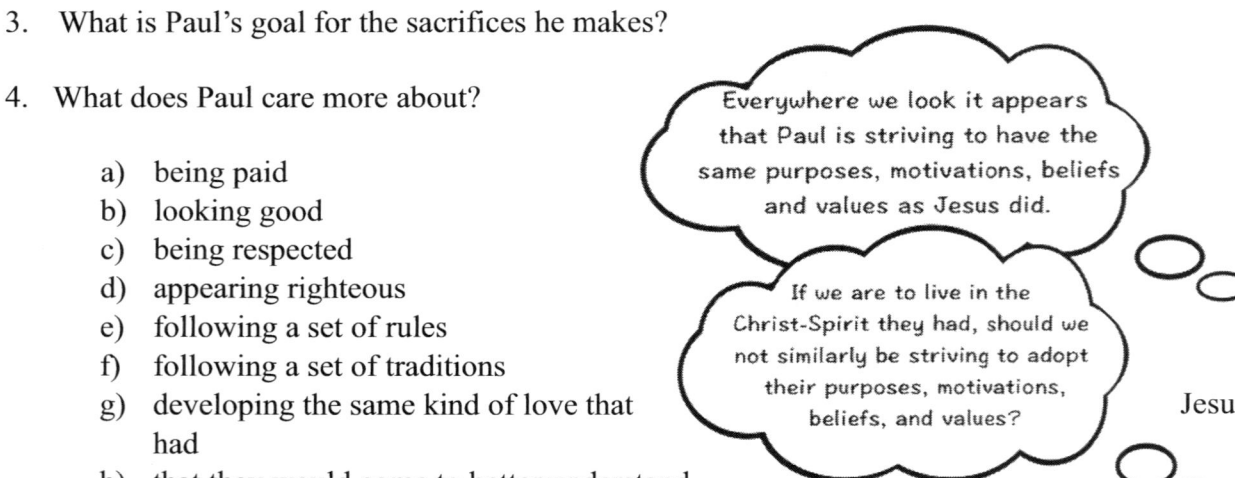

Everywhere we look it appears that Paul is striving to have the same purposes, motivations, beliefs and values as Jesus did.

If we are to live in the Christ-Spirit they had, should we not similarly be striving to adopt their purposes, motivations, beliefs, and values?

Jesus

Here is another passage that reveals Paul's heart toward his jewish brethren (who have rejected Jesus as the Christ):

> I am telling the truth in Christ, I am not lying, my conscience testifies with me in the Holy Spirit, that I have great sorrow and unceasing grief in my heart. **For I could wish that I myself were accursed, separated from Christ for the sake of my brethren**, my kinsmen according to the flesh, who are Israelites, to whom belongs the adoption as sons, and the glory and the covenants and the giving of the Law and the *temple* service and the promises, whose are the fathers, and from whom is the Christ according to the flesh, who is over all, God blessed forever. Amen. —Romans 9:1–5 NASB

5. What does Paul wish for? …And why?

6. What does Paul care more about?
   a) His own salvation
   b) The salvation of the Jewish brethren

7. What is Paul more concerned about?
    a) Getting himself to Heaven
    b) Being like Christ and expressing Christ's love to his Jewish brethren

8. Is Paul's *love for others* akin to the love we see in Christ?

> **A new commandment I give to you, that you love one another, even <u>as I have</u> <u>loved you</u>**, that you also love one another. By this all men will know that you are My disciples, if you have love for one another. —John 13:34–35 NASB

13. Does it appear that Paul is striving to do the "new commandment"?

What would Paul say?
Like Jesus, Paul has placed *the development of the Christ-Spirit* above everything else, including his own salvation. Jesus and Paul both endured extreme brutality and humiliation so that others could have a relationship with the Father. To each of them, the Kingdom/Spirit is superior to everything.

More specifically, if the Greek word "Christos" means *Christ* and *his likeness,* then we can understand why he values "Christos" above…

(a)   receiving payment
(b)   receiving respect, honor, and significance from others
(c)   comfort and certainty
(d)   his own safety and physical welfare
(e)   his own individual rights
(f)   the judgments and opinions of others
(g)   following a set of traditions and rituals
(h)   following a set of rules and regulations
(i)   physical pain, torture, and death

My God is not my traditions. My God is not my rules. My God is not the Scriptures. My God is

the Spirit that gave everything up for me. It is His Spirit that is my Lord.

Paul has placed love and service higher than everything else. He is more concerned with the development of a Christlike Spirit than anything else. He gives specific examples where he values the spreading of the gospel of Christ (Christlikeness) more than respect, comfort, physical gain, and even his own salvation.

> **He who believes in Me, as the Scripture said,**
> **'From his innermost being will flow rivers of living water.'**
> **—John 7:38 NASB**

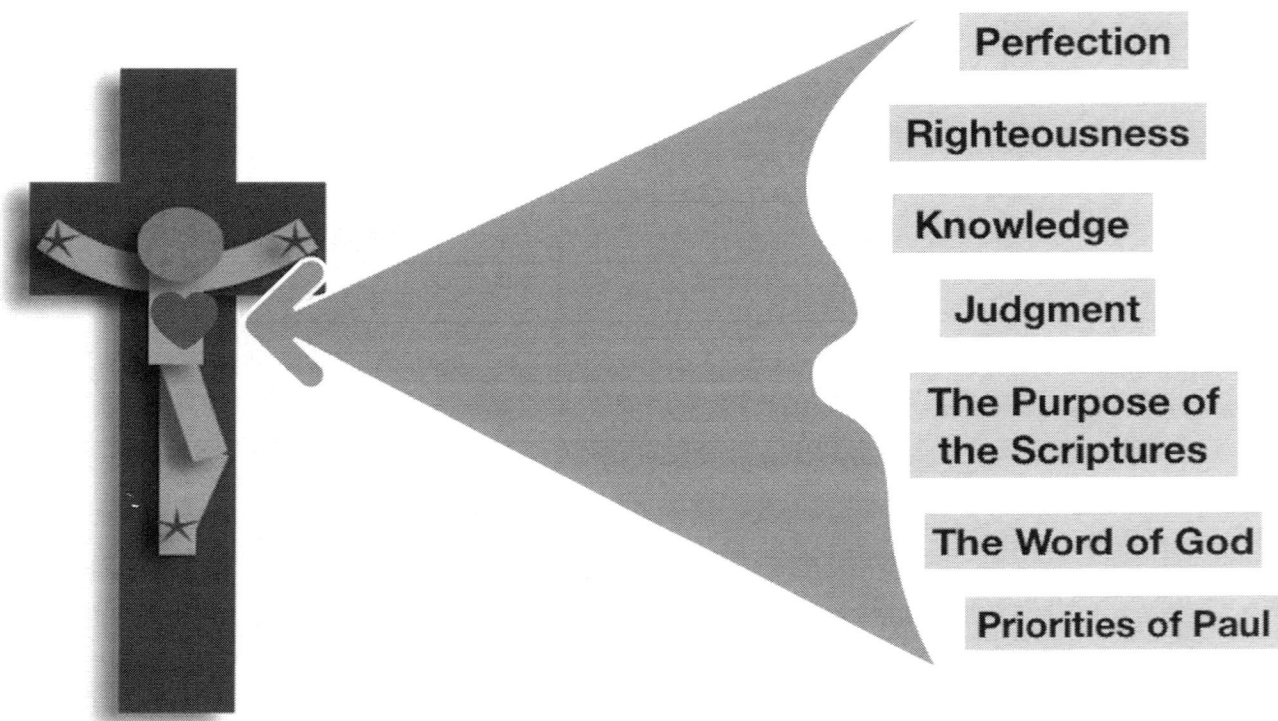

Perfection

Righteousness

Knowledge

Judgment

The Purpose of
the Scriptures

The Word of God

Priorities of Paul

**Thus far everything points to the Spirit in Christ...
Hmmm... I wonder if there is a particular rule or principle
they were trying to follow?**

What Exactly is the New Covenant?

Perry Stiltz

NEW COVENANT

"Do this in remembrance of Me"

Bread = Body
Cup = Blood

Why do we need to "examine ourselves"?

Why does Paul refer to "Judgement" and "Judging Ourselves"?

With what or whom are we comparing ourselves?

How is this related to the Communion? Or the New Covenant?

For I received from the Lord that which I also delivered to you, that the Lord Jesus in the night in which He was betrayed took bread; and when He had given thanks, He broke it and said, "This is My body, which is for you; do this in remembrance of Me." In the same way *He took* the cup also after supper, saying, "This cup is the new covenant in My blood; do this, as often as you drink *it*, in remembrance of Me." For as often as you eat this bread and drink the cup, you proclaim the Lord's death until He comes. Therefore whoever eats the bread or drinks the cup of the Lord in an unworthy manner, shall be guilty of the body and the blood of the Lord. But a man must examine himself, and in so doing he is to eat of the bread and drink of the cup. For he who eats and drinks, eats and drinks judgment to himself if he does not judge the body rightly. For this reason many among you are weak and sick, and a number sleep. But if we judged ourselves rightly, we would not be judged. But when we are judged, we are disciplined by the Lord so that we will not be condemned along with the world. So then, my brethren, when you come together to eat, wait for one another. If anyone is hungry, let him eat at home, so that you will not come together for judgment.
1Cor.11:23-34 NASB

"A New Commandment I give to you, that you love one another, even as I have loved you, that you also love one another." —John 13:34

Could Jesus' "New Commandment" be "the New Covenant"?

Would this explain why Paul writes that we need to "examine ourselves"?

Would this explain why Paul emphasizes:
a)   Love?
b)   Spiritual growth?
c)   Building each other in Christ?

What if "following Christ" was a commitment to following the Spirit in Jesus?

Could the New Covenant be the commitment to following Christ's New Commandment?
Does this fit with the other descriptions regarding the New Covenant?

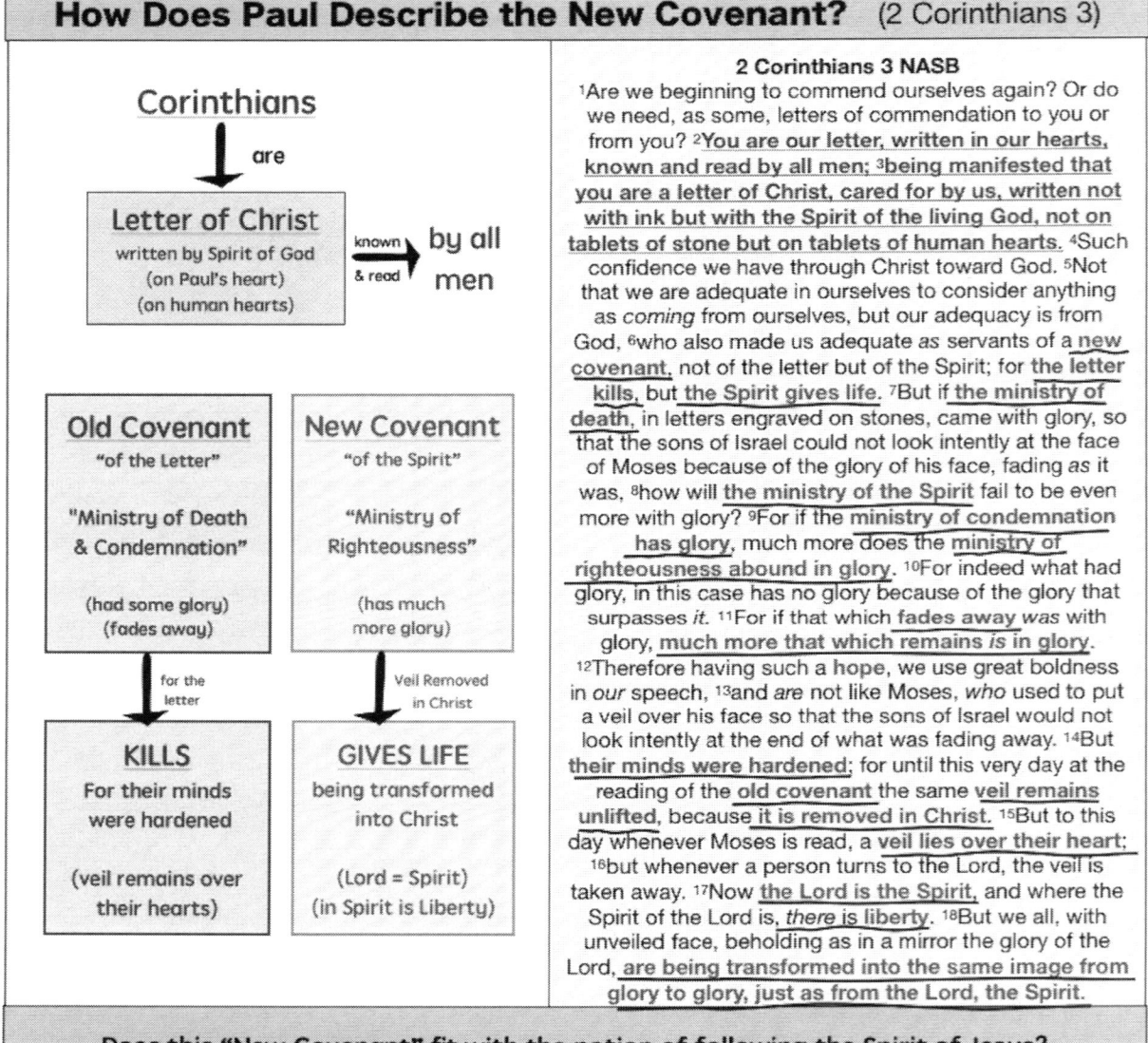

How Does Paul Describe the New Covenant? (2 Corinthians 3)

Corinthians

are

Letter of Christ
written by Spirit of God
(on Paul's heart)
(on human hearts)

known & read → by all men

Old Covenant
"of the Letter"

"Ministry of Death & Condemnation"

(had some glory)
(fades away)

for the letter ↓

KILLS
For their minds were hardened

(veil remains over their hearts)

New Covenant
"of the Spirit"

"Ministry of Righteousness"

(has much more glory)

Veil Removed in Christ ↓

GIVES LIFE
being transformed into Christ

(Lord = Spirit)
(in Spirit is Liberty)

2 Corinthians 3 NASB
[1]Are we beginning to commend ourselves again? Or do we need, as some, letters of commendation to you or from you? [2]You are our letter, written in our hearts, known and read by all men; [3]being manifested that you are a letter of Christ, cared for by us, written not with ink but with the Spirit of the living God, not on tablets of stone but on tablets of human hearts. [4]Such confidence we have through Christ toward God. [5]Not that we are adequate in ourselves to consider anything as *coming* from ourselves, but our adequacy is from God, [6]who also made us adequate *as* servants of a new covenant, not of the letter but of the Spirit; for the letter kills, but the Spirit gives life. [7]But if the ministry of death, in letters engraved on stones, came with glory, so that the sons of Israel could not look intently at the face of Moses because of the glory of his face, fading *as it was*, [8]how will the ministry of the Spirit fail to be even more with glory? [9]For if the ministry of condemnation has glory, much more does the ministry of righteousness abound in glory. [10]For indeed what had glory, in this case has no glory because of the glory that surpasses *it*. [11]For if that which fades away *was* with glory, much more that which remains *is* in glory. [12]Therefore having such a hope, we use great boldness in *our* speech, [13]and *are* not like Moses, *who* used to put a veil over his face so that the sons of Israel would not look intently at the end of what was fading away. [14]But their minds were hardened; for until this very day at the reading of the old covenant the same veil remains unlifted, because it is removed in Christ. [15]But to this day whenever Moses is read, a veil lies over their heart; [16]but whenever a person turns to the Lord, the veil is taken away. [17]Now the Lord is the Spirit, and where the Spirit of the Lord is, *there is liberty*. [18]But we all, with unveiled face, beholding as in a mirror the glory of the Lord, are being transformed into the same image from glory to glory, just as from the Lord, the Spirit.

Does this "New Covenant" fit with the notion of following the Spirit of Jesus?

Think Like Paul: Searching for the Message that Changed the World

How Does Paul Describe the New Covenant? (Hebrews 9:11-28)

Christ

(thru eternal Spirit)

the mediator of
a new covenant

Offered Himself
as sacrifice

Purifies our
conscience

(from dead works)

so ↓ that

those who
are called
may
receive an
eternal
inheritance

Hebrews 9:11-28 ESV

11But when Christ appeared as a high priest of the good things that have come, then through the greater and more perfect tent (not made with hands, that is, not of this creation) 12he entered once for all into the holy places, not by means of the blood of goats and calves but by means of his own blood, thus securing an eternal redemption. 13For if the blood of goats and bulls, and the sprinkling of defiled persons with the ashes of a heifer, sanctify for the purification of the flesh, 14how much more will the blood of Christ, who through the eternal Spirit offered himself without blemish to God, purify our conscience from dead works to serve the living God. 15Therefore he is the mediator of a new covenant, so that those who are called may receive the promised eternal inheritance, since a death has occurred that redeems them from the transgressions committed under the **first covenant**. 16For where a will is involved, **the death of the one who made it must be established.** 17For a will takes effect only at death, since it is not in force as long as the one who made it is alive. 18Therefore **not even the first covenant was inaugurated without blood.** 19For when **every commandment of the law had been declared by Moses to all the people,** he took the blood of calves and goats, with water and scarlet wool and hyssop, and sprinkled both the book itself and all the people, 20saying, **"This is the blood of the covenant that God commanded for you."** 21And in the same way he sprinkled with the blood both the tent and all the vessels used in worship. 22Indeed, under the law almost everything is purified with blood, and **without the shedding of blood there is no forgiveness of sins.** 23Thus it was necessary for the copies of the heavenly things to be purified with these rites, but the heavenly things themselves with better sacrifices than these. 24For Christ has entered, not into holy places made with hands, which are copies of the true things, but into heaven itself, now to appear in the presence of God on our behalf. 25Nor was it to offer himself repeatedly, as the high priest enters the holy places every year with blood not his own, 26for then he would have had to suffer repeatedly since the foundation of the world. But as it is, he has appeared once for all at the end of the ages to put away sin by the sacrifice of himself. 27And just as it is appointed for man to die once, and after that comes judgment, 28so Christ, having been offered once to bear the sins of many, will appear a second time, not to deal with sin but to save those who are eagerly waiting for him.

Do these descriptions fit with the notion of following the Spirit of Jesus? Or the following of Jesus' "New Commandment"?

Think Like Paul: Searching for the Message that Changed the World

Study #22: What Exactly is the "New Covenant"?

What is a Covenant?

Let's consider the *one* Old Testament reference to a "New Covenant":

> "Behold, days are coming," declares the LORD, "when I will make a **new covenant** with the house of Israel and with the house of Judah, not like the covenant which I made with their fathers in the day I took them by the hand to bring them out of the land of Egypt, My covenant which they broke, although I was a husband to them," declares the LORD."But this is the covenant which I will make with the house of Israel after those days," declares the Lord, "**I will put My law within them and on their heart I will write it**; and I will be their God, and they shall be My people. **They will not teach again, each man his neighbor and each man his brother, saying, 'Know the Lord,' for they will all know Me, from the least of them to the greatest of them,**" declares the Lord, "for I will forgive their iniquity, and their sin I will remember no more." —Jeremiah 31:31–34 NASB

A covenant is more than a contract. It is a promise to *be* a particular kind of person. When one gets married, and makes a covenant with their spouse and God, they are making a promise to *be* a godly spouse (husband or wife) to each other and before God.[25] A covenant **is a promise of being-ness.**

The Lord's Supper and the New Covenant

When Jesus initiates the New Covenant He does it at His last meal, where He refers to the bread and wine as His body and blood, and tells them to partake of it in "remembrance of Me." From the immediate context it is difficult to see how this New Covenant is any different than a ritualistic memorial. Is this remembrance the "New Covenant"? Does partaking of this memorial mean that we are apart of God's New Covenant? Or is it a reminder of some sort of deeper commitment to follow Jesus?

The Apostle John records a piece of information that could explain what the "New Covenant" actually is. In John 13, at the communion table, Jesus gives a *new* commandment:

> **A new commandment I give to you, that you love one another: just as I have loved you, you also are to love one another. —John 13:34 NASB**

Questions:
1.   Is this a commandment of being-ness?

---

[25] Similarly, Israel repeatedly broke God's covenant because they were not *being* the faithful people they agreed to be, for they were to meditate upon and apply God's principles to their own hearts.

2.   To fulfill this commandment, what would we need to remember?

I have no agenda, except to love others as Christ loved me

for that Spirit is Everything
(righteousness, perfection, the fulfillment of the Law, true knowledge, the purpose of the church, God's Message, the Holy Spirit...)

Consider Jesus' commandment in light of Paul's references to the communion and the New Covenant:

> For I received from the Lord that which I also delivered to you, that the Lord Jesus in the night in which He was betrayed took bread; and when He had given thanks, He broke it and said, "**"This is My body, which is for you; do this in remembrance of Me.**"" In the same way *He took* the cup also after supper, saying, ""This cup is the **new covenant in My blood**; do this, as often as you drink *it*, in remembrance of Me."" For as often as you eat this bread and drink the cup, you proclaim the Lord's death until He comes. —1 Corinthians 11:23-26 NASB

3. Could Jesus' commandment *be* the New Covenant? Could this "New Commandment" fit in this context?

Let's read on, and see if it fits with the subsequent verses:

> **Therefore whoever eats the bread or drinks the cup of the Lord in an unworthy manner, shall be guilty of the body and the blood of the Lord. But a man must examine himself**, and in so doing he is to eat of the bread and drink of the cup. **For he who eats and drinks, eats and drinks judgment to himself if he does not judge the body rightly.** —1Corinthians 11:27–29 NASB

Let's consider the first sentence:

> Therefore whoever eats the bread or drinks the cup of the Lord in an unworthy manner, **shall be guilty of the body and the blood of the Lord**.
> —1 Corinthians 11:23 NASB

4. According to this passage, what causes us to be "guilty of the body and the blood of the Lord"?

Previously, Paul had revealed that their communion was selfish and forgetful of the poor, and that they got together "for the worse"[26]. Their attitudes and actions were not building each other up, but were destructive. Here Paul places the guilt of the Lord's death on those who are taking

---

[26] 1Cor:11:17-22

communion in an "unworthy manner." For Paul the attitude/spirit with which we partake can be as criminal as those who physically crucified Him.

5. What is Paul's likely meaning of an "unworthy manner"?
    a) Being ungrateful
    b) Forgetting your sinful nature
    c) Forgetting those who are poor
    d) Getting drunk
    e) Forgetting the attitude/spirit of Christ

6. And why would this "unworthy manner" cause us to "be guilty of the body and blood of Christ"?
    a) Because our covenant is a promise we made to put on Christ (the Spirit of God)
    b) Because the new covenant that we follow is to "love one another as Christ loved us"
    c) Because "not putting on the spirit of Christ" = means we are not cleansed by His blood and His righteousness
    d) All of the above

7. Considering what we know about the New Testament, what is this New Covenant probably about?
    a) A promise to follow our feelings
    b) A promise to use the New Testament like it is a book of laws
    c) A promise to follow a particular style or kind of church worship
    d) A promise to love others as Christ loved us

Let us suppose that this *New Covenant* is Christ's commandment to "love one another as Christ loved us," and consider it in light of some of Paul's other passages on *law*.

> Thanks be to God through Jesus Christ our Lord! So then, on the one hand I myself with my mind am serving the **law of God**, but on the other, with my flesh the law of sin. —Romans 7:25 NASB

> There is therefore now no condemnation for those who are in Christ Jesus. For **the law of the Spirit of life** has set you free in Christ Jesus from the law of sin and death. For God has done what the law, weakened by the flesh, could not do. By sending his own Son in the likeness of sinful flesh and for sin, he condemned sin in the flesh, in order that the righteous requirement of the **law** might be fulfilled in us, who walk not according to the flesh but according to the Spirit. —Romans 8:1-4 ESV

> …To those without Law as without Law (not being without Law of God, but under *the* **law of Christ**), that I might gain *those* without Law.—1 Corinthians 9:21 LITV

Brethren, even if anyone is caught in any trespass, you who are spiritual, restore such a one in a spirit of gentleness; *each one* looking to yourself, so that you too will not be tempted. Bear one another's burdens, and thereby fulfill the **law of Christ**. —Galatians 6:1-2 NASB

8. Do these passages fit with the idea that the New Covenant is a promise to love like Christ did?

9. In second Corinthians chapter 3, we have a fairly detailed description and comparison of the new and old covenants. How does Paul describe this new covenant? Make a list:

    a)

    b)

    c)

    d)

What if we used the communion as a reminder of our commitment to: "love others as He loves us"?

What would that do to our spirits if we continually committed ourselves to that commandment?

Do these descriptions fit with the following of the New Commandment?

10. Hebrews 8 and 9 has the longest passage comparing these 2 covenants. How is this New Covenant described?

    a)

    b)

    c)

Do these descriptions fit with the following of this New Commandment?

What would Paul say?
The New Covenant is a promise to follow the Christ-Spirit (the following of Jesus' New Commandment to "love others as I have loved you.") The Lord's Supper is the partaking of this covenant, which is remembering Him and His sacrifice, while examining ourselves and considering how we may put on His Spirit.

I will measure my love with

His blood

I protest, brothers, by my pride in you, which I have in Christ Jesus our Lord, I die every day! —1 Corinthians 15:31 ESV

New Covenant: Being Christ to the World

(Symbolized in Communion)

Descriptions of the Communion in 1 Corinthians 10 & 11

- it is a participation in the body and blood of Christ (10:16-17)
- if we partake in an unworthy manner we are guilty of the body and blood of Christ (11:27)
- place to examine ourselves (11:28)
- place to judge ourselves (so that God may not judge us) (11:31)
- in this judgment we will not be condemned by the world (11:32)
- when we compare ourselves to Christ's Spirit, we are disciplined by God (11:32)

Instituting New Covenant

Take, eat; this is My body... Drink from it, all of you, for this is My blood of the covenant... Mt. 26-28

"A new commandment I give to you, that you love one another just as I have loved you, you also are to love one another. By this all people will know that you are my disciples, if you have love for one another."
—John 13:34-35

Obedience means:

"I will love others as Jesus loved me... And this is how people will know we belong to Him"
(a promise of "being-ness")

Descriptions of the Covenant in Hebrews 8 & 9

- A much more excellent "pattern" (8:5-6)
- Everyone will know God (8:11)
- God puts His laws in our minds (8:10)
- God writes His laws on our hearts (8:10)
- through a greater and more perfect tent (9:11)
- Purifies conscience (9:14)
- He is the mediator of the New Covenant (9:15)

Descriptions of the Covenant in 2 Corinthians 3

- known and read by all men (3:2)
- written on our fleshly hearts (3:3)
- it is a covenant of the spirit (3:6)
- turning to Christ = veil is taken away (3:16)
- the Lord is the Spirit (3:17)
- in it there is liberty (3:17)
- it transforms us into the Spirit of Christ (3:18)

How would Paul explain the New Covenant/Communion?

Today's Communion:
Memorial

Paul's Communion:
Memorial + Promise to follow the Spirit of Jesus

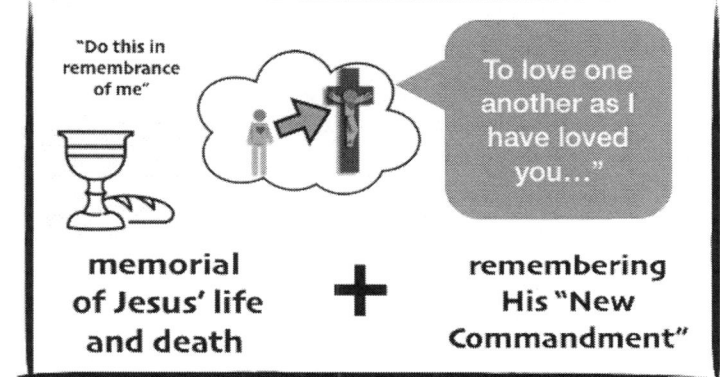

memorial of Jesus' life and death

OR

memorial of Jesus' life and death

+

remembering His "New Commandment"

"This cup is the new covenant in my blood" 1Cor. 11:25 NASB

"Whoever, therefore, eats the bread or drinks the cup of the Lord in an unworthy manner will be guilty concerning the body and blood of the Lord. Let a person examine himself, then, and so eat of the bread and drink of the cup. For anyone who eats and drinks without discerning the body eats and drinks judgment on himself." 1Cor.11:27-29 NASB

"The cup of blessing that we bless, is it not a participation in the blood of Christ? The bread that we break, is it not a participation in the body of Christ? Because there is one bread, we who are many are one body, for we all partake of the one bread." 1Cor. 10:16-17 NASB

Study #23: A Covenant of Death… for Life

Just within Paul's letters to the Corinthians we have many clues as to the significance of this "New Covenant". Let's reconsider some of Paul's descriptions of this covenant/communion:

Why did Paul write so much about death and sacrifice? It seems so morbid···

What is the value of it? How would this help us to be more like Christ?

1 Corinthians
- it is a participation in the blood of Christ (10:16)
- it is a participation of the body of Christ (10:17)
- if we partake in an unworthy manner we are guilty of the body and blood of Christ (11:27)
- it is a place to examine ourselves (11:28)
- it is a place to judge ourselves (so that God may not judge us) (11:31)
- when we compare ourselves to Christ's Spirit, we are disciplined by God (11:32)
- in this judgment we will not be condemned by the world (11:32)

2 Corinthians
- written on our fleshly hearts (3:3)
- known and read by all men (3:2)
- it is a covenant of the spirit (3:6)
- turning to Christ the veil is taken away (3:16)
- in it there is liberty (3:17)
- it transforms us into the Spirit of Christ (3:18)

> Do these descriptions fit with:
>
> …the idea that we should remember and partake of Jesus' love?
>
> …the idea that we are to measure our own love with His love?
>
> …the idea that we are to be growing in the same Spirit that Jesus had when going to the cross?
>
> … Jesus' "New Commandment" to "love one another as I have loved you"?

The New Covenant is clearly rooted in the spirit seen in Jesus. Now let's consider a couple of statements Jesus makes regarding death, sacrifice and following Him:

> And whoever does not take his cross and follow me is not worthy of me. Whoever finds his life will lose it, and **whoever loses his life** for my sake **will find it**. —Matthew 10:38-39 ESV

> And he said to all, "If anyone would come after me, **let him deny himself and take up his cross daily and follow me**." —Luke 9:23 ESV

While this "take up his cross daily and follow me" may seem strange and morbid for us today, what if Jesus was teaching them a tool or shortcut to valuing the spiritual over the physical? What if He was helping them live in the message of God? Let's examine a few more verses and try to understand Paul's notion of what the cross may represent.

For Christ did not send me to baptize but to preach the gospel, and not with words of eloquent wisdom, lest the **cross of Christ be emptied of its power**.
—1 Corinthians 1:17 ESV

Questions:
1. What power could the "cross of Christ" have? Which of the following could this cross represent:
   a) God's infinite love
   b) God's ability to change the hearts of man
   c) Our capacity to love, endure, and overcome
   d) Our capacity to affect the hearts of others
   e) All of the above

> The fear of death follows from the fear of life. A man who lives fully is prepared to die at any time.
>
> Mark Twain

2. How could "eloquent wisdom" empty the cross of its power?

I have been crucified with Christ. It is no longer I who live, but Christ who lives in me. And the life I now live in the flesh I live by faith in the Son of God, who loved me and gave himself for me. —Galatians 2:20 ESV

3. What does Paul associate with being crucified with Christ?
   a) his own death
   b) Christ living in him
   c) living by faith in the Son of God
   d) a sacrificial love (giving oneself up for another)
   e) all of the above

Always **carrying in the body the death of Jesus, <u>so that</u> the life of Jesus may also be manifested in our bodies**. For we who live are always being given over to death for Jesus' sake, **so that the life of Jesus also may be manifested in our mortal flesh**. So death is at work in us, but life in you. —2 Corinthians 4:10-12 ESV

<u>That</u> I may know him and the power of his resurrection, and may share his sufferings, **becoming like him in his death.** —Philippians 3:10 ESV

For **<u>if</u> we have been united with Him in a death** like His, we shall certainly be united with Him in a resurrection like His. —Rom. 6:5 ESV

4. What do these verses have in common? What do they associate with *suffering* and *death*?

5. What/Who lives *within* them, because of this suffering and death?

Love, death, and being spiritually alive— seem to be inextricably connected to Christ and the development of His likeness. Now let's reconsider the New Covenant:

> For I received from the Lord that which I also delivered to you, that the Lord Jesus in the night in which He was betrayed took bread; and when He had given thanks, He broke it and said, "'This is **My body**, which is for you; do this in remembrance of Me.'" In the same way *He took* the cup also after supper, saying, "'This cup is the new covenant in **My blood**; do this, as often as you drink *it*, in remembrance of Me.'" For as often as you eat this bread and drink the cup, **you proclaim the Lord's death until He comes.** —1 Corinthians 11:23-26 NASB

6. What do the bread and the cup represent? What are partaking of?

7. What are we proclaiming when we partake of this communion?

> Make room in your hearts for us. We have wronged no one, we have corrupted no one, we have taken advantage of no one. I do not say this to condemn you, for I said before that you are in our hearts, **to die together** and to live together. —2 Corinthians 7:2-3 ESV

THERE MAY BE NO SINGLE THING THAT CAN TEACH US MORE ABOUT LIFE THAN DEATH.

—ARIANNA HUFFINGTON

8. In this context of "to die together," what else does Paul mention? What is his heart revealing?

> The Spirit himself bears witness with our spirit that we are children of God, and if children, then heirs—heirs of God and fellow heirs with Christ, **provided we suffer with him** in order that we may also be glorified with him. —Romans 8:16-17 ESV

9. Why do you think Paul refers to his own suffering and death so often?

10. Why is it important to remember Christ's suffering and death?

11. How do you think Jesus prepared for his own death? At the cross what does He have to value more than anything else? What would he have to think, feel, or meditate upon when contemplating mankind (and those who want to destroy him)?

Paul's Worship

Consider Paul. He wants love and care for others to expand within and without the church. He is much more concerned about the Word (their Christlikeness), than he is about doing some formulaic concept of righteousness. Paul's idol is not some distant unknowable god. But rather, he has decided to revere the Spirit that caused Jesus to do what He did.

> But we have this measure in jars of clay, to show that the surpassing power belongs to God and not us. We are afflicted in every way; but not crushed; perplexed, but not driven to despair; persecuted, but not forsaken; struck down, but not destroyed; always carrying in the body the death of Jesus, **so that** the life of Jesus may also be manifested in our bodies. —2 Corinthians 4:7–10 ESV

Questions:

From this context, answer the following:

12. How often does Paul carry the death of Jesus?

13. Where does he keep the death of Jesus?

14. What is his purpose for carrying the death of Jesus?

15. What usually happens when people face their own mortality? How are their values and priorities affected?

I will consider it all joy when I encounter various trials, for it is in

His Spirit

that I gain endurance, which makes me perfect and complete, lacking in nothing

16. What would happen if you mentally and emotionally placed yourself in the person of Christ for a few minutes every day? How would your life be different if you emotionally connected with His mission to serve? His suffering? His compassion? His commitment? His courage? His strength? His forgiveness?…

17. How do you think those first followers were able to endure the persecutions? Which of the following sounds most like Paul's mentality?
    a) they waited for a spirit to appear
    b) a strict adherence to Paul's letters gave them strength
    c) a mental and emotional practice of remembering Christ (His mission to serve, and His commitment to love regardless of circumstances …including torture and death).

20. What would be different for you, if you came to know that you were going to die like Christ did?

21. Jesus had the ability to stop the brutality, but He didn't. What kind of resolve and love would you have to have to endure what He did?

22. What would Jesus have to believe to make that kind of sacrifice?

23. What belief has prevented you from giving Jesus' degree of love?

What would Paul say?
While Jesus equates *losing life* with *finding life*, **Paul associates becoming like Christ with growing into the spirit Jesus had *in* death. Paul was emotionally connected to Jesus' life and death. He regarded the contemplation of Jesus' death (a combination of: the *suffering he endured* and the *love that he has*) as a type of spiritual cleansing of his own sinful desires.**

Contemplating the Value of the Cross
What if developing His kind of love was the secret to overcoming lust or greed? What if it was as simple as emotionally practicing love through the toughest of situations? What if we considered the brutality Jesus suffered as our own? What if we became emotionally capable of loving and forgiving in the midst of our own destruction? What if Christ's love was their measuring stick?

> **We love because he first loved us.**
> **—1 John 4:19 ESV**

What if the secret to significant growth in Christ was growing in the suffering he endured, and the love that he decided to respond with? What if strength and courage was a product of getting comfortable with our upcoming death? What if the riches of the kingdom could come from growing in the love for those who want to destroy us?

Could real transformation be in the emotional and spiritual understanding of Christ's life and death? Could this kind of love be the door to inner strength and real freedom? Could realizing *His love for us* give us the ability and capacity to love others in the same manner?

Placing His Spirit and His love first is our *one* true answer. In fact, it is our *only* answer. The answer to all our problems is Christ. My answer (for my life's difficulties) is God's likeness within me. Your answer (for your life's difficulties) is God's likeness within you. What could possibly be more godly than that? What could possibly be more righteous that that? What could possibly be more effective to helping others see the light?

(Note: This is not a physical solution. This is a spiritual solution. This is a *using of today's difficulties* to grow in His Spirit of love and strength.)

A Mysterious Commandment

There are more than a few references to a certain commandment of the Lord, but this commandment is mysterious to us as it is not specified in their contexts.

...that you keep **the commandment** without stain or reproach until the appearing of our Lord Jesus Christ —1 Timothy 6:14 NASB

...for it would be better for them not to have known the way of righteousness, than having known it, to turn away from **the holy commandment** handed on to them. —2 Peter 2:21 NASB

So speak and so act as those who are to be judged by **the law of liberty**. —James 2:12 NASB

For **the law of the Spirit of life** has set you free in Christ Jesus from the law of sin and death —Romans 8:2 ESV

...To those without Law as without Law (not being without Law of God, but under the **law of Christ**), that I might gain those without Law. —1 Corinthians 9:21 LITV

Bear one another's burdens, and thereby fulfill the **law of Christ** —Galatians 6:2 ESV

so that in everything they may adorn **the doctrine of God** our Savior. —Titus 2:1-10 ESV

...that you should remember the words spoken beforehand by the holy prophets and **the commandment of the Lord and Savior** spoken by your apostles. —2 Peter 3:2 NASB

Hmmm.... It seems as if the writers and the recipients had an understanding of one specific commandment of the Lord... Could this mysterious commandment be the Lord's "New Commandment"? What else could they be referring to?

Facing my own death brought an instant sense of clarity and purpose.
—Tom Shadyac

Conclusions for Part 4: The New Covenant is the Christ Spirit

Paul's priorities were set on the development of the Christ-Spirit within himself and others. **The New Covenant was a promise to the following of the Christ-Spirit. It was the *putting on* and *growing into* the Spirit of Jesus.**

Paul's heart and priorities would reveal and exemplify the Christ-Spirit to those around him, and those who would receive his letters. He was so committed to this Spirit of Jesus that he would even sacrifice all that is physical (including his own life) for the sake of others. Paul follows Jesus' New Commandment of "love one another as I have loved you"[27] which Jesus gave at His last mean with His disciples (where He initiated the New Covenant). He alludes to this commitment in his letter to the Corinthians, where he tells them to *examine themselves* and *judge themselves, so that they will not be judged.*[28]

= Paul's Purpose for himself
= Paul's Purpose for the Church
= Was Commanded in Jesus'
   "New Commandment"
= New Covenant

**For in Christ Jesus neither circumcision nor uncircumcision
counts for anything, but only faith working through love.
—Galatians 5:6 ESV**

---

[27] John 13:34-35

[28] 1Corinthians 11:24-33

Part 5: How Would Paul Explain the Holy Spirit?

Study #24: The Spirit that is Holy
What would Paul say is the nature of the Spirit?

Study #25: Testing the Spirits
Comparing Paul's Holy Spirit with today's teachings.

Study #24: The Spirit that is Holy

Untangling From Today's "Holy Spirits"
There are many views regarding the Holy Spirit and how it is given or attained. Here we will try to get clarity around a couple of the Spirit's aspects to see how, or if, it may fit with the Christlikeness model of our previous studies. Again, we want to understand the letters, the language, and the ideas in the manner that they understood them. So when you read the words "Holy Spirit" remember 2 things regarding their language:

(thought bubbles) How do we get the Holy Spirit? Is it only for a few? Or is it for everyone?

Is it something that comes from prayer or baptism? Or is it something that is already in us?

How did Paul teach it? What is the role of Jesus in understanding the Holy Spirit?

1. They did not capitalize. Therefore Holy Spirit in the NT letters would look like: holy spirit.
2. "Holy" is an adjective, and describes the nature of the spirit, and therefore can be read as "the spirit that is holy" (which is the actual Greek structure).

This of course is still God's Spirit, but this practice may give us more clarity of their perspective without delving into the confusing doctrines of the Trinity- (a divided but unified God). Understanding this will make many of our more difficult passages easier to understand.

> I am not doubtful of the Holy Spirit.
>
> I am skeptical of those who profess that they are guided by Him.

In the following passages we will replace the "Holy Spirit" with "spirit that is holy" so that we may not confuse the simplicity of their meanings with today's confusing notions:

And suddenly there came from heaven a sound like a mighty rushing wind, and it filled the entire house where they were sitting. And divided tongues as of fire appeared to them and rested on each one of them. And they were all filled with the spirit that is holy and began to speak in other tongues as the Spirit gave them utterance. —Acts 2:2-4 ESV*

And do not grieve the spirit that is holy of God, by whom you were sealed for the day of redemption. —Ephesians 4:30 ESV*

Wherefore I give you to understand, that no man speaking by the Spirit of God calleth Jesus accursed: and *that* no man can say that Jesus is the Lord, but by the spirit that is holy. —1 Corinthians 12:3 KJV*

Peter *said* to them, "Repent, and each of you be baptized in the name of Jesus Christ for the forgiveness of your sins; and you will receive the gift of the spirit that is holy. —Acts 2:38 NASB*

> To be a minister of Christ Jesus to the Gentiles, ministering as a priest the gospel of God, so that *my* offering of the Gentiles may become acceptable, sanctified by the <u>spirit that is holy</u>. —Romans 15:16 NASB*

> Or do you not know that your body is a temple of the <u>spirit that is holy</u> who is in you, whom you have from God, and that you are not your own? —1 Corinthians 6:19 NASB*

Making this change (from "Holy Spirit" to "spirit that is holy") helps us understand that first century perspective in two ways. First, we are staying true to the original Greek words (πνευματος αγιου), and therefore their meanings. And second, this reordering can help us keep clear of all the misguided and incorrect associations we may have with the "Holy Spirit." While this is not crucial to this study, I have found this quite helpful in striving to understand their perspective.

From this perspective the "Holy Spirit" is not a mysterious, unclear, or random spirit, but rather it is the Spirit that we find in God, Jesus, or Paul.

Locating the Holy Spirit
As we have studied, the "Word" is Christ— the Spirit of God. It is not the Bible, and nor is it a secret message *within* the Bible. It is simply Christ (or Christlikeness). While there are not many passages that refer to the relationship between the Spirit and those who are nonbelievers, lets consider a few that appear to reveal the "location" of the Spirit.

> Jesus answered him, "Truly, truly, I say to you, unless one is born again he cannot see the kingdom of God." Nicodemus said to him, "How can a man be born when he is old? Can he enter a second time into his mother's womb and be born?" Jesus answered, "Truly, truly, I say to you, unless one is born of water and the Spirit, he cannot enter the kingdom of God. That which is born of the flesh is flesh, and **that which is born of the Spirit is spirit**. Do not marvel that I said to you, 'You must be born again.' The wind blows where it wishes, and you hear its sound, but **you do not know where it comes from or where it goes. So it is with everyone who is born of the Spirit.**"John 3:3-8 ESV

Question:
1. What does Jesus compare the "Spirit" with? What characteristic (of the Spirit) is He emphasizing in this metaphor?

On Mar's Hill, Paul speaks to *non-Christians*, where he appeals to them "as children of God," and with the suggestion that they already live in God:

> "The God who made the world and all things in it, since He is Lord of heaven and earth, **does not dwell in temples made with hands**; nor is He served by human hands, as though He needed anything, since He Himself gives to all *people* life and breath and all

things; and He made from one *man* every nation of mankind to live on all the face of the earth, having determined *their* appointed times and the boundaries of their habitation, that they would seek God, if perhaps they might grope for Him and find Him, though **He is not far from each one of us, for in Him we live and move and exist**, as even some of your own poets have said, 'For we also are His children.' "**Being then the children of God**, we ought not to think that the Divine Nature is like gold or silver or stone, an image formed by the art and thought of man… —Acts 17:23-29 NASB

Notice what he says to these *non-believers* regarding God's "location":
- God does not dwell in temples made with hands,
- He is not far from each one of us,
- In Him we live, move and exist,

Is he saying that God exists in non-believers? Is that notion found elsewhere in the New Testament? Notice how Jesus and Paul refer to the "location" of the Kingdom and Christ:

Neither shall they say, Lo here! or, lo there! for, behold, **the kingdom of God is within you**. —Luke 17:21 KJV

Here there is not Greek and Jew, circumcised and uncircumcised, barbarian, Scythian, slave, free; but **Christ is all, and in all**. —Colossians 3:11 ESV

Jesus and Paul seem to suggest that God's Spirit (Christ) is already in us, even before conversion. Now consider how Jesus describes the crowd (of presumably random followers) in what appears to be his first sermon:

You are the light of the world. —Matthew 5:14 ESV

He does not say "you are darkness, and will someday become the light." He simply says "You are the light of the world." Hmmm…. Okay…. Now consider the language Paul uses in recalling his own conversion:

But when **God**, who had set me apart *even* from my mother's womb and called me through His grace, **was pleased to *reveal His Son** in me so that I might preach Him among the Gentiles, I did not immediately consult with flesh and blood. —Galatians 1:15-16 NASB (*note: reveal = apokaluptō: to take the cover off)

Did you get that?… God was pleased to "take the cover off" His son (in Paul)!
…And notice how Jesus equates being a child of God (or the devil) with particular attributes:

Blessed are the peacemakers, for they shall be called **sons of God**. —Mathew 5:9 NASB

You are of *your* father the devil, and you want to do the desires of your father. He was a murderer from the beginning, and does not stand in the truth because there is no truth in him. Whenever he speaks a lie, he speaks from his own *nature,* for he is a liar and the father of lies. —Luke 8:44 NASB

Jesus and Paul know that we all have the potential to be either a child of God or the devil. And they associate "being a son" with the following of their attributes.

Questions:
2. Does God's Spirit sound like something you have or you don't? Or does it seem like something we can develop, grow into, or uncover?

3. If the Spirit of God is already in us (though it may be covered by lies and the cares of this world), then does this fit with study #13 where Paul refers to the word of God as being Christ-in-you?

4. Read Mark 12:13-17 regarding taxes to Caesar, and answer the following:
    a) Whose image is on the coin?
    b) What belongs to Caesar?
    c) Whose image is on man?
    d) What belongs to God?

5. Do you think assuming the best in others (seeing the Christ in them) would help in evangelism? Why or why not?

There is no more "us and them", there is only

Christ

who is all, and in all

What would Paul say?
1. The Spirit is like the wind, as we cannot see it, but only its effects.
2. The Spirit of God (and the devil) already resides within all of us.
3. We are sons of God as we align ourselves with His character/Spirit.
4. And thus, the Spirit is something we can grow into.

You've always had the power my dear, you just had to learn it for yourself.
—Glinda (Wizard of Oz)

How would Paul explain the "Holy Spirit"?
How would he explain the Spirit to non-believers?

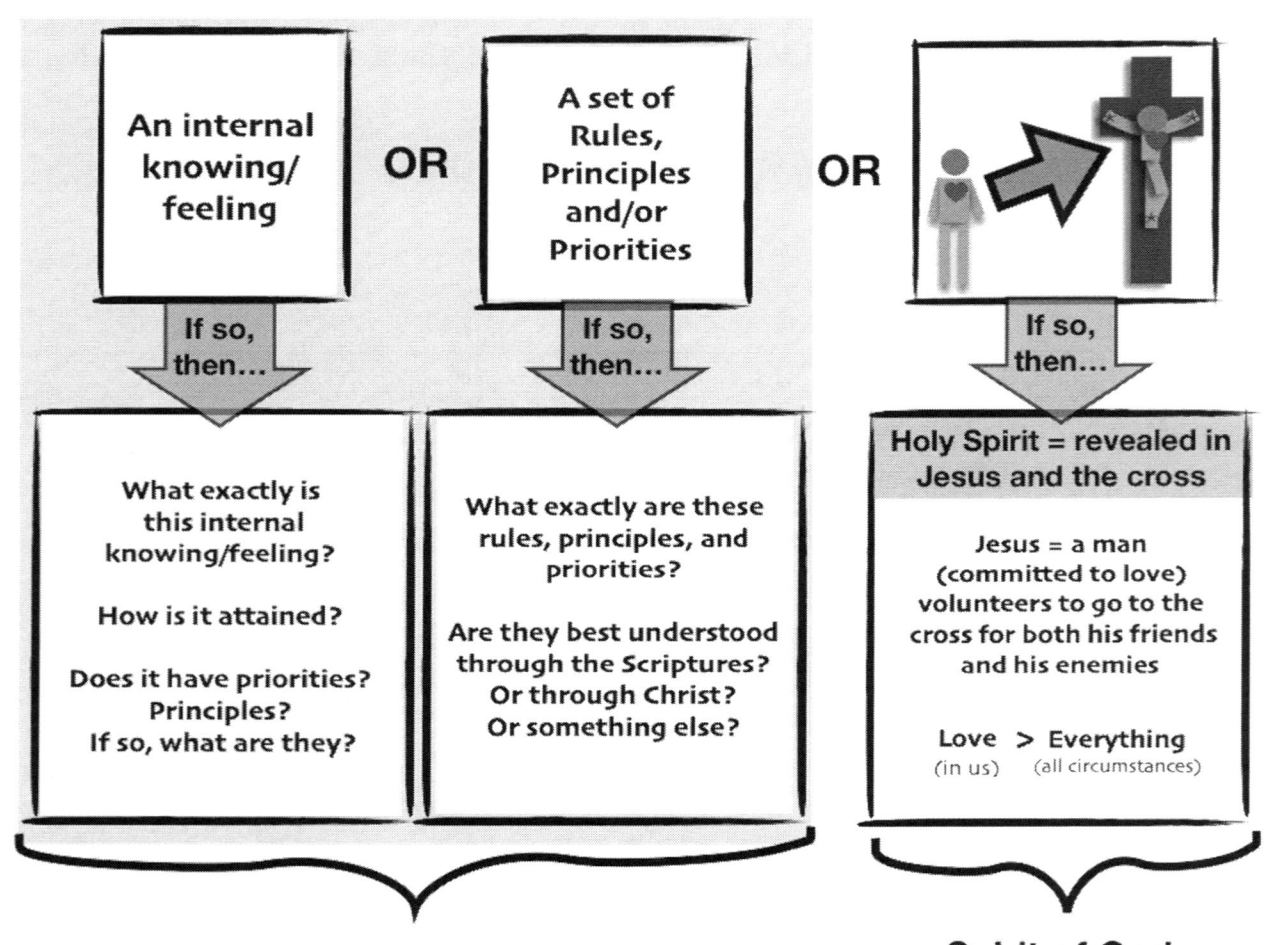

An internal knowing/ feeling

OR

A set of Rules, Principles and/or Priorities

OR

If so, then…   If so, then…   If so, then…

What exactly is this internal knowing/feeling?

How is it attained?

Does it have priorities? Principles? If so, what are they?

What exactly are these rules, principles, and priorities?

Are they best understood through the Scriptures? Or through Christ? Or something else?

Holy Spirit = revealed in Jesus and the cross

Jesus = a man (committed to love) volunteers to go to the cross for both his friends and his enemies

Love > Everything
(in us)   (all circumstances)

Spirits are unclear and ambiguous
(especially to non-Christians)
How do they relate to Christ?

Spirit of God revealed
(poured out upon all flesh —Joel 2:28)

Study #25: Testing the Spirits

Let us briefly consider what we've already determined
from our previous studies:

- *Perfection* and *fulfilling the Law* are in loving others.
- Knowledge and righteousness are in Christ's Spirit.
- Christianity is conforming to Christ.
- The purpose of the Bible is to lead us to Christ's Spirit.
- The Message of God is Christ's Spirit.
- Paul has the same purpose as Jesus, which is the teaching and spreading of God's Spirit.
- The Covenant is a promise to following Jesus' Spirit.

What kind of spirit did Paul consider holy?

How can we discern between a holy spirit and an unholy one?

Each of these point to something that John already knew: **Christ is everything**.

So what is Christlikeness? How does a Christlike spirit compare with the Holy Spirit that we teach today?

1 John 4:1-2 admonishes,

> Beloved, **do not believe every spirit, but test the spirits to see whether they are from God**, because many false prophets have gone out into the world. By this you know the Spirit of God: every spirit that confesses that Jesus Christ has come in the flesh is from God. NASB

To figure this out, let us determine the qualities of the spirits of today, by considering some common concepts and attributes of the "Holy Spirit."

While there are vastly different ways we may understand the "Holy Spirit," there are a couple of predominant themes in Christianity today. Here we will consider the two major divisions. I have labeled them: a "feeling spirit," and a "rules spirit" (Though churches and individuals mix and match these, certain qualities are common). After exploring these two *tendencies*, we will compare them with the Christlikeness evident in Jesus and Paul.

The Feeling Spirit

In John's day many teachers believed that Jesus did not come in the flesh but only in the Spirit, which explains his emphasis on Christ's fleshly appearance. Today, one of our major teachings seems to equate the Holy Spirit with an internal feeling or "knowing". The vagueness and subjectiveness of this spirit make it virtually impossible to determine its characteristics, and thus it's veracity. Its subjective nature and unclear purpose has caused many people to "know" or "feel" it in different ways. This tends to lead to confusion and doubt with both believers and nonbelievers, as there is usually is no clear distinction between this "Holy Spirit" and ones emotions. This inability to have clarity around the nature or purpose of this spirit has led many to think that Christians are illogical or flighty.

Some of the weaknesses of this feeling/knowing spirit are:

- There appears to be no clear or concise definition or standard.
- Since this spirit is an internal "feeling" it is unverifiable.
- An unclear spirit makes it difficult to distinguish between other spirits.
- Its actions can often seem unlike the spirit that we find in Jesus or Paul.
- Its emotional and sometimes illogical nature creates doubt and skepticism for both Christians and non-christians (which does not cause others to glorify God).
- Typically, there is no clear explanation on:
    - how the Spirit is attained,
    - how it works within us,
    - its purpose,
    - or how we can distinguish it from feelings or emotions.

> Does the experience of confidence, joy, and peace mean that you have the Holy Spirit?
>
> How can we really be sure?

Question:
1. Do any of these resemble the Spirit evident in Jesus and Paul?

The Rules/Logic Spirit

While some have equated the Holy Spirit with a feeling or a knowing, others have equated it with the following of a particular set of rules and examples. These churches focus on the Bible and Bible Study (this is my training). They believe that the Bible is *the* 'word of God', and strive to follow its rules and patterns. In my experience, they tend to avoid discussions regarding the Holy Spirit as they don't feel comfortable with its subjective nature.

The weaknesses of this "rules spirit" do not stem from the desire for reason and logic, but rather the inaccurate thinking that the physical Bible is *the* "message of God," and thus is today's standard. This thinking leads to valuing the Bible above everything else. Most of these studies expose some fallacy of this approach.

Some of the difficulties/weaknesses of this "rules mindset" are:

- It makes NT references to the Spirit difficult to comprehend, or unnecessary and irrelevant.
- This mindset, in conjunction with the notion that the 'Bible is the word of God', has created the concept that the Bible is alive, and that we are to conform to it, rather than learn and transform into the perfect Spirit it proclaims.
- There is little understanding of *how* the Spirit works today.
- It reduces or minimizes the need to understand the Spirit of Christ.
- It suggests that right and wrong can be determined by observation, which encourages the passing of judgment on others.
- It often creates a rigidity that is uninviting to prospective converts.
- (For a more complete list refer to: Concluding Thoughts on the Word)

Question:

2. Do any of these resemble the Spirit or mindset of Jesus or Paul?

These "weaknesses" may not apply to the Holy Spirit you have been taught. These are just some of the characteristics I've noticed… Ultimately, what matters is that we are striving to follow the Spirit we find in Christ… For it is through Him that God poured out *His* Spirit.

Comparing and Contrasting the Spirits

While there are variety of views on the Spirit, these are just a couple of the common themes. And as to which one to follow, we rarely try to quantify the differences. My effort here is to compare and contrast today's thinking with what we've come to learn regarding the mindset/Spirit of Christ as seen in both Jesus and Paul.

The following chart is not perfect, and nor is it complete, as they are just notes and distinctions that I have observed. **The goal here is to get us to think.** This is not meant to be a judgment or criticism, but rather a tool to help us contemplate and contrast today's common notions of "Spirit" with the Spirit that led both Jesus and Paul.[29]

While it seems that there is little reason to criticize the spirits found in Jesus and Paul (if not blasphemous), it also seems that when we look closely at today's notions of the "Spirit" there are some significant shortcomings. Let us revisit John's advice and consider what specifically it is that he wants the readers to compare their spirits with:

> Beloved, do not believe every spirit, but test the spirits **to see whether they are from God**, because many false prophets have gone out into the world. —1 John 4:1 NASB

John expects them to know God's character. He expects them to compare the spirits with His Spirit. To a traditional Jew, who is now a follower of Christ, God is not some illogical, flighty, or random individual. He is infinite wisdom, infinite love, and infinitely good. John knew Jesus. He knew the being who chose to endure physical hell for the benefit of others. He knew that Jesus' spirit was *of God*. That was John's standard. And here he seems to expect the readers to compare their spirits with God's Spirit.

**The church exists to train its member through the practice of the presence
of God to be servants of others, to the end that Christlikeness
may become common property.
—William Adams Brown**

---

[29] (Note: I may not be familiar with the "Spirit" that you have been taught, so some or all may not apply)

Getting Clarity with the Spirits		
	Feeling Spirit	**Rules Spirit**	**Christ-Spirit** (Paul's Perspective)
What is most important?	?!?!? "Holy Spirit"	Bible/reason/rules	Spirit of God/Jesus (love, joy, peace···)
What is the goal in teaching?	?!?!? "Holy Spirit"	Bible knowledge	the development of "Christ in you"
What do they follow?	?!?!? "Holy Spirit"	scriptural examples	Spirit revealed in Jesus
What is Righteousness? How do we become righteous?	?!?!?	?!?!?	living in Christ's Spirit (love, joy, peace···)
What is the New Covenant?	?!?!?	?!?!?	A promise to put on the Spirit of Jesus
What is the Law of Christ?	?!?!?	?!?!?	"Love one another as I have loved you" Jn.13:34
How do they typically teach others about God?	emphasize love and grace;	emphasize judgment	through own spirit of kindness & love (Christ's Spirit)
What is the Nature of the Holy Spirit?	?!?!?	?!?!?	love, joy, peace, courage··· (the spirit of Christ)
Evidence for having the Holy Spirit?	?!?!? "I just know it" (subjective)	?!?!?	Demonstrating Spirit of Jesus (His purpose, love, joy, peace···)
Emphasis in assembly?	"Holy Spirit"	"Correct Worship"; Aligning with Scriptures	Remembering and encouraging Christ(likeness) (Aligning with Christ)
Outsiders may describe churches as...	emotional or illogical	legalistic or dead	Followers of Jesus (John 13:34–35)

Yes in Him

While God's Spirit is obviously good, let's consider another passage that may help us understand their approach to the Spirit:

> Therefore, I was not vacillating when I intended to do this, was I? Or what I purpose, do I purpose according to the flesh, so that with me there will be yes, yes and no, no at the same time? But as God is faithful, **our word to you is not yes and no**. For the Son of God, Christ Jesus, who was preached among you by us— by me and Silvanus and Timothy—**was not yes and no, but is yes in Him**. For as many as are the promises of God, **in Him they are yes**; therefore also through Him is our Amen to the glory of God through us. Now He who establishes us with you in Christ and anointed us is God, who also sealed us and gave us the Spirit in our hearts as a pledge. —2 Corinthians 1:17–22 NASB

Associating a person to a particular mindset or attribute is not unusual today. In our culture Leonardo Da Vinci is connected with creativity, Hitler with racism and evil, and comparing someone to Einstein is calling them intelligent(unless it's sarcastic). Similarly, Christ would also have been connected with a particular attribute. Let's consider what they may have associated to Him and His life.

Questions:

3. Considering the *life and death of Jesus*, what would they have associated with Christ?

4. When we compare their notions of the Spirit with some of the teachings we find today, there is some disparity in meanings and applications. What specifically do you think "yes in Him" meant to those in the first century?

5. Does this passage in first Corinthians suggest that we can choose to be "yes in Him"? Or that we have **no** ability to choose Him?

6. What values or virtues are "of God"?

7. What would Jesus have to believe about others in order to endure what He did?

8. If Christianity is truly centered around Christ, then shouldn't we be striving to understand Him?

God!
Help me to adopt
your values,
and your priorities,
so that

may be alive and
powerful within me

9. If Christ really is our answer, then shouldn't the question of "What is the Holy Spirit?" be answered by looking at His Spirit?

10. What attitude or belief could you adopt, in order to become more like God's Spirit?

11. What current belief would you need to forget, in order to become more like Christ?

What would Paul say?
Christ is not just a name we proclaim, He is a spirit we embody. His Spirit is comprised of humility, forgiveness, compassion, peace, joy, courage, confidence, determination and the like.

The spirit we find in Jesus of Nazareth is God's Spirit. He is not only the messenger, He is the message itself. His spiritual likeness is our wisdom, knowledge, power and righteousness. His spiritual likeness is our purpose, our path, and our goal. He not only reveals God's Spirit, He reveals the image we were designed to be. And His ability to endure the worst of circumstances with the Spirit of God is the faith He left for us (enduring nails while loving the nailer). That Spirit is the "correct" Spirit. That spirit is the one that is holy. That spirit was their answer to everything.

**God!
Help me love as you
loved. Help me see**

your Spirit

**of love, joy, peace,
and courage within
myself and others,
as that is the Spirit
we find in your
perfect Son**

**Never be afraid to ask a question, especially if you fear it's answer.
—Harry Lewis**

Final Thoughts

A Brief Summary

Paul's "Christ is Everything" Faith
 10 Distinctions on how their faith was different

God's Ultimate Commandment (and Demonstration)

Reconsidering the New Covenant and the Bible

My Personal Challenge to You

A Brief Summary

To recap, let us *briefly* summarize what we have learned:

- Through the Christ-Spirit we may become God's image on earth. That Spirit is both our path and our goal, and it will cover us in the day of judgment.(Studies #1-5)

- The purposes of the Scriptures are to teach, lead, remind, and encourage us into being the likeness of God (Christ). (Studies #6-10)

- God's message = Christ, or Christ in you (His "New Commandment") (Studies #11-20)

- Paul "follows Christ" by adopting His Spirit, particularly His love for others. (Study #21)

- The New Covenant is the promise to follow Christ's likeness. (Study #22)

- The New Testament writers taught, emphasized and exemplified Christ's ability to love and die (for others). (Study #23)

- The Holy Spirit is the Spirit we find in Jesus— a likeness of God that is within each of us. The characteristics and priorities of Jesus reveal the Spirit we were created *to be*. (Studies #24-25)

Spirit of Christ in You

= the Way, the Truth, and the Life
= the Righteousness of God
= the Goal of the Church
= the Purpose of the Bible
= the Message of God
= the Purpose of Paul
= the New Covenant
= the Holy Spirit

Paul's "Christ is Everything" Faith

Here are some of the more notable differences between the faith of today and those in the first century. In these conclusions, I think we can start to see how they were Christ-centered, and where we have become unclear with our terminology and purposes and have conflated them with our traditions, rules and practices. Here are the 10 major differences:

1. For Paul, Christianity wasn't a religion, it was a following of Christ's Spirit. "Following Christ" in the early church was more than a realization of His Deity. He was seen as a pathway back to God. He was seen as God's image in humanity, and the model of who we are supposed to be. Growing into His likeness was the way back to a relationship with the Creator. Christ (which can also mean "Christlikeness") was more of a "way" of being, than a religion. (Studies #1-5)

> I am the way, the truth, and the life: no man cometh unto the Father, but by me. —John 14:6 KJV

Paul had clarity around the roles of Jesus and His Spirit. He saw Christ's Spirit as the literal answer for everything.

2. The Scriptures lead us to the Christ-Spirit (God's ultimate message). The Old Testament Scriptures conveyed spiritual principles through laws, regulations, stories, wisdom, poetry, history, warnings and visions. They were written for the purposes of leading people to understanding and developing the Spirit of Christ(the Word/Message of God).

> Therefore the Law has become our tutor to lead us to Christ, so that we may be justified by faith. —Galatians 3:24 NASB

The Word-that-became-flesh was the Spirit revealed in the person of Jesus. Christ was the ultimate embodiment and fulfillment of God's spiritual teachings. The New Testament letters were explicitly written for the expressed purpose of teaching, reminding and encouraging the church to grow in this Christ-Spirit-likeness.[30] (They were not written to be some sort of "new standard," but rather were written to point to the standard—the Christ-Spirit.) (Studies #6-10)

> The goal of our instruction is love from a pure heart, a good conscience, and a sincere faith. —1 Timothy 1:5 NASB

3. The Christ-Spirit (Holy Spirit) is the goal. Jesus taught that "you are a son of the devil if you follow the devil." He also taught that "you are a son of God if you love your enemies" (#1). Today we have an array of different "Holy Spirits." Paul was squarely centered on helping the church develop *the Spirit revealed in Jesus.* (#23-24)

---

[30] Many of the NT letters contain specific instructions to specific churches, who had specific problems and concerns. Those specifics were always centered on growth and the development of the Christ-Spirit within those individuals.

However, you are not in the flesh but in the Spirit, if indeed the Spirit of God dwells in you. But **if anyone does not have the Spirit of Christ, he does not belong to Him**.
—Romans 8:9 NASB

My children, with whom **I am again in labor until Christ is formed in you.**—Galatians 4:19 NASB

For Christ is the end (goal) of the law for righteousness to everyone who believes. —Romans 10:4 NASB

Today's notions of the Holy Spirit are vague and unclear, and sometimes even unlike Christ. John states that we should test the spirits to see if they are *from* God.

Beloved, do not believe every spirit, **but test the spirits to see whether they are from God**, because many false prophets have gone out into the world. —1John 4:1 NASB

God's Spirit was not seen as random, flighty or emotional. His Spirit (a.k.a. the Holy Spirit) was revealed in the person of Jesus.

It will come about after this that **I will pour out My Spirit on all mankind**; and your sons and daughters will prophesy, your old men will dream dreams, your young men will see visions. **Even on the male and female servants I will pour out My Spirit in those days**. —Joel 2:28-29 NASB

Jesus the Christ was someone who we could grow to be like, rather than a distant unknowable being. He was the embodiment of all that was *of God*. And it was through growing into His Spirit that we come to receive the blessing of Christ.

Today most have reverence for His incredible Spirit, but tend to forget that we too were made in the Creator's image. We see His amazing ability to love through the cross, but forget that **his followers committed themselves to this same Spirit**, even in the face of their own destruction.

I have been crucified with Christ; and **it is no longer I who live, but Christ lives in me**; and the *life* which I now live in the flesh I live by faith in the Son of God, who loved me and gave Himself up for me. —Galatians 2:20 NASB

4. They believed that "growing in Christ" was an essential part of following Him.
"Following Christ" was, at its core, a striving to be more like Him. (Today we emphasize Christ's part in everything, and that there is nothing that we can do to earn salvation. While that is true, its emphasis has caused some to *not* realize that "faith in Christ" had been equated with growing in Christ's spiritual likeness.) The Corinthians were people who claimed to follow

Christ, but were doing little to be like Him. Paul rebukes them for their lack of growth, and repeatedly warns them about falling away.

> But I, brothers, could not address you as spiritual people, but as people of the flesh, as infants in Christ. I fed you with milk, not solid food, for you were not ready for it. And even now you are not yet ready, for you are still of the flesh.—1Corinthians 3:1-3 ESV

> But I am afraid that as the serpent deceived Eve by his cunning, your thoughts will be led astray from a sincere and pure devotion to Christ. —2 Corinthians 11:3 NASB

> For in the case of those who have once been enlightened and have tasted of the heavenly gift and have been made partakers of the Holy Spirit, and have tasted the good word of God and the powers of the age to come, **and *then* have fallen away**, it is impossible to renew them again to repentance, since they again crucify to themselves the Son of God and put Him to open shame. —Hebrews 6:4-6 NASB

Remember, these are groups of people who have not had our denominational teachings, but rather have been taught to *build each other up in Christ*, and that His Spirit is *the goal* and *righteousness itself*. So when Paul makes a statement like this one in Hebrews 6, what exactly would they have understood? The inference is not difficult: "following Christ" is a growing to be more like Him. (Studies #1-5)

5. John and Paul refer to God's message as Christ's Spirit (Christ-in-you).

Today's gospel message is typically some mixture of:
a) a series of facts about Jesus,
b) following the teachings/patterns of New Testament,
c) personal feelings about the Holy Spirit,
d) and vague notions of "love,"
e) and being a "good" person.

The "Word of God," as those in the first century would have understood it, is simply the Spirit of Jesus (the embodiment of God's spiritual principles). Which is why Jesus says:

> **'From his innermost being will flow rivers of living water.**'—John 7:38 NASB

And why John and Paul equate His Spirit with the 'Word of God'.

> And the **Word became flesh**, and dwelt among us, and we saw His glory, glory as of the only begotten from the Father, full of grace and truth.—John 1:14 NASB

> Of *this church* I was made a minister according to the stewardship from God bestowed on me for your benefit, so that I might fully **carry out** the *preaching of* **the word of God…** **which is Christ in you**, the hope of glory. **We proclaim Him, admonishing every man**

and teaching every man with all wisdom, so that we may present every man complete in Christ. —Colossians 1:25, 27-28 NASB

To those in the first century, God's message was a spirit. The Spirit seen in Jesus was God's message to humanity. And this would be the apostles' message to the world. This Christ-in-you message came from realizing the perspective of Jesus (a man who chooses to go to a cross (because He loves all, even His enemies)). Paul wrote letters to encourage the church to live in the Christ-Spirit. And he strove to teach "the word" (the Spirit of Christ) through its work in Jesus and himself.

6. The Christ-Spirit is truly God's answer to everything. The first century writers were squarely centered on Christ and how He is the source for everything. They called Him the Word, the Truth, their foundation, and "all things that pertain to life and godliness" (Today, we often use these terms to describe the Bible).

> His divine power has granted to us **all things that pertain to life and godliness, through the knowledge of Him** who called us to his own glory and excellence—2Peter 1:3 ESV

In the first century, they were not pointing the church to their own letters. They always pointed directly to the all-encompassing answer Himself—Christ. Their answers were in this Being—this God-likeness-on-earth-Being. That Spirit was their answer. That Spirit was *the* message. And that Spirit was *the all-encompassing-everything* to those prophets of the first century.

> For I decided to know nothing among you except Jesus Christ and him crucified. —1Corinthians 2:2 ESV

They had Christ as their reference point, not a collection of letters. They looked to the man who conquered humiliation, torture and death. They looked to His Spirit(the development of Jesus spiritual likeness within themselves) for the answers and resources they needed, for He was the one being who was able to overcome every injustice and every sin. This Christ-Spirit was the Way, the Truth and the Life.

7. Through the Christ-Spirit we can become the righteousness of God. We tend to categorizing actions as "right" or "wrong," while they simply looked to increase the Christ-Spirit in people. God's notion of righteousness is simply the adapting of His Spirit.

> For our sake he made him to be sin who knew no sin, **so that in him we might** become **the righteousness of God**. —2 Corinthians 5:21 ESV

Today, we have been taught that the Bible (their letters) is our standard, and have difficulties with explaining what exactly is rightness, while they just saw this Christ-Spirit as righteousness itself. (Study #4)

8. For Paul, Christ(likeness) is the real thing, and everything else is in service to the development of the Christ-Spirit. Paul was singularly focused on the development of the Christ-Spirit within each and every follower. Everything he did and taught was in service to the Christ-Spirit, for this God-likeness within would be the only thing that would endure.

> For **no man can lay a foundation other than the one which is laid, which is Jesus Christ**…each man's work will become evident; for the day will show it because it is *to be* revealed with fire, and the fire itself will test the quality of each man's work. —1Corinthians 3:11, 13 NASB

Today, we tend to emphasize our doctrines, traditions, rules, or the participating in a particular church. But when Paul teaches these notions, he always mentions them in the context of *encouraging the recipients to greater spiritual growth* (a.k.a. Christlikeness).

> Therefore no one is to act as your judge in regard to food or drink or in respect to a festival or a new moon or a Sabbath day—**things which are a *mere* shadow** of what is to come; but **the substance belongs to Christ**. —Colossians 2:16-17 NASB

God, Christ, the Law, and the prophets have always been pointing us toward this Christ-Spirit within… This was the goal and purpose for everything. This Christ-Spirit was the substance.[31] God has always wanted us to be *His image on earth*. This is *why* we were created. And this is what Christ came to restore. (Studies #1-25)

9. Communing with Christ is an aligning our spirits with His Spirit. Today our partaking of the Communion tends to be a ritualistic remembering of Jesus and His sacrifice. For the disciples of Christ this was more than a cognitive remembrance. It was an emotional understanding of the life and death that He endured, while also being a reminder and reaffirmation of their own promises to follow Him… For they knew the commandment He gave at that last meal:

> A new commandment I give to you, that you love one another, even as I have loved you, that you also love one another. By this all men will know that you are My disciples, if you have love for one another. —John 13:34-35 NASB

This "Law of Christ" given at the communion would become their covenant with God. It could only be followed with a committed effort and promise of their own: "to love others as He loved me." As we see in Paul's letter to the Corinthians, several notions that do not make sense if the communion was simply a remembering of Him and His sacrifice.

> For as often as you eat this bread and drink the cup, you proclaim the Lord's death until He comes. Therefore **whoever eats the bread or drinks the cup of the Lord in an**

---

[31] Today, in large part, we have confused the "substance" of Christ with the "shadows" of particular traditions or works.

unworthy manner, shall be guilty of the body and the blood of the Lord. <u>But a man</u> <u>must examine himself</u>, and in so doing he is to eat of the bread and drink of the cup. For he who eats and drinks, eats and drinks judgment to himself if he does not judge the body rightly. For this reason many among you are weak and sick, and a number sleep. **<u>But if we judged ourselves rightly, we would not be judged</u>. But when we are judged, we are disciplined by the Lord so that we will not be condemned along with the world.** —1Cor.11:26-32 NASB

Today's notions of a memorial do not adequately explain Paul's references to: "examining yourself," "judging yourself," and then a "judgment" that is guilty of the "body and the blood" of Jesus. Why would one need to "examine himself," if it simply was a memorial? How would "judging ourselves" prevent us from being judged? And what does that have to do with the supper or communion? Why is it in *this* context? Paul's severity is difficult to explain if the communion was just simply a remembering of His sacrifice… But if Christianity is a commitment to the New Commandment, then we can start to see how the Christ-Spirit is everything to those first messengers of the good news. (Study #22)

10. The New Covenant is a commitment to following the New Commandment. Today we typically describe the "New Covenant" as little more than a "covenant of grace". While "grace" is an accurate descriptor, it tells us virtually nothing regarding any specific terms, conditions or expectations. What exactly is a covenant? Is there a difference between a contract and a covenant? And what exactly is this New Covenant with God?

The emphasis of the New Testament points us clearly toward one thing: Growth in Christ's likeness. For those in the first century there is no New Testament. There is only the person of Jesus. There is only Christ, and everything we receive from God flows *through Him*… So could Jesus' "New Commandment" be God's covenant? Or His only commandment? Could it be the summation of all of God's precepts and expectations?[32] (Study #22)

---

[32] I know this seems overly simple… But ask yourselves… Does this New Commandment fit? Does it cause you to understand and grow in Christ's Spirit? Does it fit with the emphases, purposes, and specific instructions of the New Testament authors? Does it fit with the purpose for the Old Testament, and its prophecies? Does it fit with the teachings that "in Christ" there are abundant spiritual riches? Does it fit with their instructions to be humble, honest and forgiving? Does it fit with their teachings on being "slaves to Christ," "free in Christ" and "united in Christ"? Could this be the key to everything? Could this be the message that transformed the world?

This *New Commandment = Law of Christ* notion did not become apparent to me until I had thoroughly understood how the Christ-Spirit was everything(Studies #1- 21) to the first century authors.

 Note: If you have been trained into a fundamentalist mentality, you likely will feel the need to examine and reexamine these studies to make sure they are accurate. I invite you to critically consider these passages/studies, and explain to me where I misused a context or taught something incorrectly… But I ask that you consider these passages humbly and honestly and with the Spirit and care of Christ Himself.

God's Ultimate Commandment (and Demonstration)

When we considered Paul's emphasis and priorities, it appears that "faith" or *being led by the Spirit* is the result of an alignment with the priorities and characteristics of Jesus Himself. We find in Paul a spirit that values love and service above everything else, even his own life, just as Jesus did. We find in Paul a reliance and emphasis on "Christ" in every imaginable way. Not just Christ as the God-image that came to earth, but Christ as spiritual likeness that we are to grow into. Everything that Paul teaches seems to be pointing us directly at one goal— the growing of the Spirit of Jesus within each of us (a.k.a. Christ).

One of the major roots of today's divisions and problems is simply a lack of clarity and purpose. We are entrenched in vague purposes and terminology which may, or may not, fit with the Christianity of the first century. We are often unclear with our terms, like "Word," "faith" and "Holy Spirit," which has given rise to people developing their own interpretations, and their own faiths... Which again, may or may not, be akin to the faith that Jesus taught and exemplified.

Essentially, Paul had one reference point whereas today we may have two, three, or more. The three major reference points of today are:
- Jesus Christ,
- The Bible (and our rules for interpretation),
- and the "Holy Spirit" (however we define, or feel it).

The first century believer did not have the New Testament... but they didn't need one. They had Jesus. They had a real-life person as their reference point. They had a person that had God's Spirit. They saw Jesus as the one person who truly reveals God's nature. They saw this man (who goes to a cross) as the founder and creator of a new faith. They saw a spiritual path back to the Creator Himself. Jesus didn't do this by setting up a new list of ordinances, but rather by choosing the ultimate demonstration. They drank from the purity of this message. They gathered their faith from *the* source—Christ.

Are we drinking from the pureness of that Spirit? Or are we gathering our faith downstream of our ancestral religions? Let's compare the Christ-centeredness of the NT authors, and the Bible-centeredness of today. (See Chart)

One is clearly centered on bringing Christ's likeness to earth, while the other is so vague that each of us could have our own private interpretation. Their focus on Christ's likeness is clear, while today's teachings are unclear, if not confusing.

> And I will give them one heart, and put a new spirit within them. And I will take the heart of stone out of their flesh and give them a heart of flesh, that they may walk in My statutes and keep My ordinances and do them. Then they will be My people, and I shall be their God.
>
> Ezekiel 11:19-20 NASB

How the "Bible = the Word of God" Notion
Has Led Us to Ambiguity and Confusion

	Bible = God's Message	Christ = God's Message
What is the "Word of God"?	The Bible	Christ's Spirit
What is the New Testament?	Word of God	letters of encouragement in Christ (likeness)
What is the Purpose of the New Testament?	Instruction Manual	Teach/remind recipients of Christ (likeness)
What is our standard?	Bible	Spirit in Jesus
What is our goal?	???	Christ's likeness
Purpose of man?	???	To be the image of God
What is the New Covenant?	???	To love one another as He loved us (Growing in Christlikeness)
Emphasis in teaching?	???	Spirit of Jesus
What specifically is our way back to God?	???	Following Christ's likeness
How do we receive righteousness?	???	Through Christ (valuing, growing and identifying with His spiritual likeness)
What is the Holy Spirit?	???	Spirit of God/Christ
What is love?	???	Serving others for the sake of Christ(likeness)
Leads the church to···	Ambiguity and Confusion (private interpretations of Scripture)	Being recognized as followers of Christ (John 13:34–35)

Let's piece together some of the facts of Jesus' last 24 hours, and consider the perspective of the disciples that were with Him:

- Jesus has His last meal with His disciples.
- Jesus initiates a New Covenant.
- This covenant is a communion that reminds them of Jesus' body and blood.
- Jesus gives His disciples a "New Commandment."
- This New Commandment is to "love one another as I have loved you."
- Jesus prays that God's Spirit be in the disciples (as it is in Him).
- Jesus is captured, mocked, beaten severely, and nailed to a cross.
- Jesus has the ability to call down angels to stop the brutality…. but doesn't.
- Jesus dies.

In other words…
At the cross, Jesus demonstrates the glory and likeness of God, by revealing the depth of His love. Jesus suffered and went to His death with every ability to stop his ordeal— but He doesn't… There was something more important. There was you and me. There was the Creator that the world needed to see, and a Spirit that needed to be revealed.

So, on the night before He was to demonstrate His commitment to "love" itself…
Jesus gives His followers *His commandment*:

This was His *one* commandment, and for the disciples the following of this New Commandment trumped everything. There was no secondary principle. This "Law of Christ" would represent the entirety of "following Christ," and it would be the purpose and goal for everything else the apostles would profess.

This commandment would be the reason for all of their instructions and all of their sacrifices. And this mental and spiritual practice of "loving others as He loved me" would prepare them for their own persecution and martyrdom.

Their personal creed of: "I will love you as Christ loved me" was different than any previous laws or commands, for it demanded a growing understanding and realization of two spiritual questions[33]:

God,
help me live by

Your Message

Love one another as I loved you

1. How much did Christ/God love me?
2. How can I love others like that?

It was not *something to do*. It was *a Spirit to be*. It was a change in identity. It was developing a set of beliefs and motivations that are *of* the Father, and revealed in Jesus. This Christ-Spirit would be His message, His purpose, and His goal for us.

so that others may know I am a disciple of your Son

The messengers(a.k.a. apostles) didn't put their energy into building churches, worship teams, or printing Bibles. They placed their value on the one and only thing that makes any difference in the spiritual quality of peoples lives—Christ— the development of His Spirit. They didn't place their trust into traditions or rules. They placed their trust in His likeness, and the growing of that likeness (in themselves and others). Their focus was singularly set on Christ—the "God-image" that is within each of us.

> For I decided to know nothing among you except Jesus Christ and him crucified.
> —1 Corinthians 2:2

---

[33] Can you see how the contemplation of these 2 questions can help us fulfill the two great commandments?

Reconsidering the New Covenant and the Bible

Now that we have a clearer notion of the "New Covenant," let's reconsider the emphasis of the New Testament writers. Does this New Commandment/Covenant explain **why** they wrote what they wrote?

A.   <u>**The New Testament authors emphasized:**</u>
- Christ and remembering Him
- Living in the Spirit (or Holy Spirit)
- Love, humility, joy, peace, compassion, forgiveness…(and other attributes of Christ)
- Growth and the building up of each other in Christ
- Enduring tribulations as Christ did (including death)

B.   <u>**The New Testament writers did NOT emphasize:**</u>
- A specific set of traditions, rituals, and ceremonies that the church must follow
- A specific set of rules, laws, and regulations that need to be obeyed
- A specific set of activities that are necessary for proper worship (singing, preaching…)
- A specific set of actions (works) of righteousness

Some Final Questions:

1. Does their emphasis(**A**) fit in with Jesus' New Commandment? (explain)

2. Does their **lack** (of emphasis) of certain teachings(**B**) support the idea that:
the New Commandment = New Covenant? (explain)

3. Why do you think the NT authors emphasized certain teachings, and not others?

4. Does this New Commandment….

a) Help us see God's love for us?

b) Fit with Paul's letters, and their stated purposes?

c) Fit with Peter's and John's letters, and their purposes?

d) Fit with the New Testament as a whole?

e) Fit with Jesus' parables regarding the Kingdom?

f) Help us understand how Jesus is "the Way"?

g) Help us understand the communion, and its purpose?

we have overcome
the world

h) Give us clarity about our own purpose?

i) Explain the growth of the early church?

j) Explain how Christ is God's answer to sin?

k) Help us understand the "will of God"?

l) Give us confidence about living in the Holy Spirit?

m) Help us understand what it means to "live in Christ" and "walk in the light"?

n) Help us understand Paul and Peter's emphasis on death?

o) Help us understand the disciples' faith in the midst of persecution?

p) Encourage us in the midst of our own trials and tribulations?

q) Explain the manner in which we are "children of God" and a "new creation"?

r) Explain the "law of Christ," the "law of liberty," and the "law of the Spirit of life"?

s) Give us clarity about the righteousness, perfection, and judgment of Christ?

t) Help us understand the love, joy, peace and patience of God?

u) Help us understand the "riches of Christ"?

v) Help us understand the concept of liberty and being "free in Christ"?

w) Help us understand what it means to be "united in Christ"?

x) Help us in our ministry and evangelism? If so, how?

y) Help us understand how Jesus is the author and finisher of our faith?

z) Help us see how Christ is God's answer to *everything*?

5. Can you see how following Christ's command would...

1. Require us to try to understand how much He loves us?
2. Help us see our own value?
3. Help create deeper relationships?
4. Help mend severed relationships?
5. Help us overcome anxiety and depression?
6. Help us understand the struggles of others?
7. Help people who are suffering?
8. Help those who are enduring persecution?
9. Help people struggling with addiction?
10. Be available to people of all education levels and literary abilities?

But What If This Is Wrong...

But what if this New Commandment is *not* the New Covenant, and every other conclusion in these studies are false, misleading or inaccurate.... Then, as followers of Christ, we still need to determine...

1. What exactly is the New Covenant?
2. What exactly is God's message?
3. What exactly is the "Word of God"?
4. How did those in the first century "follow Christ"?
5. How should we be "following Christ"?
6. What exactly is righteous, and righteousness?
7. What is the purpose of the New Testament?
8. What is the ultimate purpose/goal for specific New Testament instructions?
9. How and why did the early church grow so fast?
10. What precisely is the purpose of man?
11. How, exactly, is Jesus the "Way"?
12. What exactly is the Kingdom, and how was/is it revealed?
13. What is the "new creation" that we are supposed to be?
14. What makes a spirit "holy"?
15. How would we know if we have the Holy Spirit?
16. What is the "law of Christ"? And the "law of liberty"?
17. What does it mean to be "united in Christ"?
18. What does it mean to be "slaves to Christ"?
19. What does it mean to be "free in Christ"?
20. What exactly did the first century believers consider to be "faith in Christ"?
21. What exactly is "walking in the light"?
22. What exactly is the will of God?...

But,
even if *everything*
in these studies is incorrect…

…Shouldn't we
be striving
to follow His
"New Commandment"
anyway?

Shouldn't that
be first and foremost
in our hearts and minds?

Paul's Vision for the Church

Message?

> **Christ in You**
> Col.1:25-29

Faith?

> **Same faith Jesus had**
> 1Cor.2:16; Heb.12:2; 1Pet.4:1;1Jn. 1:7

Purpose?

> **Everyone growing to be more like Jesus**
> Rom. 8:9; Eph. 4; 2Cor.13:5; 1Tim.1:5

Results?

> **ONE** body, Spirit, hope, Lord, faith, baptism, God, and Father of all, who is over all and through all and in all. Eph. 4:4-6

in

God's Image on Earth:
Love, joy, peace, humility, hope, compassion, courage, strength, gratitude, boldness...

Think Like Paul: Searching for the Message that Changed the World

www.ThinkLikePaul.com

My Personal Challenge to You

For the Doubtful:

1. For 6 months, explore the possibility of living by this "New Covenant" of Christlikeness (i.e. strive to live by the "I will love you, as Christ loved me" principle).

2. Study the passages in this book exegetically with an open heart, and tell me where I'm incomplete or are misusing a passage. (But please use reason and exegetical principles)

For the Convicted:

3. Commit yourself to the "New Covenant" (i.e. strive to live by the "I will love you, as Christ loved me" principle).

4. Minimize or eliminate emphasis on traditions, rules, and feelings that do not encourage Christlikeness.

5. Make Christlikeness your purpose. Commit yourself to growing in the love, joy, peace, strength, courage, and forgiveness that is found in Jesus and our infinite Creator. Remind yourself (and others) of the image of God that is within each of us. Be a conduit of the compassion, forgiveness, and other blessings that have been afforded to you from God. And offer those blessings to others.

6. Remember that we are to walk Christ's path. Mentally and emotionally prepare ourselves to love others in the most difficult of circumstances. Remind ourselves that we are not here to "get things," or to be comfortable, or to be certain about the world. We are here to be an abundant Spirit, to trust the Infinite, and to die in HIs likeness… *regardless* of any and all circumstances. And as Christ prepared himself for death, we too are here to prepare ourselves for our own destruction by continually reexamining our own devotion to His New Commandment.

7. See the Christ-Spirit in yourself and others. Encourage and reinforce the Christ-Spirit in all. Adore and worship that Spirit. And remind us all of the Creator who made us in His image.

8. Replace judgment (on yourself and others) with understanding and compassion. And *know* that the infinitely wise Creator is truly fair, just, and compassionate, even when we are not.

9. Invite others to this kind of "following Christ." (God's message of "Christ in you")

www.ThinkLikePaul.com

www.ThinkLikePaul.com

Homework

for

Studies #1-25

www.ThinkLikePaul.com

Homework #1: Knowing Him

Therefore from now on we recognize no one according to the flesh; even though we have known Christ according to the flesh, yet now we know Him in this way no longer. – 2 Corinthians 5:16

1. If we don't know Jesus according to the flesh (physical), in what manner do we know Christ?

2. Jesus dying on the cross is/was a
   a) Physical reality
   b) Spiritual reality
   c) Both

3. What do you think was more impactful to those first followers?
   a) A man being crucified
   b) The realization of what Jesus and the crucifixion represents

4. What does the crucifixion of Jesus represent?

5. What do you think *"knowing Christ"* meant to Paul?

6. What do you think is more impactful in our teaching others about God/Christ? (rank from 1-7)

   _____Telling others about a man who died by crucifixion

   _____Telling them that the Son of God died for their sins

   _____Telling them they need to go to church

   _____Telling them that they are going to Hell

   _____Showing others our changed spirit

   _____Telling them of the love of God

   _____Having the care and love for them that Christ had for us (willing to die for them)

7. How much does God love mankind?

8. How much should we love mankind?

9. How should we know and recognize others?

Homework #2: Fulfilling the Law

1. How did Jesus 'fulfill the Law'?

2. In regards to fulfilling the Law, what specific actions did Jesus take?

3. What actions did He **not** take, that make His life and death so extraordinary?

4. From what we know about Paul, in what manner do you think he modeled Christ? (answer the following with: yes or no)
   a) Having His compassion
   b) Adherence to a set of laws
   c) A desire to serve
   d) Not retaliating
   e) A willingness to sacrifice oneself for another
   f) A commitment to building up others

5. How do you think Paul would describe the love he sees in Christ?

6. Is it possible to be loved and not know it?

7. Do you know people who don't know God's love?

8. Does God love sinners? Did He love us before we repented? Why?

9. What lies might prevent people from feeling or appreciating their own value?

10. How would our lives be better if we understood God's love for us?

11. What lie have prevented you from feeling or appreciating the love God has for you?

12. Who would you be if you did not believe that lie? (Give 3 aspects of how you and your life would be different)

Homework #3: Judge Righteous Judgment

And there was much muttering about him among the people. While some said, "He is a good man," others said, "No, he is leading the people astray." Yet for fear of the Jews no one spoke openly of him. About the middle of the feast Jesus went up into the temple and began teaching. The Jews therefore marveled, saying, "How is it that this man has learning, when he has never studied?" So Jesus answered them, "My teaching is not mine, but his who sent me. If anyone's will is to do God's will, he will know whether the teaching is from God or whether I am speaking on my own authority. The one who speaks on his own authority seeks his own glory; but the one who seeks the glory of him who sent him is true, and in him there is no falsehood. Has not Moses given you the law? Yet none of you keeps the law. Why do you seek to kill me?" The crowd answered, "You have a demon! Who is seeking to kill you?" Jesus answered them, "I did one work, and you all marvel at it. Moses gave you circumcision (not that it is from Moses, but from the fathers), and you circumcise a man on the Sabbath. If on the Sabbath a man receives circumcision, so that the law of Moses may not be broken, are you angry with me because on the Sabbath I made a man's whole body well? Do not judge by appearances, but judge with right judgment." –John 7:12-24 ESV

From the context, answer the following:

1. Why were some passing judgment on Jesus?

2. Where did Jesus get his teaching?

3. Why do some speak on their own authority?

4. How does Jesus describe the person who seeks God's glory?

5. Was Jesus' healing on the Sabbath righteous?

6. According to the Old Testament, was it permissible to heal on the Sabbath?

7. What makes Jesus' healing righteous?

Homework #4 The Righteousness of Christ

Contemplate the perspective of the first followers. (Refer to Study #19)

1. In what manner would they have considered Jesus righteous? Was He righteous because of some specific action? Was He righteous because of what He taught? Or was He righteous because He had the same spirit, mindset, and purpose of the Father? Or is it due to something else?

2. In what manner is Jesus like God?

3. What kinds of things are a 'shadow'?

4. What is the 'substance'?

5. What makes an act good or bad?

6. Are religious systems good, bad, or neither?

7. Do you know people who equate Christianity with a religious system? How can we help those who fall into this mentality?

8. Can we make traditions or the *following of rules* more important than Spirit?

9. What happens when a church places more emphasis on traditions than Spirit?

10. What happens when a church places more emphasis on rules than Spirit?

11. What do you think God is more interested in? A church that is devoted to:
    1. traditions
    2. rules
    3. growing in the likeness of Christ

12. Which is more encouraging? And why?

www.ThinkLikePaul.com

Homework #5: What is our Relationship with Christ?

Using the **NASB** fill in the blanks.

1. **2Cor 3:18** But we all, with unveiled face, beholding as in a mirror the glory of the Lord, are being _____ into the same image from glory to glory, just as from the Lord, the Spirit.

2. **2Cor 5:14** For the love of Christ _____ _____.

3. **Rom 8:9** However, you are not in the flesh but in the _____, if indeed the Spirit of God dwells in you. But if anyone does not have the Spirit of _____, he does not belong to Him.

4. **Heb 1:1** God, after He _____ long ago to the fathers in the prophets in many portions and in many ways,

5. **Heb 1:2** in these last days has _____ to us in His Son, whom He appointed heir of all things, through whom also He made the world.

6. **Heb 1:3** And He is the radiance of His glory and the _____ _____ of His nature, and upholds all things by the word of His power.

7. **Heb 12:2** fixing our eyes on Jesus, the _____ and _____ of faith, who for the joy set before Him endured the cross, despising the shame, and has sat down at the right hand of the throne of God.

8. **1Pe 1:14** As obedient children, do not be _____ to the former lusts *which were yours* in your ignorance,

9. **1Pe 1:15** but like the Holy One who called you, be _____ yourselves also in all *your* behavior;

10. **1Pe 1:16** because it is written, "YOU SHALL BE _____, FOR I AM HOLY."

11. Does this sound like a "Church of Christlikeness"? Why or Why not?

12. Give contextual answers to how the following instructions helped grow Christlikeness in the first century.

Instructions	How may these instructions relate to the development of Christlikeness?
Partaking of communion (1Cor.11)	
Singing (Col.3)	
Speaking in tongues (1Cor.12)	
Assembling together (Heb.10)	
Wearing head coverings (1Cor.11)	
Getting married (1Cor. 7)	
Not getting married (1Cor. 7)	

www.ThinkLikePaul.com

Homework #6: The Role of Knowledge

Use the given contexts to answer the following questions:

> For this reason also, since the day we heard *of it*, we have not ceased to pray for you and to ask that you may be filled with the **knowledge** of His will in all spiritual wisdom and understanding, so that you will walk in a manner worthy of the Lord, to please *Him* in all respects, bearing fruit in every good work and increasing in the **knowledge** of God; strengthened with all power, according to His glorious might, for the attaining of all steadfastness and patience; joyously giving thanks to the Father, who has qualified us to share in the inheritance of the saints in Light. —Colossians 1:9-12 NASB

1. In Colossians chapter 1, what kind of knowledge does Paul pray for them to be filled with?

2. Why does Paul want them to have this knowledge? (Give four reasons from the text)

   a.

   b.

   c.

   d.

> I thank my God always, making mention of you in my prayers, because I hear of your love and of the faith which you have toward the Lord Jesus and toward all the saints; *and I pray* that the fellowship of your faith may become effective through the **knowledge of every good thing which is in you** for Christ's sake. For I have come to have much joy and comfort in your love, because the hearts of the saints have been refreshed through you, brother. —Philemon 1:4-7 NASB

3. Paul wants them to become *"effective through the knowledge of every good thing which is in you."* What are the good things in you? Could he be referring to the word of God (the Spirit of Christ)?

4. After considering these verses, what does Paul consider real knowledge?
   a) Genealogies
   b) Old Testament
   c) New Testament
   d) Laws
   e) The plan of salvation
   f) A particular set of traditions
   g) Christ (the Spirit)

   For I determined to know nothing among you except Jesus Christ, and Him crucified. —1 Corinthians 2:2 ESV

5. From this verse, what 3 concepts is Paul determine to know?

6. What role do biblical facts have in this "knowledge"? Explain.

**What we are after is the root and not the branches.
The root is the real knowledge;
the branches are the surface knowledge.
Real knowledge breeds body feel and personal expression;
surface knowledge breeds mechanical conditioning
and imposing limitation and squelches creativity.
—Bruce Lee**

Homework #7: The Role of the Scriptures

"And how from infancy you have known the Holy Scriptures, which are able to make you wise <u>for</u> salvation through faith in Christ Jesus. All Scripture is God-breathed and is useful for teaching, rebuking, correcting and training in righteousness, <u>so that</u> the servant of God may be thoroughly equipped for every good work." –2 Timothy 3:15-17 NIV

1.   What are the Scriptures able to do?

2.   From the context, what specific writings/scriptures is Paul referring to?

3.   Faith is in _____
      a) Christ/Christlikeness
      b) my works
      c) my knowledge
      d) Scriptures

4.   'Faith in Christ Jesus' is probably a reference to:
      a) believing that Jesus is the Christ, the Son of God
      b) believing that Jesus rose from the dead
      c) believing that Christ/Christlikeness is our one path back to God
      d) all of the above

5.   Scripture is useful for teaching, rebuking, correcting, training in _____
      a) righteousness
      b) Christ/Christlikeness
      c) religiousness
      d) condemning others

6.   What would Timothy probably think that this "righteousness" is a reference to?
      a) Christ/Christlikeness
      b) Following the Old Testament
      c) something else _____

7.   According to this passage the goal of scripture is:
      d) to help us be thoroughly equipped for every good work
      e) have a spiritual weapon
      f) something else _____

8.   How would Timothy know what is a 'good work'?

Homework #8: The Scriptures Relationship with Christ

Connect the purposes of the letters with Christ/Christlikeness.

The Purpose of the Letters	How Does the purpose relate to Christ/ Christlikeness?
1 Timothy 1:5	Christ(likeness) is loving others from a pure heart, good conscience and sincere faith.
1 Corinthians 4:14-16	
2 Corinthians 2:3-4	
2 Corinthians 2:8-9	
Romans 15:14-16	
Ephesians 3:4-6	
1 Timothy 3:14-16	
John 20:31	
1 John 2:7-8	
1 John 2:21	
2 John 1:4-6	

www.ThinkLikePaul.com

Homework #9: Religiousness vs. Christlikeness

Use a dictionary to define the following:

Religion:

Christlikeness:

Consider James thoughts on religion:

> If anyone thinks himself to be religious, and yet does not bridle his tongue but deceives his *own* heart, this man's religion is worthless. Pure and undefiled religion in the sight of *our* God and Father is this: to visit orphans and widows in their distress, *and* to keep oneself unstained by the world. —James 1:26-27 NASB

1. Is James' thoughts on pure religion closer to today's definition of *religion* or *Christlikeness*?

2. How do you think the Pharisees would have defined "pure religion"?

3. What do you think Paul would define as "pure religion"?

4. Would you say Jesus was religious? Why or why not?

5. What is the difference between today's concepts of a "religion" and the first century concept of "faith". Make a list:

Religion	Faith

Homework #10: Christ = the Spirit of God in Man

If Christ (Christos) can be interpreted as:
A. the physical person of Jesus, or
B. the Spirit (of God) that he had;

… Then circle the likely meaning for "Christ":

Therefore if you have been raised up with <u>Christ</u> (**Jesus** or **Spirit**), keep seeking the things above, where <u>Christ</u> (**Jesus** or **Spirit**) is, seated at the right hand of God. Set your mind on the things above, not on the things that are on earth. For you have died and your life is hidden with <u>Christ</u> (**Jesus** or **Spirit**) in God. When <u>Christ</u> (**Jesus** or **Spirit**), who is our life, is revealed, then you also will be revealed with Him in glory. Therefore consider the members of your earthly body as dead to immorality, impurity, passion, evil desire, and greed, which amounts to idolatry. For it is because of these things that the wrath of God will come upon the sons of disobedience, and in them you also once walked, when you were living in them. But now you also, put them all aside: anger, wrath, malice, slander, *and* abusive speech from your mouth. Do not lie to one another, since you laid aside the old self with its *evil* practices, and have put on the new self who is being renewed to a true knowledge according to the image of the One who created him— *a renewal* in which there is no *distinction between* Greek and Jew, circumcised and uncircumcised, barbarian, Scythian, slave and freeman, but <u>Christ</u> (**Jesus** or **Spirit**) is all, and in all. So, as those who have been chosen of God, holy and beloved, put on a heart of compassion, kindness, humility, gentleness and patience; bearing with one another, and forgiving each other, whoever has a complaint against anyone; just as the Lord forgave you, so also should you. Beyond all these things *put on* love, which is the perfect bond of unity. Let the peace of <u>Christ</u> (**Jesus** or **Spirit**) rule in your hearts, to which indeed you were called in one body; and be thankful. Let the word of <u>Christ</u> (**Jesus** or **Spirit**) richly dwell within you, with all wisdom teaching and admonishing one another with psalms *and* hymns *and* spiritual songs, singing with thankfulness in your hearts to God. Whatever you do in word or deed, *do* all in the name of the Lord Jesus, giving thanks through Him to God the Father. Colossians 3:1-17 NASB

Now consider the perspective of those first century Christians, who were familiar with the *life* and *death* of Jesus.

1. What was his major accomplishment?
   a) dying on a cross
   b) loving all people (including His enemies) more than anything else

2. What does the cross represent to the first century followers:
   a) weakness
   b) love
   c) something else:_____

From the previous passage, explain the following phrases:

3. *"if you have been raised up with Christ"*

4. *"Christ who is our life"*

5. *"Christ is all and in all"*

6. *"Let the peace of Christ rule in your hearts"*

7. What is the *"word of Christ"? And how does it dwell in us?*

Any transition serious enough to alter your definition of self will require not just small adjustments in your way of living and thinking but a full-on metamorphosis.
-Martha Beck

Homework #11 The Word in the Gospel of John

For each context, list the descriptions of the 'word', and determine which definition(s) may best fit. Is he referring to a *literal word*, a *message*, the *Spirit*, or a *writing or scripture*? How many of the following could mean both "message" and "Spirit"?

Example

So Jesus said to the Jews who had believed Him, "If you abide in my **word,** you are truly my disciples, and you will know the truth, and the truth will set you free." —John 8: 31-32

1. **Notes on the 'word':**

it is something we 'abide in'

= discipleship

= know the truth

= will be set free

2. **Which best fits for this "word"?**

A. ~~literal word~~ ?????

B. message **OK**

C. Spirit **OK**

D. ~~writing/scripture~~

Jesus answered them, "Truly, truly, I say to you, everyone who practices sin is a slave to sin. The slave does not remain in the house forever; the son remains forever. So if the Son sets you free, you will be free indeed. I know that you are offspring of Abraham; yet you seek to kill me because my <u>word</u> finds no place in you. I speak of what I have seen with my Father, and you do what you have heard from your father." — John 8:34-38

3. **Notes on the 'word':**

4. **Which best fits for this "word"?**

A. literal word

B. message

C. Spirit

D. writing/scripture

Jesus answered, "I do not have a demon, but I honor my Father, and you dishonor me. Yet I do not seek my own glory; there is One who seeks it, and he is the judge. Truly, truly, I say to you, if anyone keeps my <u>word</u>, he will never see death." —John 8:49-51

5. **Notes on the 'word':**

6. **Which best fits for this "word"?**

A. literal word

B. message

C. Spirit

D. writing/scripture

 www.ThinkLikePaul.com

Jesus answered, "If I glorify myself, my glory is nothing. It is my Father who glorifies me, of whom you say, 'He is our God.' But you have not known him. I know him. If I were to say that I do not know him, I would be a liar like you, but I do know him and I keep his <u>word</u>. Your father Abraham rejoiced that he would see my day. He saw it and was glad." —John 8:54-56

7. **Notes on the 'word':**

8. **Which best fits for this "word"?**
   A. literal word
   B. message
   C. Spirit
   D. writing/scripture

This was to fulfill the **word** of Isaiah the prophet which he spoke: "LORD, WHO HAS BELIEVED OUR REPORT? AND TO WHOM HAS THE ARM OF THE LORD BEEN REVEALED?" –John 12:38

9. **Notes on the 'word':**

10. **Which best fits for this "word"?**
   A. literal word
   B. message
   C. Spirit
   D. writing/scripture

Jesus answered and said to him, "If anyone loves Me, he will keep My **word**; and My Father will love him, and We will come to him and make Our abode with him. He who does not love Me does not keep My **words**; and the **word** which you hear is not Mine, but the Father's who sent Me." –John 14:23-24

11. **Notes on the 'word':**

12. **Which best fits for these "word"s?**
   A. literal word
   B. message
   C. Spirit
   D. writing/scripture

13. Could the "word" have a dual meaning of "message" and "Spirit" in some of these passages?

www.ThinkLikePaul.com

Homework #12: The Word in the Letters of Peter and James

For each context, list the descriptions of the 'word', and determine which definition(s) may best fit. How many of the following could mean both "message" and "Spirit"?

Therefore, putting aside all malice and all deceit and hypocrisy and envy and all slander, like newborn babies, long for the pure milk of the **word,** so that by it you may grow in respect to salvation, if you have tasted the kindness of the Lord. And coming to Him as to a living stone which has been rejected by men, but is choice and precious in the sight of God, you also, as living stones, are being built up as a spiritual house for a holy priesthood, to offer up spiritual sacrifices acceptable to God through Jesus Christ. For *this* is contained in Scripture: "BEHOLD, I LAY IN ZION A CHOICE STONE, A PRECIOUS CORNER *stone,* AND HE WHO BELIEVES IN HIM WILL NOT BE DISAPPOINTED." This precious value, then, is for you who believe; but for those who disbelieve, "THE STONE WHICH THE BUILDERS REJECTED, THIS BECAME THE VERY CORNER *stone,*" and, "A STONE OF STUMBLING AND A ROCK OF OFFENSE"; for they stumble because they are disobedient to the **word,** and to this *doom* they were also appointed. 1 Peter 2:1-8 NASB

1. **Notes on the 'word':**

2. **Which best fits for these "word"s?**
   A. literal word
   B. message
   C. Spirit
   D. writing/scripture

And I will make every effort so that after my departure you may be able at any time to recall these things. For we did not follow cleverly devised myths when we made known to you the power and coming of our Lord Jesus Christ, but we were eyewitnesses of his majesty. For when he received honor and glory from God the Father, and the voice was borne to him by the Majestic Glory, "This is my beloved Son, with whom I am well pleased," we ourselves heard this very voice borne from heaven, for we were with him on the holy mountain. And we have the prophetic **word** more fully confirmed, to which you will do well to pay attention as to a lamp shining in a dark place, until the day dawns and the morning star rises in your hearts, knowing this first of all, that no prophecy of Scripture comes from someone's own interpretation. For no prophecy was ever produced by the will of man, but men spoke from God as they were carried along by the Holy Spirit. 2 Peter 1:15-21ESV

3. **Notes on the 'word':**

4. **Which best fits for this "word"?**
   A. literal word
   B. message
   C. Spirit
   D. writing/scripture

Do not be deceived, my beloved brothers. Every good gift and every perfect gift is from above, coming down from the Father of lights with whom there is no variation or shadow due to change. Of his own will he brought us forth by the **word** of truth, that we should be a kind of first fruits of his creatures. James 1:16-18 ESV

5. **Notes on the 'word':**

6. **Which best fits for this "word"?**
   A. literal word
   B. message
   C. Spirit
   D. writing/scripture

Know this, my beloved brothers: let every person be quick to hear, slow to speak, slow to anger; for the anger of man does not produce the righteousness of God. Therefore put away all filthiness and rampant wickedness and receive with meekness the implanted **word,** which is able to save your souls. But be doers of the **word**, and not hearers only, deceiving yourselves. For if anyone is a hearer of the word and not a doer, he is like a man who looks intently at his natural face in a mirror. For he looks at himself and goes away and at once forgets what he was like. But the one who looks into the perfect law, the law of liberty, and perseveres, being no hearer who forgets but a doer who acts, he will be blessed in his doing. If anyone thinks he is religious and does not bridle his tongue but deceives his heart, this person's religion is worthless. Religion that is pure and undefiled before God, the Father, is this: to visit orphans and widows in their affliction, and to keep oneself unstained from the world. James 1:19-27 ESV

7. **Notes on the 'word':**

8. **Which best fits for these "word"s?**
   A. literal word
   B. message
   C. Spirit
   D. writing/scripture

9. Could the "word" have a dual meaning of "message" and "Spirit" in some of these passages?

www.ThinkLikePaul.com

Homework #13: The Word in Paul's Letters (Part 1)

For each context, list the descriptions of the 'word', and determine which definition(s) may best fit. How many of the following could mean both "message" and "Spirit"?

For I could wish that I myself were accursed and cut off from Christ for the sake of my brothers, my kinsmen according to the flesh. They are Israelites, and to them belong the adoption, the glory, the covenants, the giving of the law, the worship, and the promises. To them belong the patriarchs, and from their race, according to the flesh, is the Christ, who is God over all, blessed forever. Amen. But it is not as though the **word** of God has failed. For not all who are descended from Israel belong to Israel. —Romans 9:3-6 ESV

1. **Notes on the 'word':**

2. **Which best fits for this "word"?**
   - A. literal word
   - B. message
   - C. Spirit
   - D. writing/scripture

For Moses writes about the righteousness that is based on the law, that the person who does the commandments shall live by them. But the righteousness based on faith says, "Do not say in your heart, 'Who will ascend into heaven?'" (that is, to bring Christ down)"or 'Who will descend into the abyss?'" (that is, to bring Christ up from the dead). But what does it say? "The **word** is near you, in your mouth and in your heart" (that is, the **word** of faith that we proclaim); because, if you confess with your mouth that Jesus is Lord and believe in your heart that God raised him from the dead, you will be saved. For with the heart one believes and is justified, and with the mouth one confesses and is saved. For the Scripture says, "Everyone who believes in him will not be put to shame. "—Romans 10:5-11ESV

3. **Notes on the 'word':**

4. **Which best fits for these "word"s?**
   - A. literal word
   - B. message
   - C. Spirit
   - D. writing/scripture

How then will they call on Him in whom they have not believed? How will they believe in Him whom they have not heard? And how will they hear without a preacher? How will they preach unless they are sent? Just as it is written, "HOW BEAUTIFUL ARE THE FEET OF THOSE WHO BRING GOOD NEWS OF GOOD THINGS!" However, they did not all heed the good news; for Isaiah says, "LORD, WHO HAS BELIEVED OUR REPORT?" So faith *comes* from hearing, and hearing by the **word** of Christ. —Romans 10:14-17 NASB

5. **Notes on the 'word':**

6. **Which best fits for this "word"?**
   A. literal word
   B. message
   C. Spirit
   D. writing/scripture

Which definition best fits for the following?

7. For to one is given **the word of wisdom** through the Spirit, and to another **the word of knowledge** according to the same Spirit; —1 Corinthians 12:8 NASB

   A. literal word   B. message   C. Spirit   D. writing/scripture

8. by which also you are saved, if you hold fast the **word** which I preached to you, unless you believed in vain. —1 Corinthians 15:2 NASB

   A. literal word   B. message   C. Spirit   D. writing/scripture

9. But as God is faithful, our **word** to you is not yes and no. —2 Corinthians 1:18 NASB

   A. literal word   B. message   C. Spirit   D. writing/scripture

10. Could the "word" have a dual meaning of "message" and "Spirit"?

It is no longer I who live, but Christ who lives in me.
—Galatians 2:20 ESV

Homework #14: The "Word" in Hebrews

Here are the other references to the "'word" in Hebrews. Which of the following meanings/definition(s) fit with these specific passages in the book of Hebrews? How many of the following could mean both "message" and "Spirit"?

1. **Heb 1:3** And He is the radiance of His glory and the exact representation of His nature, and upholds all things by the **word** of His power. When He had made purification of sins, He sat down at the right hand of the Majesty on high…

    A. literal word   B. message   C. Spirit   D. writing/scripture

2. **Heb 2:2** For if the **word** spoken through angels proved unalterable, and every transgression and disobedience received a just penalty…

    A. literal word   B. message   C. Spirit   D. writing/scripture

3. **Heb 4:2** For indeed we have had good news preached to us, just as they also; but the **word** they heard did not profit them, because it was not united by faith in those who heard.

    A. literal word   B. message   C. Spirit   D. writing/scripture

4. **Heb 5:13** For everyone who partakes only of milk is not accustomed to the **word** of righteousness, for he is an infant.

    A. literal word   B. message   C. Spirit   D. writing/scripture

5. **Heb 6:5** and have tasted the good **word** of God and the powers of the age to come…

    A. literal word   B. message   C. Spirit   D. writing/scripture

6. **Heb 7:28** For the Law appoints men as high priests who are weak, but the **word** of the oath, which came after the Law, appoints a Son, made perfect forever.

    A. literal word   B. message   C. Spirit   D. writing/scripture

7. **Heb 11:3** By faith we understand that the worlds were prepared by the **word** of God, so that what is seen was not made out of things which are visible.

    A. literal word   B. message   C. Spirit   D. writing/scripture

8. **Heb 13:7** Remember those who led you, who spoke the **word** of God to you; and considering the result of their conduct, imitate their faith.

    A. literal word   B. message   C. Spirit   D. writing/scripture

9. **Heb 13:22** But I urge you, brethren, bear with this **word** of exhortation, for I have written to you briefly.

    A. literal word   B. message   C. Spirit   D. writing/scripture

10. Could the "**word**" have a dual meaning of "message" and "Spirit"?

www.ThinkLikePaul.com

Homework #15: The Word in Paul's Letters (Part 2)

Which definition(s) best fits for "word" in each of these passages? How many of the following could mean both "message" and "Spirit"?

1. **Gal 5:14** For the whole Law is fulfilled in one **word,** in the *statement,* "YOU SHALL LOVE YOUR NEIGHBOR AS YOURSELF."

    A. literal word   B. message   C. Spirit   D. writing/scripture

2. **Gal 6:6** The one who is taught the **word** is to share all good things with the one who teaches *him.*

    A. literal word   B. message   C. Spirit   D. writing/scripture

3. **Eph 4:29** Let no unwholesome **word** proceed from your mouth, but only such a **word** as is good for edification according to the need *of the moment,* so that it will give grace to those who hear.

    A. literal word   B. message   C. Spirit   D. writing/scripture

4. **Phil 1:14** and that most of the brethren, trusting in the Lord because of my imprisonment, have far more courage to speak the **word** of God without fear.

    A. literal word   B. message   C. Spirit   D. writing/scripture

5. **Phil 2:16** holding fast the **word** of life, so that in the day of Christ I will have reason to glory because I did not run in vain nor toil in vain.

    A. literal word   B. message   C. Spirit   D. writing/scripture

6. **Col 1:5** because of the hope laid up for you in heaven, of which you previously heard in the **word** of truth, the gospel.

    A. literal word   B. message   C. Spirit   D. writing/scripture

7. **Col 3:16** Let the **word** of Christ richly dwell within you, with all wisdom teaching and admonishing one another with psalms *and* hymns *and* spiritual songs, singing with thankfulness in your hearts to God.

    A. literal word   B. message   C. Spirit   D. writing/scripture

8. **Col 3:17** Whatever you do in **word** or deed, *do* all in the name of the Lord Jesus, giving thanks through Him to God the Father.

    A. literal word   B. message   C. Spirit   D. writing/scripture

9. **Col 4:3** praying at the same time for us as well, that God will open up to us a door for the **word,** so that we may speak forth the mystery of Christ, for which I have also been imprisoned;

    A. literal word   B. message   C. Spirit   D. writing/scripture

Homework #16: Jesus' Word (Gospel of Matthew)

Which definitions for the "word" does Jesus (through Mathew's gospel) use most?

1. **Mt 8:8** But the centurion said, "Lord, I am not worthy for you to come under my roof, but just say the **word** and my servant will be healed.

    A. literal word   B. message   C. Spirit   D. writing/scripture

2. **Mt 8:16** When evening came, they brought to Him many who were demon-possessed; and He cast out the spirits with a **word**, and healed all who were ill.

    A. literal word   B. message   C. Spirit   D. writing/scripture

3. **Mt 12:32** "Whoever speaks a **word** against the Son of Man, it shall be forgiven him; but whoever speaks against the Holy Spirit, it shall not be forgiven him, either in this age or in the *age* to come.

    A. literal word   B. message   C. Spirit   D. writing/scripture

4. **Mt 12:36** "But I tell you that every careless **word** that people speak, they shall give an accounting for it in the day of judgment.

    A. literal word   B. message   C. Spirit   D. writing/scripture

5. **Mt 13:19** "When anyone hears the **word** of the kingdom and does not understand it, the evil *one* comes and snatches away what has been sown in his heart. This is the one on whom seed was sown beside the road.

    A. literal word   B. message   C. Spirit   D. writing/scripture

6. **Mt 13:22** "And the one on whom seed was sown among the thorns, this is the man who hears the **word**, and the worry of the world and the deceitfulness of wealth choke the **word**, and it becomes unfruitful.

    A. literal word   B. message   C. Spirit   D. writing/scripture

7. **Mt 13:23** "And the one on whom seed was sown on the good soil, this is the man who hears the **word** and understands it; who indeed bears fruit and brings forth, some a hundredfold, some sixty, and some thirty."

    A. literal word   B. message   C. Spirit   D. writing/scripture

8. **Mt 15:6** he is not to honor his father or his mother.' And *by this* you invalidated the **word of God** for the sake of your tradition.

    A. literal word   B. message   C. Spirit   D. writing/scripture

9. How does Jesus predominantly use the "word"?

www.ThinkLikePaul.com

Homework #17: A Better Covenant

2 Corinthians 3 NASB

> Are we beginning to commend ourselves again? Or do we need, as some, letters of commendation to you or from you? You are our letter, written in our hearts, known and read by all men; being manifested that you are a letter of Christ, cared for by us, written not with ink but with the Spirit of the living God, not on tablets of stone but on tablets of human hearts.
>
> Such confidence we have through Christ toward God. Not that we are adequate in ourselves to consider anything as *coming* from ourselves, but our adequacy is from God, who also made us adequate *as* servants of a new covenant, not of the letter but of the Spirit; for the letter kills, but the Spirit gives life.
>
> But if the ministry of death, in letters engraved on stones, came with glory, so that the sons of Israel could not look intently at the face of Moses because of the glory of his face, fading *as* it was, how will the ministry of the Spirit fail to be even more with glory? For if the ministry of condemnation has glory, much more does the ministry of righteousness abound in glory. For indeed what had glory, in this case has no glory because of the glory that surpasses *it*. For if that which fades away *was* with glory, much more that which remains *is* in glory.
>
> Therefore having such a hope, we use great boldness in *our* speech, and *are* not like Moses, *who* used to put a veil over his face so that the sons of Israel would not look intently at the end of what was fading away. But their minds were hardened; for until this very day at the reading of the old covenant the same veil remains unlifted, because it is removed in Christ. But to this day whenever Moses is read, a veil lies over their heart; but whenever a person turns to the Lord, the veil is taken away. Now the Lord is the Spirit, and where the Spirit of the Lord is, *there* is liberty. But we all, with unveiled face, beholding as in a mirror the glory of the Lord, are being transformed into the same image from glory to glory, just as from the Lord, the Spirit.

Use the preceding passage to answer the following questions:

1. What/Who is Paul's letter?

2. Where is this letter written?

3. Who reads this letter?

4. The Corinthians are a letter of _____.

5. This letter was not written with ink, but with what?

6.   What is the letter written on?

7.   What gives life?

8.   What kills?

9.   What was engraved in stone?

10.   What is the ministry of death and condemnation?

11.   How does Paul describe the new covenant?

12.   What is the Lord?

In each of the following determine whether or not the word could have a dual meaning of both "message" and "Spirit"?

13. **1Th 1:6** You also became imitators of us and of the Lord, having received the **word** in much tribulation with the joy of the Holy Spirit…   **Yes** or **No**

14. **1Th 4:15** For this we say to you by the **word** of the Lord, that we who are alive and remain until the coming of the Lord…   **Yes** or **No**

15. **2Th 3:1** Finally, brethren, pray for us that the **word** of the Lord will spread rapidly and be glorified, just as *it did* also with you…   **Yes** or **No**

16. **2Ti 2:9** for which I suffer hardship even to imprisonment as a criminal; but the **word** of God is not imprisoned.   **Yes** or **No**

17. **2Ti 2:15** Be diligent to present yourself approved to God as a workman who does not need to be ashamed, accurately handling the **word of truth**.   **Yes** or **No**

18. **2Ti 4:2** preach the **word**; be ready in season *and* out of season; reprove, rebuke, exhort, with great patience and instruction.   **Yes** or **No**

19. **Tit 1:3** but at the proper time manifested, *even* His **word**, in the proclamation with which I was entrusted according to the commandment of God our Savior…   **Yes** or **No**

20. **Tit 1:9** holding fast the faithful **word** which is in accordance with the teaching, so that he will be able both to exhort in sound doctrine and to refute those who contradict.   **Yes** or **No**

21. **Tit 2:5** *to be* sensible, pure, workers at home, kind, being subject to their own husbands, so that the **word** of God will not be dishonored.   **Yes** or **No**

> MY FLESH ALSO WILL LIVE IN HOPE.
>
> ACTS 2:26

Homework #18: The Word According to John (Part 2)

In each of the following determine whether or not the word *could* have a dual meaning of both "message" and "Spirit/Christ"? (circle Yes or No)

1. **1Jn 1:1** What was from the beginning, what we have heard, what we have seen with our eyes, what we have looked at and touched with our hands, concerning the **word of Life**— (Yes or No)

2. **1Jn 1:10** If we say that we have not sinned, we make Him a liar and His **word** is not in us. (Yes or No)

3. **1Jn 2:5** but whoever keeps His **word**, in him the love of God has truly been perfected. By this we know that we are in Him.   (Yes or No)

4. **1Jn 2:14** I have written to you, fathers, because you know Him who has been from the beginning. I have written to you, young men, because you are strong, and the **word of God** abides in you, and you have overcome the evil one. (Yes or No)

5. **1Jn 3:18** Little children, let us not love with **word** or with tongue, but in deed and truth. (Yes or No)

6. **Rev 1:2** who testified to the **word of God** and to the testimony of Jesus Christ, *even* to all that he saw. (Yes or No)

7. **Rev 1:9** I, John, your brother and fellow partaker in the tribulation and kingdom and perseverance *which are* in Jesus, was on the island called Patmos because of the **word of God** and the testimony of Jesus. (Yes or No)

8. **Rev 3:8** 'I know your deeds. Behold, I have put before you an open door which no one can shut, because you have a little power, and have kept My **word**, and have not denied My name. (Yes or No)

9. **Rev 3:10** 'Because you have kept the **word** of My perseverance, I also will keep you from the hour of testing, that *hour* which is about to come upon the whole world, to test those who dwell on the earth. (Yes or No)

10. **Rev 6:9** When the Lamb broke the fifth seal, I saw underneath the altar the souls of those who had been slain because of the **word of God**, and because of the testimony which they had maintained; (Yes or No)

11. **Rev 12:11** "And they overcame him because of the blood of the Lamb and because of the **word** of their testimony, and they did not love their life even when faced with death. (Yes or No)

12. **Rev 20:4** Then I saw thrones, and they sat on them, and judgment was given to them. And I *saw* the souls of those who had been beheaded because of their testimony of Jesus and because of the **word of God**, and those who had not worshiped the beast or his image, and had not received the mark on their forehead and on their hand; and they came to life and reigned with Christ for a thousand years. (Yes or No)

Homework #19: More Practice on the "Word" (Acts)

Do these verses regarding "**the word**" seem to have a spiritual component? Could some of them have a dual meaning of both "message" and "Christ's commandment"? (circle Yes or No)

1. **Acts 6:4** "But we will devote ourselves to prayer and to the ministry of **the word**." (Yes or No)

2. **Acts 6:7** **The word of God** kept on spreading; and the number of the disciples continued to increase greatly in Jerusalem, and a great many of the priests were becoming obedient to the faith. (Yes or No)

3. **Acts 8:14** Now when the apostles in Jerusalem heard that Samaria had received **the word of God**, they sent them Peter and John… (Yes or No)

4. **Acts 8:25** So, when they had solemnly testified and spoken **the word of the Lord**, they started back to Jerusalem, and were preaching the gospel to many villages of the Samaritans. (Yes or No)

5. **Acts 10:36** "**The word** which He sent to the sons of Israel, preaching peace through Jesus Christ (He is Lord of all)– (Yes or No)

6. **Acts 11:1** Now the apostles and the brethren who were throughout Judea heard that the Gentiles also had received **the word of God**. (Yes or No)

7. **Acts 13:46** Paul and Barnabas spoke out boldly and said, "It was necessary that **the word of God** be spoken to you first; since you repudiate it and judge yourselves unworthy of eternal life, behold, we are turning to the Gentiles. (Yes or No)

8. **Acts 13:48** When the Gentiles heard this, they *began* rejoicing and glorifying **the word of the Lord**; and as many as had been appointed to eternal life believed. (Yes or No)

9. **Acts 15:7** After there had been much debate, Peter stood up and said to them, "Brethren, you know that in the early days God made a choice among you, that by my mouth the Gentiles would hear **the word** of the gospel and believe. (Yes or No)

10. **Acts 15:36** After some days Paul said to Barnabas, "Let us return and visit the brethren in every city in which we proclaimed **the word of the Lord**, *and see* how they are." (Yes or No)

11. **Acts 16:6** They passed through the Phrygian and Galatian region, having been forbidden by the Holy Spirit to speak **the word** in Asia; (Yes or No)

12. **Acts 18:5** But when Silas and Timothy came down from Macedonia, Paul *began* devoting himself completely to **the word**, solemnly testifying to the Jews that Jesus was the Christ. (Yes or No)

13. **Acts 19:20** So **the word of the Lord** was growing mightily and prevailing. (Yes or No)

14. **Acts 20:32** "And now I commend you to God and to **the word** of His grace, which is able to build *you* up and to give *you* the inheritance among all those who are sanctified. (Yes or No)

Homework #20: How Does the Word of Christ Dwell in Us?

Let the word of Christ dwell in you richly, teaching and admonishing one another in all wisdom, singing psalms and hymns and spiritual songs, with thankfulness in your hearts to God. —Colossians 3:16 ESV

Is the "word of Christ" a reference to the gospel? Is Paul referring to the New Testament? Consider the context:

Put to death therefore what is earthly in you: sexual immorality, impurity, passion, evil desire, and covetousness, which is idolatry. On account of these the wrath of God is coming. In these you too once walked, when you were living in them. **But now you must put them all away: anger, wrath, malice, slander, and obscene talk from your mouth. Do not lie to one another, seeing that you have put off the old self with its practices and have put on the new self, which is being renewed in knowledge after the image of its Creator.** Here there is not Greek and Jew, circumcised and uncircumcised, barbarian, Scythian, slave, free; but Christ is all, and in all.

Put on then, as God's chosen ones, holy and beloved, compassion, kindness, humility, meekness, and patience, bearing with one another, and if one has a complaint against another, forgiving each other; as the Lord has forgiven you, so you also must forgive. And above all these put on love, which binds everything together in perfect harmony. And let the peace of Christ rule in your hearts, to which indeed you were called in one body. And be thankful. **Let the word (message) of Christ dwell in you richly,** teaching and admonishing one another in all wisdom, singing psalms and hymns and spiritual songs, with **thankfulness in your hearts to God.** And whatever you do, in word or deed, do everything in the name of the Lord Jesus, giving thanks to God the Father through him. —Colossians 3:1-17 ESV

Notice the earthly things we are to put to death:
- Sexual immorality
- Impurity
- Passion
- Evil desire
- Covetousness
- Anger
- Wrath
- Malice
- Slander
- Obscene talk
- Lying

- Divisions based upon race, circumcision, slave or free

Now notice how he describes us and the "new self" that is 'Being renewed in knowledge after the image of the Creator':
- Having the identity of Christ (Christ is all, and in all).
- Being God's chosen ones, holy and beloved
- Putting on compassion
- Putting on kindness
- Putting on humility
- Putting on meekness
- Putting on patience
- Bearing with one another
- Forgiving those on both sides of a complaint
- Putting on love above all, which binds everything together in perfect harmony
- Allowing the peace of Christ to rule in our hearts
- Being thankful
- Letting the word (message) of Christ dwell in us richly, singing hymns ... with thankfulness in our hearts.

> Thou hast loved righteousness, and hated iniquity; therefore God, *even* thy God, hath anointed thee with the oil of gladness above thy fellows.
>
> Heb. 1:9 KJV

Questions:

1. Do you see a theme? What is it?

2. Does Paul give any specific actions?

3. Does anything in this passage suggest that Paul's letter is "the word"?

4. Does anything suggest that past letters *are* "the word of God"? Or that future letters *are going to be* "the word of God"?

5. In verse 15 Paul writes, "And let the peace of Christ rule in your hearts," where "rule" has the concept of govern or arbitrate. How can Christ *govern* our hearts or our lives now? What exactly does that mean?

6. Reread the context. Could the "word of Christ" be the "Spirit of Christ," or His commandment to "love one another as I have loved you"?

7. What best fits with this context? What would have those in Colossae have thought is the "word of Christ"?

8. How can we let the word of Christ dwell within us?

Conclusion:
"Let the word (message) of Christ dwell in you richly," contextually appears to be a reference to the putting on the spiritual attributes of Jesus (this could also be a reference to the depth of love that placed himself on the cross).

Our Spiritual Father Wants Us to Have a Spiritual Answer
The message of Christ/God is spiritual (having to do with the Spirit). This is why striving to keep the law can not save. This is why Paul has to rebuke churches for not living by a Spirit of faith and love. This is also why the Law can still be considered good and holy, but not perfect (Study #1). And this is why this new covenant of Christ's likeness is so much greater. (Studies #21-25)

**We know the truth,
not only by the reason,
but also by the heart.
–Blaise Pascal**

Homework #21: Paul's Motivation

Using the NASB, fill in the blanks.

1. **Col 3:3** For you have died and your life is _____ with Christ in God.

2. **Col 3:4** When Christ, who is our_____, is revealed, then you also will be revealed with Him in glory.

3. **Gal 4:19** My children, with whom I am again in labor until Christ is formed in

   _____

4. **Eph 4:24** and put on the _____, which in *the likeness of* God has been created in righteousness and holiness of the truth.

5. **Eph 5:1** Therefore be imitators of _____, as beloved children;

6. **1Co 2:16** For WHO HAS KNOWN THE MIND OF THE LORD, THAT HE WILL INSTRUCT HIM? But we have the mind of _____.

7. **2Co 3:3** being manifested that you are a _____ ____ _____, cared for by us, written not with ink but with the _____ of the living God, not on tablets of stone but on tablets of _____.

8. **2Co 3:17** Now the Lord is the _____, and where the Spirit of the Lord is, *there* is liberty.

9. From what you now know about Paul, what seems to motivate Paul the most? (Rank the 5 most important)

   _____ Money
   _____ Respect
   _____ Friendships
   _____ Getting to heaven
   _____ Not going to hell
   _____ God's love for him
   _____ Loving others
   _____ Imitating Christ
   _____ Something else: _____

10. If it is important to Paul, should it be important to us? How can we use this information to better teach the Spirit?

> For the love of Christ controls us, because we have concluded this: that one has died for all, therefore all have died. —2 Corinthians 5:14 NASB

To put on the Spirit of Christ (that we see in Jesus and Paul), to endure the hardships and continue to love like they did, what would you have to believe about …

11. Life?

12. Suffering?

13. Criticism/humiliation?

14. Death?

www.ThinkLikePaul.com

Homework #22: The New Covenant

Now for this very reason also, applying all diligence, in your faith supply moral excellence, and in *your* moral excellence, knowledge, and in *your* knowledge, self-control, and in *your* self-control, perseverance, and in *your* perseverance, godliness, and in *your* godliness, brotherly kindness, and in *your* brotherly kindness, love. For if these *qualities* are yours and are increasing, they render you neither useless nor unfruitful in the true knowledge of our Lord Jesus Christ. For he who lacks these *qualities* is blind *or* short-sighted, having forgotten *his* purification from his former sins. Therefore, brethren, be all the more diligent to make certain about His calling and choosing you; for as long as you practice these things, **you will never stumble**; for in this way the entrance into the **eternal kingdom** of our Lord and Savior Jesus Christ **will be abundantly supplied to you**. —2 Peter 1:5-11 NASB

1. According to this passage, what will cause us to 'never stumble'?

2. According to this passage what has to happen for the "eternal kingdom" to be abundantly supplied for us?

3. For the 1st century Christians, what did it mean to "follow Christ"?

4. What are the spiritual implications of the Lord's Supper?

5. What is the difference between a covenant and a contract?

6. What is the New Covenant?

7.   What if we spiritually and emotionally partook of the blood and the body of Christ(God's Spirit)? Would that help us with our tribulations today?

8.   If you were going to create a Lord's Supper service that remembers Christ and reinforces the New Covenant (our promise to love like Christ), what would that look like?

9.   Explain how observing the Communion and the New Covenant can help us acquire some of the traits we see in Christ:

10. Could God's Word(Message) and the New Covenant be the same thing? Explain how they relate to each other.

Our lives begin to end the day we become silent about things that matter.
—Martin Luther King Jr.

Homework #23:

1. Who was Benedict Arnold? What is the one thing he is known for? What does it mean to compare someone to call someone "Benedict Arnold"?

2. Who was Adolf Hitler? What is the one thing he is known for? What does it mean to call someone "Hitler" today?

3. Who was Albert Einstein? What is the one thing he is known for? What does it mean to call someone "Einstein" today?

4. What is the one thing Christ is known for? What does Paul likely mean when he refers to Christ living himself and others?

5. How can we grow in Christ's likeness? How can we help others grow into his likeness?

6. What daily habits can help us remember the spirit we find in Jesus? (list 3 habits)

7. If Christ (the Spirit of God) is the Word, and He states that His commandment is to "love one another as I have loved you," then would (or would not) following this commandment be... "Being led by the Holy Spirit"?

8. Is there a difference between the Word, the Holy Spirit, and the following of the New Commandment? If so, then…. What is that difference?

9. Could loving people the way Jesus did be "living in the Holy Spirit"?

10. Sometimes people say "We can't be like Christ." Did Paul ever write anything like that? Or did he see and encourage the "Christ" within people?

11. If you were trying to encourage your child to be a great musician, would you ever tell him "you can't be like Beethoven"? How do our beliefs affect our children?

Death smiles at us all, all a man can do is smile back.
—Marcus Aurelius

Homework #24: Filled with the "Fullness of God"

In Paul's letter to the Ephesians, he tells the church how they may be filled with "all the fullness of God."

> For this reason I bow my knees before the Father, from whom every family in heaven and on earth is named, that according to the riches of his glory He may grant you to be strengthened with power through His Spirit in your inner being, (a) so that Christ may dwell in your hearts through faith—(b) that you, being rooted and grounded in love, (c) may have strength to comprehend with all the saints what is the breadth and length and height and depth, and to know the love of Christ that surpasses knowledge, (d) that you may be filled with all the fullness of God. —Ephesians 3:14-19 ESV

Notice how these ideas are connected with each other.

1. What two ideas does <u>(a) so that</u> connect?

2. What two ideas does <u>(b) that you</u> connect?

3. What two ideas does <u>(c) may have</u> connect?

4. What two ideas does <u>(d) that you</u> connect?

For in Him dwelleth all the fullness of the Godhead bodily. —Colossians 2:9 ASV

5. The Spirit here is connected to what ideas?

6. Does this sound like something Paul wants them to grow into?

7. Where else does Paul (or any writer) tell us how we may attain the *fullness of God*? Do you think he is exaggerating? Is he referring to a particular trait? Why would Paul write that?

www.ThinkLikePaul.com

Homework #25: What Can Christ Do Today?

Answer the following questions with regard to evangelism:

1. How would teaching Christ (as God's message) be different than teaching the Bible and its 31,102 verses (as God's message)?

2. What does Christ teach us about our potential?

3. What may Christlikeness teach us about God's riches? Or an abundant life?

4. Would a deeper understanding of the love and suffering of Christ help us have more compassion and patience for those enslaved in sin?

5. Do you think people would be interested in a spiritual being who supplies us with the spiritual resources that we see in Christ?

Answer the following with regard to contentions and divisions within the church:

6. What would happen if my main goal was to develop the Spirit of Christ? What if our main goal as a church was to develop the Christ Spirit within each other?

7. How does Christ see us? What if we actually saw each other as Christ see us? What if we believed more in their greatness, than their current feelings of inadequacy?

Answer the following with regard to our inward psychological/emotional struggles:

8. Could a church that truly immerses itself into Christ (His life, spirit, psychology, values and emotions) be able to handle the trials and tribulations of this life?

9. Could a church that believes in the infinite spiritual resources within be the remedy for depression? Fear? Anger? Doubt? Feelings of inadequacy?

10. Could an individual who really developed the beliefs of Jesus be able to endure ALL things?

www.ThinkLikePaul.com

Glossary & Charts

Bible—The term "Bible" is not used within the Bible, but is a term that was developed after the first century to refer to a collection of letters written by people who were led by the Spirit. Purpose: Old Testament point us toward Christ, with the New Testament reminding and teaching us about Christ(the Messiah and growing into his likeness).

Christ (Christos)—the Son of God; the image of God (that man was designed to be); christlikeness; the Alpha and Omega; God's message to humanity; righteousness of God; the Mediator between God and man; the spiritual pathway back to God; the exact representation of God Himself...

Christianity or "Following Christ"—transforming oneself into the Spirit found in Christ.

Church— are those who have been "called out" of the world's mindset. They are those who have been drawn back to their spiritual Father. They are the "assembled group" who help each other grow up to be more like Christ. **Purpose:** Build each other up in Christ.

Communion—The Lord's Supper is a reminder of Christ and the New Covenant. It is a reminder of his heart (his love, courage, strength, joy and wisdom...), and his unwavering commitment to us. (See New Covenant).

Discipline within the church— If there were those who were proclaiming Christ, but were arrogantly living a life against his likeness, they were rebuked, and potentially separated from the church. But it was all done for the purpose of showing how a fleshly spirit/purpose is incompatible with Christ, *so that* they may realign their spirit with God's Spirit(Christ).

Faith—Faith is trusting that God will take care of us regardless of circumstances. Abraham's faith was a knowing that "God will provide" when there are no visible provisions. It is rooted in our knowledge of God's power, love, and presence.

Faith in Christ—is trusting the notion that Christ is from God Himself, and that His Spirit(heart/mindset) is our path back to the Creator.

Holy Spirit—The "Holy Spirit" is a spirit that is *of* God. It is the Spirit that is revealed in Jesus the Christ.

Judgment— We are going to be judged by Christ and what is within our hearts. And as we have put on Christ (likeness), we will be clothed on judgment day, where our sin will be covered.

Kingdom— The striving to follow Christ's Spirit is making Christ your king, and being in His kingdom. It is the process of 'going onto perfection', and growing more and more into His likeness (love, joy, peace, forgiveness, compassion, courage, hope...).

Knowledge— The New Testament divides knowledge into two basic categories:

1. Knowledge of Christ: love of God, growth, encouragement, spiritual wisdom...(the embodiment of God's spiritual wisdom).

www.ThinkLikePaul.com

2. Knowledge used for personal gain: information used to bind, control, pass judgment on others, or used without regard to the souls of others.

Love (Agape)— The realization of God's unconditional love (revealed in Jesus). It is care for others that is greater than circumstances. It is stronger than (the fear of) rejection, humiliation, separation, physical pain, and even torture and death.

New Covenant— a promise to follow His likeness, and specifically His commandment of "love one another as I have loved you."

Perfection— Perfection is loving your enemies as God does. As it is seen in Jesus, it is a commitment to love regardless of circumstances. (Study #1)

Repentance— Changing of one's mindset/heart into alignment with Christ's (God).

Righteousness— living with the same spirit(mindset and purpose) of Jesus/God. (Study #4)

Roles and authority in the church—The different roles within the church were for the purpose of helping others grow in Christ's likeness. The only authority anyone had was in helping others to become more like Christ. Everything was done for that one purpose.

Sin— where we have "missed the target"; areas where we are not like Christ.

Son of God— Jesus is "*the* son of God" as he is the first man born of the Spirit. We are "sons of God" as we follow Christ —the striving to put on His likeness. (In Matthew 5 Jesus equates being a "son of God" with loving our enemies as God does.)

Spirit—The spirit we find in God and Jesus. Living in His Spirit (the Holy Spirit) is living with His mindset (priorities, beliefs, values, attitudes and purposes).

Word—has two predominant uses in the New Testament: "a message" and "Christ-Spirit." (Often seems to mean both)

"The Word" (of God)—is used as a metonym (an expression) for "the Spirit of God working within us," which is the embodiment of God's spiritual precepts.

Taking Inventory

What exactly have we been taught? Are we just following the thinking of those who taught us? To better understand the faith of the first century, we should first be clear with the our current notions of "following Christ." The following questions will help us consider and get clarity with our current concepts of what it means to "follow Christ":

Assessing Our Current Hierarchy of Beliefs

1. Which traditions are "right"? Or cause us to be "right"?

2. Which traditions are "wrong"? Or cause us to be "wrong"?

3. How do you(or your church) determine what is "right" or "correct"?

4. When you teach the Bible, what are your rules for interpretation?

5. Who determined the rules?

6. What is the difference between a religion and a faith?

7. When you teach "Christ," what specifically are you teaching?

8. How would you explain "faith", or "following Christ"?

9. What passages/concepts do you teach when speaking with non-christians?

10. Do you emphasize facts about His life? Or parables He taught?

11. Do you emphasize spiritual principles? Or His spiritual likeness?

12. Do you emphasize commandments? Or church? Or rules?

13. And if so, what commandments? What church? What rules?

14. When you teach the Holy Spirit, what exactly do you teach?

15. What has to happen for one to receive the Holy Spirit?

16. How would one determine whether or not they have the Holy Spirit?

17. What specifically is the New Covenant?

18. What is/are a Christian's guiding principle(s) for making decisions?

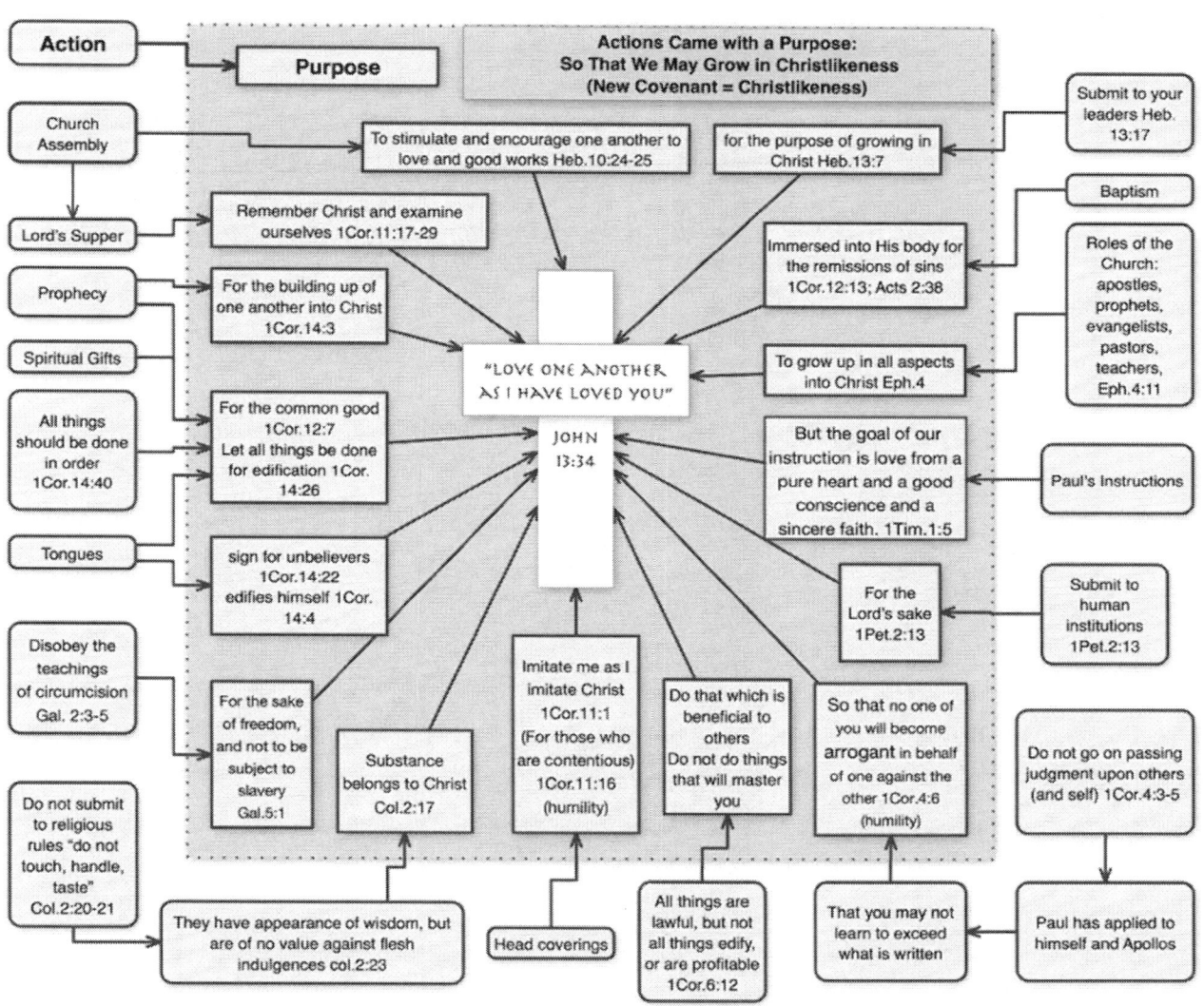

Action → **Purpose**

Actions Came with a Purpose:
So That We May Grow in Christlikeness
(New Covenant = Christlikeness)

Church Assembly → To stimulate and encourage one another to love and good works Heb.10:24-25

Lord's Supper → Remember Christ and examine ourselves 1Cor.11:17-29

Prophecy → For the building up of one another into Christ 1Cor.14:3

Spiritual Gifts

All things should be done in order 1Cor.14:40 → For the common good 1Cor.12:7 Let all things be done for edification 1Cor. 14:26

Tongues → sign for unbelievers 1Cor.14:22 edifies himself 1Cor. 14:4

Disobey the teachings of circumcision Gal. 2:3-5 → For the sake of freedom, and not to be subject to slavery Gal.5:1

Do not submit to religious rules "do not touch, handle, taste" Col.2:20-21 → They have appearance of wisdom, but are of no value against flesh indulgences col.2:23

"LOVE ONE ANOTHER AS I HAVE LOVED YOU" JOHN 13:34

for the purpose of growing in Christ Heb.13:7 ← Submit to your leaders Heb. 13:17

Immersed into His body for the remissions of sins 1Cor.12:13; Acts 2:38 ← Baptism

To grow up in all aspects into Christ Eph.4 ← Roles of the Church: apostles, prophets, evangelists, pastors, teachers, Eph.4:11

But the goal of our instruction is love from a pure heart and a good conscience and a sincere faith. 1Tim.1:5 ← Paul's Instructions

For the Lord's sake 1Pet.2:13 ← Submit to human institutions 1Pet.2:13

Substance belongs to Christ Col.2:17

Imitate me as I imitate Christ 1Cor.11:1 (For those who are contentious) 1Cor.11:16 (humility) ← Head coverings

Do that which is beneficial to others Do not do things that will master you ← All things are lawful, but not all things edify, or are profitable 1Cor.6:12

So that no one of you will become arrogant in behalf of one against the other 1Cor.4:6 (humility) ← That you may not learn to exceed what is written ← Paul has applied to himself and Apollos ← Do not go on passing judgment upon others (and self) 1Cor.4:3-5

One Purpose: God's Likeness in Man
(a.k.a. Christ/Kingdom)

Christ's Relationship with the Law and Scriptures

He came to fulfill the Law (Mt. 5:17)
He is the end(goal) of the Law (Rom.10:4)
The Law is our tutor to lead us to Christ (Ga.3:24)
Scriptures teach us about the mindset that Christ had (Rom.15:3-5)
Scriptures can make us wise for salvation through faith in Christ (2Tim.3:15)

Conclusion:
Christ(likeness) is our goal

Christ's Relationship to God

He is the exact representation of God
He is the message/word of God
He is the righteousness of God
He is the wisdom of God
He is the power of God
He is the glory of God
He is the lamb of God
He is the son of God
He is God with us

Conclusion:
Christ is our key to knowing and relating to God

Forms of Christ

Spirit in Jesus
Spiritual substance that sustained people in OT (1Cor.10:1-4; 1Pet.1:10-11)
Spirit that is alive in Paul (Gal.2:20)
Spirit that we can grow into (Gal.4:19; 2Cor.13:5; 2Cor.5:21)
Christ = real substance (Col. 2:16-17)

Conclusion:
Christ = Spirit of God in man

Prophecies of a Spiritual Kingdom

God's Spirit would be poured out (Joel 2:28)
New Covenant would be written on our hearts (Jer.31:31-33)
All people would know Him (Jer.31:34)
God will be on his throne (2Sam.7:12-17)
Messiah has the keys to David's house (Isa.22:22)

Conclusions:
1. God's Spirit has been poured out though Christ;
2. the new law is written on our hearts;
3. and everyone would know Him

Christ: the Likeness of God (in mankind)

Purpose for Activities & Spiritual Gifts

Communion = remember Him & examine ourselves (1Cor.11)
Baptism = put to death the old man, and being born again to a newness of life (Gal.6:4)
Assembly = building each other up in Him; stimulate one another to love and good works (Eph.4:15; Heb.10:24-25)
Gifts of the Spirit = for the common good; edification of the church (1Cor.12,14)

Conclusion:
Build one another up in Him

Followers Relationship with World

We are the light of the world (Mt.5:14)
We are the salt of the earth (Mt.5:13)
we are a letter of Christ (2Cor.3.3)
We give off the aroma of Christ (2Cor.2:14-15)
People glorify God thru our good works (Mt.5:16)
We are minister of reconciliation (2Cor.5:18)
We preach Christ (spirit of God)
We are the righteousness of God to others (2Cor.4:21)
We become the likeness of God (Gal.4:19)
We love them like Christ loved us (Jn.13:34-35)

Conclusion:
We are here to be God's likeness

Christ's Relationship with Followers

He is the light of men (Jn.1:4)
He is the bread of life (Jn. 6:35)
He is God's message to mankind (Jn.1:1)
He authored our faith (Heb.12.2)
Our Lord is the Spirit (Rom.8:9)
Christ is formed within us (Gal.4:19)
We are a letter of Christ (2Cor.3.3)
Be imitators of God (Eph.5:1)
He is our life (Col.3:4)
Put on the likeness of God (Eph.4:24)
We have the mind of Christ (1Cor.2:16)
God now speaks to us through Christ (Heb.1:1-3)
We may become the righteousness of God (2Cor.5:21)
He is the image we are being transformed into (2Cor.3:18)
We are to test ourselves to see if He is in us (2Cor.13:5)
He is the finisher of our faith (Heb.12:2)

Conclusion:
We are to be transforming into God's likeness

Roles of Apostles and Prophets

Witnesses to Christ (1Pet.5:1)
Have the Spirit of Christ (Rom.15:19)
Ministers of Christ (Rom.15:16)
Minister of reconciliation (2Cor.5:18)
Have authority to build others up in Christ (not for tearing down) (2Cor.13:10; Gal.4:19)
Determined to know nothing but Jesus and Him crucified (1Cor.2:2)
Love others like Christ loved them (Jn.13:34-35)
The goal of their instruction is love (1Tim.1:5)
Controlled by the love of Christ (2Cor.5:14)

Conclusion:
They were witnesses and messengers of Christ's likeness

www.ThinkLikePaul.com

Think Like Paul: Searching for the Message that Changed the World	Pharisees' Paradigm	Paul's Paradigm
How is "Righteousness" attained?	adherence to Scriptures (according to their religious system)	developing and growing into Christ's Spirit (Study #4)
What is "True Knowledge"?	knowing the Scriptures (according to their religious system)	developing and growing into Christ's Spirit (study #6)
What is "Fulfilling the Law"?	obedience to every Scripture (according to their religious system)	love (Spirit of Jesus) (study #2)
What is the Purpose of the Scriptures?	manual for life and Godliness (according to their religious system)	to lead us to Christ's Spirit, so that we may have the same Spirit (studies #6-10)
What is the Purpose of Man?	obey the Scriptures (according to their religious system)	be the image of God (Spirit of Jesus) (study #5)
What is Most Important?	their religious system (rules, traditions, being "right"...)	Christ (developing Spirit of Jesus)
What is "God's Solution"?	obedience to Scriptures (in accordance to their religious system)	Christ (developing Spirit of Jesus in mankind)

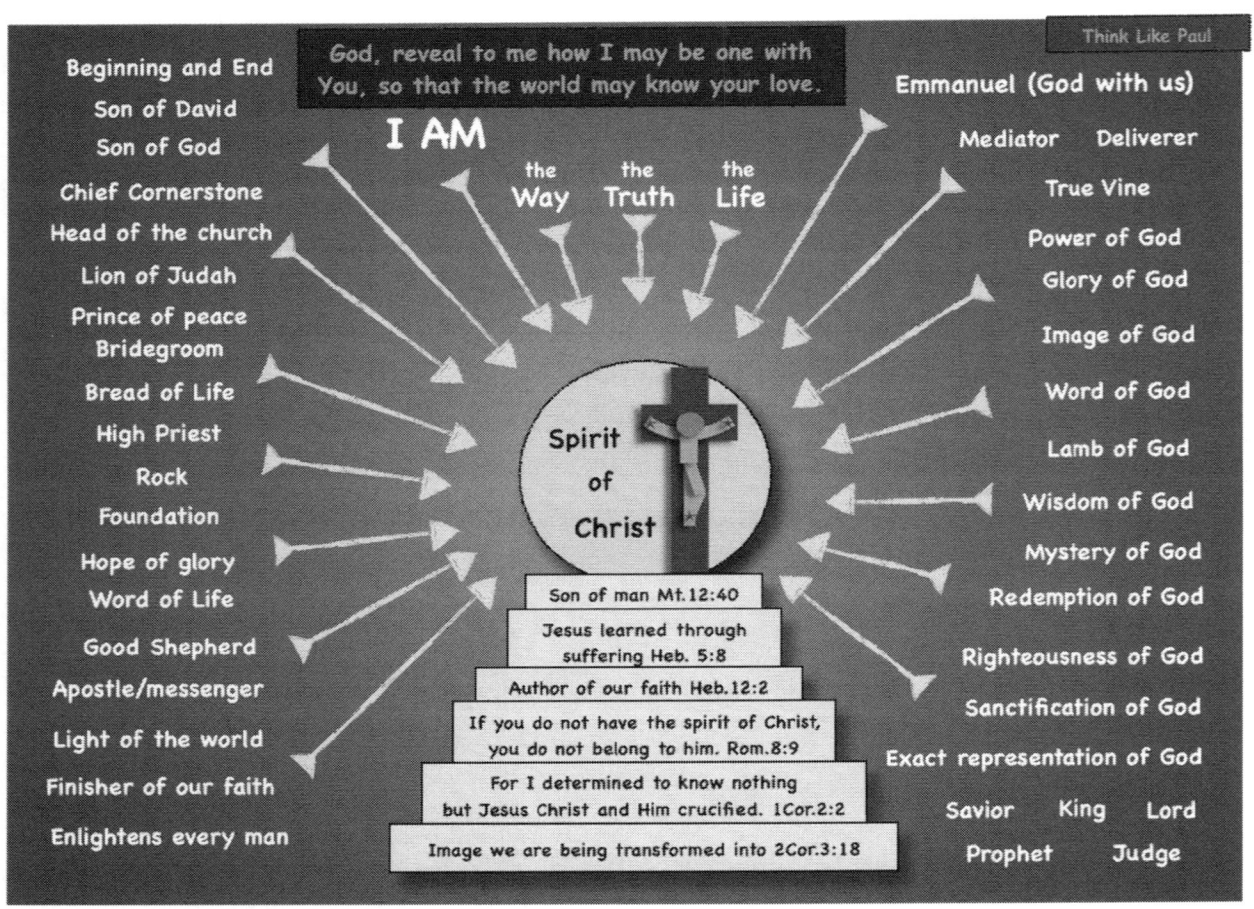

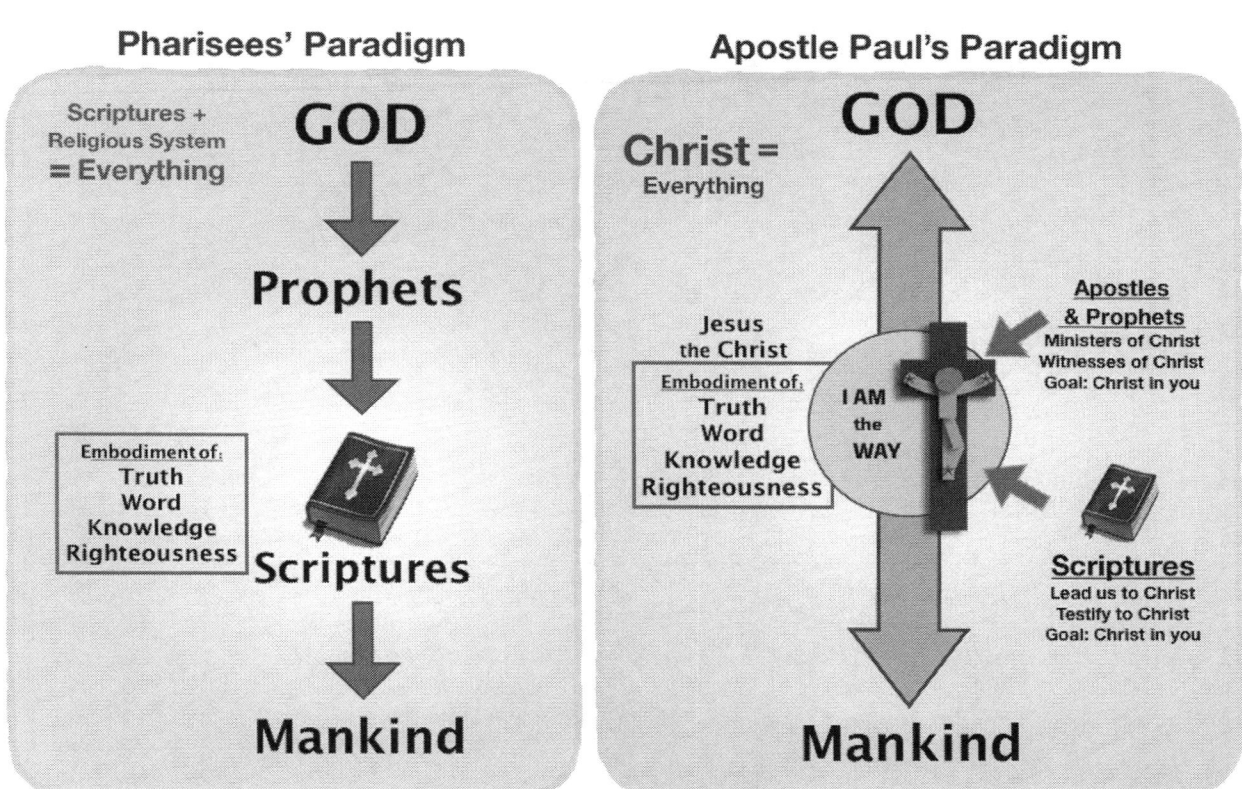

Pharisees' Paradigm

Scriptures +
Religious System
= Everything

GOD

↓

Prophets

↓

Embodiment of:
Truth
Word
Knowledge
Righteousness

Scriptures

↓

Mankind

Apostle Paul's Paradigm

Christ =
Everything

GOD

Jesus
the Christ
Embodiment of:
Truth
Word
Knowledge
Righteousness

I AM
the
WAY

**Apostles
& Prophets**
Ministers of Christ
Witnesses of Christ
Goal: Christ in you

Scriptures
Lead us to Christ
Testify to Christ
Goal: Christ in you

Mankind

Think Like Paul: Searching for the Message that Changed the World
by Perry Stiltz

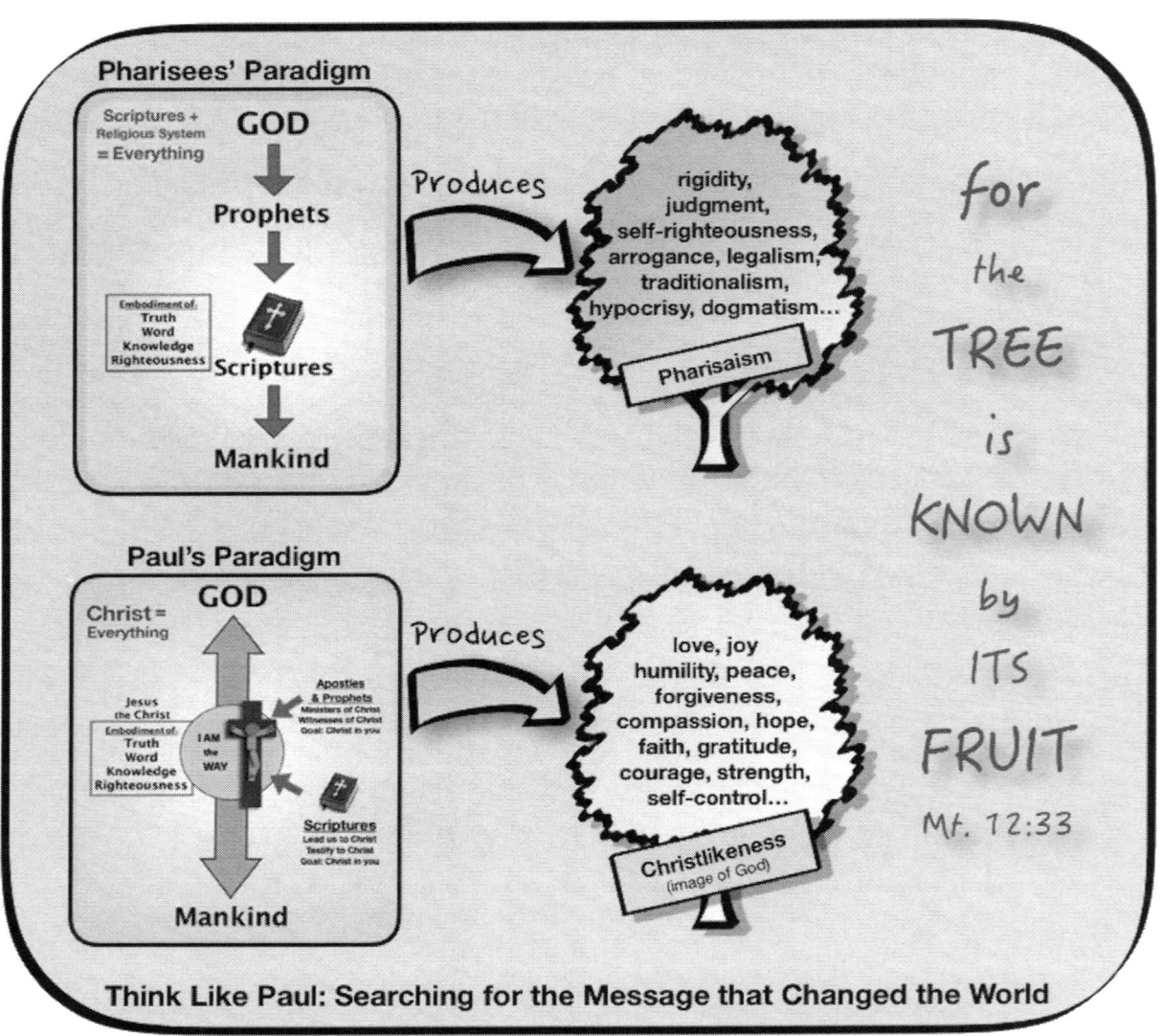

Think Like Paul: Searching for the Message that Changed the World

The Word Causes Followers to be One with...

The night before He goes to the cross,

Jesus Prays that:

1. Disciples have His joy,
2. Disciples are kept from evil,
3. **Disciples are sanctified in the truth** (= God's word)

Sanctified = made holy

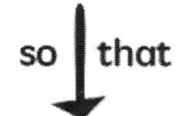

so | that

4. **Disciples and future believers are ONE with Christ (& God)**

so | that

5. the world may **know Christ,** & know that God **loved** the world (just as God loved Jesus)

Jesus Prays to God
(John 17:13-26 NASB)

But now I come to You; and these things I speak in the world so that they may have My joy made full in themselves. I have given them **Your word**; and the world has hated them, because they are not of the world, even as I am not of the world. I do not ask You to take them out of the world, but to keep them from the evil *one*. They are not of the world, even as I am not of the world. **Sanctify them in the truth; Your word is truth.** As You sent Me into the world, I also have sent them into the world. For their sakes I sanctify Myself, that they themselves also may be sanctified in truth. I do not ask on behalf of these alone, but for those also who believe in Me through their **word**; that they may all be one; even as You, Father, *are* in Me and I in You, that they also may be in Us, so that the world may believe that You sent Me. The glory which You have given Me I have given to them, that they may be one, just as We are one; I in them and You in Me, that they may be perfected in unity, so that the world may know that You sent Me, and loved them, even as You have loved Me.

God, may we be one with Christ and You, so that others may know You love them...

Think Like Paul: Searching for the Message that Changed the World

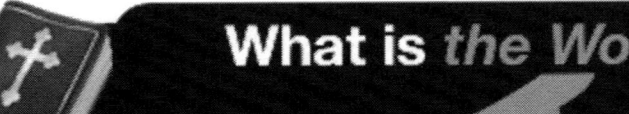

What is *the Word*?

Today's Paradigm Word = Scriptures		Paul's Paradigm Word = Spirit of Christ
Scriptures are living and active and can judge the intentions of the heart	"the word of God is living and active…" (Heb.4:12)	Spirit of Christ/God is living and active and can judge the intentions of the heart
the Bible is our weapon against the enemy	"the sword of the Spirit, which is the word of God" (Eph.6:17)	the Spirit of Jesus (in you) is our weapon against the enemy
preach the Bible	"Preach the word" (2 Tim. 4:2)	preach Christ (the Spirit of Jesus in you)
the Bible will nourish us	"pure milk of the word" (1Pet.2:2)	the Spirit we find in Jesus (going to the cross) will nourish us
faith comes from reading/hearing the Bible	"Faith comes by hearing, and hearing by the word of God" (Rom. 10:17)	faith comes from hearing/ understanding the Spirit of Christ (in you)
????	"Washing of water by the word" (Eph.5:26)	loving your wife (and others), as Christ loved the church, can change their hearts
accurately handling the Bible	"accurately handling the word of truth" (2Tim. 2:15)	accurately handling the Spirit of Christ (in you)
????	"for it is sanctified by means of the word of God and prayer" (1Tim.4:5)	having the 'Spirit of Christ (in you)' during prayer sanctifies things
????	"adulterating the word of God" (2Cor.4:2)	deceit and craftiness adulterates the Spirit of Christ (in you)
the seed is the Scriptures	"the seed is the word of God" (Lk. 8:11)	the seed is the Spirit of God
the Pharisees made void the Scriptures	"you have made void the word of God" (Mt. 15:6)	the Pharisees made void the Spirit of God
message of God (unspecific)	"the word of God continued to increase" (Acts 6:7)	Spirit of Christ (message of God)
message of God (unspecific)	"the word of the Lord has sounded forth from you" (1Thes.1:8)	Spirit of Christ (message of God)

Think Like Paul: Searching for the Message that Changed the World   Perry Stiltz

www.ThinkLikePaul.com

More *Word* Passages

Mt. 15:6	you have made void the word of God	the Pharisees made void the Spirit of God (in them)
Lk. 8:11 (Mt.13-18-23; Lk.4:14-20)	the seed is the word of God	the seed is the Spirit of God
John 1:1	In the beginning was the Word, and the Word was with God, and the Word was God.	Word = Christ
John 1:14	And the Word became flesh, and dwelt among us	Word = Christ
Acts 6:4,7	devote ourselves... to the ministry of the word; the word of God continued to increase	Spirit of Christ (message of God)
Acts 13:5	to proclaim the word of God	Spirit of Christ (message of God)
Rom. 10:17	Faith comes by hearing, and hearing by the word of God	faith comes from hearing/ understanding the Spirit of Christ (in you)
Gal. 6:6	who is taught the word is to share all good things	Spirit of Christ (message of God)
Col. 3:16	Let the word of Christ richly dwell within you	let the message of Christ richly dwell within you
2Tim. 2:15	accurately handling the word of truth	accurately handling the Spirit of Christ (in you)
2Tim. 4:2	Preach the word	preach Christ (the Spirit of Jesus in you)
1Pet. 1:23	for you have been born again not of seed which is perishable but imperishable, that is, through the living and enduring word of God.	They were "born through" the living and enduring Word of God
1Pet. 1:27	but the word of the Lord remains forever, and this word is the good news that was preached to you.	"remains forever" "good news" "previously preached"
1Pet. 2:2	pure milk of the word	the Spirit we find in Jesus (going to the cross) will nourish us
1Pet. 2:8	a stone of stumbling and a rock of offence —who are stumbling at the word.	They stumbled over Jesus (as the message)
Rev. 19:13	He is clothed in a robe dipped in blood, and the name by which he is called is The Word of God.	Word = Christ

Think Like Paul: Searching for the Message that Changed the World   Perry Stiltz

Made in the USA
Lexington, KY
08 December 2018